Reviews of *Ada, The Enchantress of Numbers*

"Beyond stereotypes"
Wired

"Excellent and thoughtful"
Annals of the History of Computing

"Toole lets Ada speak for herself through letters to colleagues, family and friends which bring Ada to life with an intimacy a biography never could."
Alice Polesky, *San Francisco Chronicle*

"Ada Lovelace: The World's First Hacker . . . Toole did research for more than eight years, burying herself in British archives and libraries to narrate and edit this extraordinary collection of letters written by Ada Lovelace. Not only do they outline Ada's ingenuity for the sciences, but they also enlighten us on all aspects of Lady Lovelace's multidimensional life: her passionate desire to flourish in a "man's world," her battle with drug addiction and chronic sickness, and her efforts as a mother and wife. Lovelace also had a reputation as a wild gambler and a lover. What can tell us more truthfully about Ms Lovelace's life than letters from the Lady herself?"
Carla Sinclair, *Net Chick*

"Ada Lovelace has a mythic resonance for our digital age: reverent visits to Ada's grave now outnumber pilgrimages to the grave of her father, the poet Byron. Betty Alexandra Toole's revelatory book gives us the sad, evocative and all–too–human story of the woman behind the Ada myth."
Bruce Sterling, co-author of the *Difference Engine*
and author of *Hacker Crackdown*

". . . Ada was one of the first to write programs of instructions for Babbage's Analytical Engines, the famous precursors to the modern digital computer. Beautiful, charming, temperamental, an aristocratic hostess, mathematicians of the time thought her a splendid addition to their number. Babbage warmly appreciated her worth, and the value of the felicitous account she wrote of his Analytical Engines and their potential scope of application.

"The story of Ada's life and of her relationship with Babbage has been sadly distorted, and Dr Toole, who has in my view an unrivaled knowledge of Ada's life, here gives us the opportunity to set the record straight. By this Dr Toole helps clarify not only Ada's personal life, but also an important early stage of the computer revolution. . . . I warmly welcome the publication of this critical selection of Ada's letters."
Dr Anthony Hyman, author of *Charles Babbage,
Pioneer of the Computer* (Oxford/Princeton)

"Daughter of Lord Byron, companion and partner of Charles Babbage, Ada was one of the most picturesque characters in the history of technology. . . Ada's letters are some of the classic founding documents of cybernetics and computer science, written nearly a century before ENIAC . . .
Howard Rheingold, author of *Vir~~~~~~~~~~~~~~~~~~~~~ies*

"Dr Toole has written a brilliant an~~~~~~~~~~~~~~~~~~~~~~~~~~~~~th not only of Lovelace's genius but al~~~~~~~~~~~~~~~~~~~~~~~n-tial and inspiring book, one that cros~~~~~~~~~~~~~~~~~~~~~~"
L~~~~~~~~~~~~~~e

~~~~~ing Ada

The Countess of Lovelace

Daughter of the late Lord Byron

ADA

THE ENCHANTRESS OF NUMBERS

PROPHET
OF THE
COMPUTER AGE

A Pathway to the 21st Century

Betty Alexandra Toole, Ed.D.

STRAWBERRY PRESS
MILL VALLEY, CALIFORNIA

ISBN 0-912647-18-3
Library of Congress Number 97-062562

Published by
STRAWBERRY PRESS
227 Strawberry Drive
Mill Valley, CA 94941

Correspondence and orders should be sent to:

adatoole@well.com, or

Critical Connection
P.O. Box 452
Sausalito, CA 94966
FAX 415-388-2328

Cover designed by Leah Schwartz and Robert Cooney
Book designed by Robert Cooney
Composition in Times Europa by Archetype Typography
Printed in Canada
Logo by Leah Schwartz

Cover: Portrait of Augusta Ada Byron, Lady Lovelace, by A. E. Chalôn, circa
1838, courtesy of the Trustees of the British Museum. Back cover portrait of
Charles Babbage by William Brockedon FRS, 1840, courtesy of the National
Portrait Gallery; photographs of Analytical Engine and Charles Babbage,
1833, courtesy of the Science Museum; and frontispiece, portrait of Ada
Byron, Lady Lovelace, circa 1838, part of a series by A. E. Chalôn, courtesy of
the Trustees of the British Museum.

"The truth is easy to kill, but a lie well told lasts forever."

Mark Twain

To Esther and Dave, and to all who touch these pages, with the hope that the fortune in the Chinese cookie is as accurate as the words of Mark Twain: "Time is precious, but truth is more precious than time."

for

"No one knows what almost <u>awful</u> energy & power lie yet undevelopped in that <u>wiry</u> little system of mine."

Ada Byron, Lady Lovelace

TABLE OF CONTENTS

ACKNOWLEDGMENTS

This book is the result of more than twenty years of addiction to Ada. It represents eight years of research, and along the way many people have helped me. For a complete listing of those who helped me make the first edition reality, please see the acknowledgments in *Ada, The Enchantress of Numbers: A Selection from the Letters of Lord Byron's Daughter and Her Description of the First Computer*.

I would like to acknowledge first both my parents, who encouraged my interest in mathematics and science and taught me the concept that truth is by far the most important element in one's personal life. The structure of learning that was imparted to me at the University of Chicago reinforced that concept – how important it is not to confuse truth with mind-set or distort truth through the medium of expression. The structure of this book – part biography, part letters – gives readers the opportunity to come to their own conclusions on the basis of the information presented. As an educator, I have found the most effective way to get to the "heart of the matter" is to involve students in a way that gives them the power to determine what is truth and what is not.

This paperback edition is a revised and abridged version of the original, *Ada, The Enchantress of Numbers: A Selection from the Letters of Lord Byron's Daughter and Her Description of the First Computer*. My thanks go again to publisher Herman Schwartz, M.D., of Strawberry Press; Leah Schwartz for the cover design; Rima and John Outram for putting up with me through the years, as well as allowing me to use their marvelous Macs; Judy Rodich for her excellent editing and proofreading; Jennifer Thompson for the index; and Robert Cooney for the book design. The librarians and staff at the Bodleian Library were helpful beyond the call of duty, especially Colin Harris and Mary Clapinson. And special thanks go to my friends who have seen that I am as "detestably persevering" as Ada feared she was: Melanie McGrath; Paul Wilmshurst; Avril Couris; Marilyn Jacobs; Elma Dangerfield, the major force behind the Byron Society; and Anthony Hyman, Babbage's biographer.

I am most indebted to the Earl of Lytton and his literary agent, Gerald Pollinger, for permission to research and publish these letters from the Lovelace-Byron Collection on deposit at the Bodleian Library, Oxford University. My thanks go to the British Library for Ada's letters to Babbage (specific mention in Appendix I). The pictures on the cover are acknowledged on the copyright page. John Murray, Don Palermo, Derek Wise, and Andrew Nicholson were most kind in allowing me to use material that has not been catalogued and to quote from those letters. In addition, my thanks go to the Nottingham Library-Newstead Abbey, and Pamela Wood for the letter in that collection. Last, I am most grateful to Colonel Gross, U.S.A.F., for his help in annotating Ada's Notes, Chapter 12, so that they are specifically meaningful to the users of *Ada,* the software language.

Betty Alexandra Toole
November 6, 1997

"Forget this world and all its troubles and if possible its multitudinous Charlatans — every thing in short but the Enchantress of Numbers."

Charles Babbage, 1843

FAMILY TREE OF AUGUSTA ADA BYRON, LADY LOVELACE

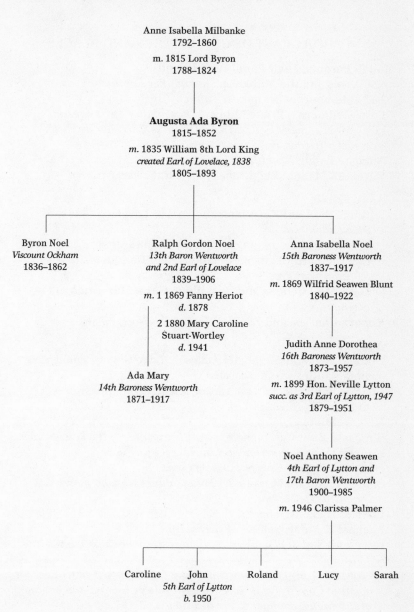

Anne Isabella Milbanke
1792–1860

m. 1815 Lord Byron
1788–1824

Augusta Ada Byron
1815–1852

m. 1835 William 8th Lord King
created Earl of Lovelace, 1838
1805–1893

Byron Noel
Viscount Ockham
1836–1862

Ralph Gordon Noel
*13th Baron Wentworth
and 2nd Earl of Lovelace*
1839–1906

m. 1 1869 Fanny Heriot
d. 1878

2 1880 Mary Caroline
Stuart-Wortley
d. 1941

Ada Mary
14th Baroness Wentworth
1871–1917

Anna Isabella Noel
15th Baroness Wentworth
1837–1917

m. 1869 Wilfrid Seawen Blunt
1840–1922

Judith Anne Dorothea
16th Baroness Wentworth
1873–1957

m. 1899 Hon. Neville Lytton
succ. as 3rd Earl of Lytton, 1947
1879–1951

Noel Anthony Seawen
*4th Earl of Lytton and
17th Baron Wentworth*
1900–1985

m. 1946 Clarissa Palmer

Caroline   John   Roland   Lucy   Sarah
5th Earl of Lytton
b. 1950

A SHORT CAST OF CHARACTERS AND PLACES

Ada's Parents, Their Family and Friends
The Noels and the Milbankes: *her mother's family*
Lady Melbourne: *her mother's aunt*
Lord Melbourne, Prime Minister: *her mother's first cousin*
Mary Montgomery, Selina Doyle, Francis Carr: *her mother's spinster friends, or "Three Furies"*
Augusta Leigh: *her father's half-sister*
Elizabeth Medora Leigh: *one of Augusta's seven children*

Ada's Family
William, the Lord King, later the Earl of Lovelace: *Ada's husband*
Hester, Charlotte, *and* Locke King: *William's sisters and brother*
Byron, the Lord Ockham, Annabella, and Ralph: *Ada and William's children*
Greene, Miss Cooper, and Dr William Carpenter: *children's attendants and tutors*
Robert, Charles, and Edward Noel: *Ada's Noel cousins*

Ada's Friends
Olivia (Livy) and Annabella Acheson: *Lady Gosford's daughters*
Joanna Baillie: *popular novelist*
Charles Babbage: *mathematician, scientist, and inventor of Calculating Engines*
Herschel Babbage: *his son*
Sir David Brewster: *pioneer in optics, inventor of the kaleidoscope*
Andrew Crosse: *experimenter in electricity*
John and Robert Crosse: *Andrew's sons*
Sophia Frend De Morgan: *Dr Frend's daughter, who married Augustus De Morgan*
Charles Dickens: *novelist*
Michael Faraday: *pioneer of electricity*
Reverend Samuel Gamlen: *Ada's minister, who married Ada and William*
Woronzow Greig: *Mrs Somerville's son from her first marriage, went to Cambridge University with Ada's husband and became Ada's friend, confidant, and attorney*

Sir John Cam Hobhouse: *Lord Byron's closest friend*
Anna Jameson: *author, helped out with Medora, Augusta Leigh's daughter*
Dr James Phillips Kay, later Sir Kay-Shuttleworth: *knighted for contribution to the establishment of public education in Great Britain*
Frederick Knight: *publisher, Somerset neighbor*
Dr Locock: *Ada's doctor and friend*
Malcolm and Nightingale: *Ada's so–called "sporting friends"*
Harriet Martineau: *scientific reporter*
Hugh Montgomery: *nephew of Mary Montgomery*
Mary Somerville: *translated LaPlace's work from French*
Fanny Smith: *later Fanny Noel, illegitimate niece of Selina Doyle, married Edward Noel*
Mary and Martha Somerville: *daughters of the prominent scientist Mary Somerville*
Sir Gardner Wilkinson: *Egyptologist*
Lord and Lady Zetland: *owners of the horse Voltigeur*

Teachers and Tutors
Dr William Frend: *Lady Byron's tutor, who helped Ada as well*
Dr William and Mary King: *Lady Byron's friends who lived in Brighton and associated with the Brighton Cooperative*
Miss Lawrence: *a Liverpool educator*
William Turner: *shorthand tutor*
Mary Somerville: *prominent scientist*
Miss D' Espourria, *harp teacher*
Augustus De Morgan: *leading mathematician, logician, and actuary*
Professor Faia: *voice teacher*

Homes
As a child: *Bifrons, Mortlake and Fordhook*
After her marriage, in London: *St James's Square, Manchester Square, Grosvenor Place, Cumberland St, 6 Great Cumberland Place*
In Surrey: *Ockham, East Horsley Towers*
In Somerset: *Ashley Combe, Porlock, Minehead*

Horses
Sylph, Dubby, Flirt, Tam O'Shanter
Racing Horses: *Flying Dutchman, Voltigeur, Teddington*

TIME-LINE

YEAR	EVENT
1641	Blaise Pascal develops one of the first calculating machines
1784	Augusta Mary Byron (Lord Byron's half sister) is born
1788	Lord Byron (Ada's father) is born
1791	Charles Babbage (Ada's closest friend) is born
1792	Anne Isabella (Annabella) Milbanke (Ada's mother) is born
1793	Start of the Napoleonic Wars
1804	J. M. Jacquard invents apparatus to automate looms
1805	William King (Ada's husband) is born
1811	The Luddites fight industrialization
1812	Lord Byron's maiden speech before Parliament Lord Byron's first major poetical work, *Childe Harold*, is published
1815	Lord Byron and Annabella Milbanke wed (January 2) Augusta Ada Byron is born in London (December 10) Battle of Waterloo and the end of the Napoleonic Wars Steamers on the Thames
1816	Lord and Lady Byron separate (January 16) Lord Byron leaves England (April 25)
1822	Lady Noel (Lady Byron's mother) dies
1824	Lord Byron dies in Greece (April 19)
1828	Ada designs a flying machine
1829	Ada gets the measles and becomes an invalid
1832	Parliament passes Reform Bill, which expanded political power
1833	Ada slowly recovers and is presented at court Ada meets Charles Babbage and his Difference Engine
1834	Babbage conceptualizes the Analytical Engine
1835	Ada weds William King (July 8)
1836	Ada's first child, Byron, is born (May 12)

1837   Ada's second child, Anne Isabella (Annabella), is born
       (September 22)
       Victoria crowned – The Victorian Era begins

1838   William and Ada become Earl and Countess of
       Lovelace (June 30)

1839   Ada's third child, Ralph Gordon, is born (July 2)

1840   Lord Lovelace becomes Lord Lieutenant of Surrey
       Babbage goes to Italy to discuss the Analytical Engine
       Ada begins studying mathematics with De Morgan

1841   Lady Byron reveals Ada's "Most <u>Strange</u> and
       <u>Dreadful</u> History"

1842   Ada returns after a nine-month absence to her
       mathematical studies
       L. F. Menabrea's description of the Analytical Engine
       is published in Switzerland (October)

1843   Ada's translation and Notes are published (August)

1844   Ada visits the Crosse household in late November

1850   Ada visits her father's ancestral home, Newstead Abbey

1851   The Great Exhibition, Queen Victoria's ball, and
       Derby Day

1852   Ada dies (November 27)

1860   Lady Byron dies (May 16)

1862   Byron, now the Viscount Ockham, dies

1871   Charles Babbage dies (October 18)

1890   Hollerith of the United States uses the punch card for
       sorting and tabulating information for the United
       States Census

1893   Lord Lovelace dies (December 29)

1931   Vannevar Bush of MIT builds the first "modern large
       analog" computer

1946   ENIAC – First digital computer built

1974   Proposal by military for a common high-order
       computer language

1975   First iteration of the language called Strawman, second
       iteration called Woodenman

1978   A winning language selected after extensive review

1980   Language named "Ada" in her honor

1984   "Ada" becomes a trademark of the United States
       Department of Defense

Introduction

The proper study of mankind is man.
Alexander Pope

ADA, THE ENCHANTRESS OF NUMBERS: *Prophet of the Computer Age* is a revised and abridged selection from the letters of Lord Byron's daughter and her description of the first computer. It is a pathway to the 21st century, for it is part biography, part letters, and in many ways is similar to finding information on the Internet and receiving email. These letters are the literary remains of a remarkable 19th century woman, sometimes called the first programmer, who foresaw the impact of the computer age.

I think her letters and her description of the first computer are pure gold, and obviously I am not alone. Some people have mined and transformed excerpts from these letters so that Ada has emerged as her father's daughter, "mad and bad." She has been characterized in the novel, *The Difference Engine,* as the "Queen of Engines"; she has been used as the main character in a virtual reality movie, *Conceiving Ada*; and most likely she was the inspiration for Thomasina in Tom Stoppard's *Arcadia.* Her name has been a trademark of the U.S. Department of Defense, which named a computer language *Ada* in her honor. Yet, despite all of this the "real Ada" is illusive, mysterious, and very human.

Why has she evoked three biographies and inspired characterizations in plays, novels, and a virtual reality movie? Why was a modern computer language named after a Victorian lady whose short life spanned the years 1815-1852? Why have her skills become part of a secondary mathematics textbook?

At the very least, Ada was a fascinating human being who saw things in an unusual way. That is no surprise since she was connected to two great geniuses – her father, the romantic poet

Lord Byron, and Charles Babbage, the mathematician and scientist. Her claim to current fame is that for a short time Ada was Babbage's voice to the world. She described his greatest accomplishment, the Analytical Engine, and the intellectual birth of the computer revolution.

The picture on the cover of this book is not a demure Victorian lass but a lady with a prominent and expansive jaw, on which Ada thought the word mathematics might be inscribed. She sought to know the world of ideas: of mathematics, science, mesmerism, and music. She also loved to ice skate, spin dreams of foreign places while riding on her horse through the English countryside, and at times wished to "annihilate her metaphysical daughter." Perhaps because she had a famous father, she was a very shy and private person. During long lonely hours, she was tormented by many problems that we confront today – being brought up as an only child in a one-parent family, loneliness, incest, motherhood, high expectations, career, drug addiction, gambling, and infidelity.

Ada's speculations from childhood on reveal that she refused to be boxed in time and place. She saw the need for a mathematical and scientific language that incorporated imagination. Many of her ideas, from flying machines to a molecular universe, were not the foundation of work in the field; however, they reveal that she was a synthesizer and a prophet of the computer age.

How we process information in the "information age" is critical to all of us today. Many contemporary books explore the right-left brain dichotomy and describe physics, science, and the world of machines to fit that concept. Danah Zohar, in her book, *The Quantum Self*, describes what it means to live in a quantum world: "The creative dialogue between mind and matter is the physical basis of human creativity."[1] Ada foreshadowed the 21st century throughout her life. She did an intriguing cosmic dance that blended imagination and facts; daily life and the meaning of it all; the potential and the limits of technological innovation; and analysis and metaphysics. Ada's path was not poetry or science, but poetical science.

Ada's Heritage and Her Path: Poetical Science

How did I become captivated by Ada? A chapter of my doctoral dissertation at the University of California at Berkeley dealt with the history of calculating devices, and as part of my research I went to visit the Science Museum in London. Next to a model of Charles Babbage's Analytical Engine, now heralded by many as the first computer, was the portrait of a lovely Victorian lady, Augusta Ada Byron, Lady Lovelace, Lord Byron's daughter, who wrote a description in 1843 of Babbage's plans for the Analytical Engine. This strange combination of poetry and science intrigued me! It was this critical combination that enabled Ada not only to see the value of Babbage's plans, but to predict some of the ramifications of those ideas. Ada, just like her father, had the ability to use imagination and metaphor to evaluate accurately a concept or an idea. She applied this talent to the description of a technological innovation that still has meaning today. It is essential that poets and scientists get to the heart of the matter simply, succinctly, and successfully. Today we need such skills to determine the value of everything from the printed word to the computer printout: poetical or analog skills in a digital world.

At the beginning of the Industrial Revolution, the rivalry between poetry and science resulted in the separation of the theories of objectivism and subjectivism.[2] The allies of objectivism were scientific truth, digital skills, and reason. In contrast, subjectivism came to be associated with analog skills, emotions, imagination, intuitive insight, and "higher truth." With the development of technology and its dehumanizing influence, which Byron so ardently complained about in his maiden speech before Parliament, the Romantic poets left reason, science, and technology to the empiricists. For Ada, these philosophical frameworks were not abstract intellectual arguments but the battleground of her life. Her mother and father, though both members of the British aristocracy, could not have been more different in background, temperament, and point of view.

Ada's mother, Lady Byron, was born Anne Isabella (Annabella) Milbanke on 17 May 1792 after her parents had been married for 15 years. She was an only child. Her mother, Lady Judith Milbanke, though caring, was a domineering and independent woman. She took an avid interest in her husband's parliamentary career. She detested women who were mere "cyphers."

When Annabella was a teenager, she was so precocious that her parents hired Dr William Frend as a tutor. Dr Frend had been banished from Cambridge for publishing a pamphlet advocating peace. He gave Annabella a course of study similar to that of a Cambridge student. She completed the fourth book of Euclid, wrote a penetrating criticism of Francis Bacon's *The Advancement of Learning*, and studied the works of the philosopher David Hume and the writings of Jonathan Swift. Annabella especially enjoyed the strength of the characters and the methodical development of the plots in the works of Jane Austen. Austen's novels dealt primarily with courtship, and when Annabella was eighteen that was her primary concern.

Annabella spent a great deal of time analyzing herself and defining her values. She had such high standards that she dismissed various suitors for being "too silken" or having insanity in their families. Elizabeth Barrett Browning described Annabella as walking straight not from strength, but from stiffness. The Duchess of Devonshire described her as an "icicle."

George Gordon, the future Lord Byron, was born in London on 22 January 1788. The nicknames of his ancestors warn immediately that they were not country patricians. His grandfather was an admiral in the Navy and for many of his escapades on the sea was known as "Foul Weather Jack." Byron's great uncle, the fifth Lord Byron, was known as the "Wicked Lord." He was convicted of manslaughter, but pleading his privilege as a lord, was not punished. He spent the rest of his life as a recluse at Newstead Abbey, the family estate near Nottingham.

Lord Byron's father, Captain John Byron, was a dashing, debonair gambler always a step ahead of his creditors. He was known as "Mad Jack" and disowned by "Foul Weather Jack." "Mad Jack's" first marriage was to the divorced wife of Lord Carmarthen. In 1783 they had a daughter, Augusta. When his wife died, "Mad Jack" squandered her fortune. He then went to the Spa at Bath and successfully wooed another heiress, Miss Catherine Gordon of Gight, who traced her ancestors back to King James I. Soon after their marriage, George Gordon, the future Lord Byron, was born with a club foot. Catherine took her son to Aberdeen, Scotland to live. "Mad Jack" managed to gamble and spend her fortune as well and went to Paris to escape his creditors. He died when his son was three years old. Byron's vague memory of his parents' relationship was that they often were involved in raging battles.

Byron's life was no better. He did not have the upbringing of a lord or scholar. He attended a day school in Aberdeen and was teased and tormented about his club foot. However, everything changed when he was ten years old. His uncle died, and he became the sixth Lord Byron, Baron Byron of Rochdale.

Byron's mother took him to London and hired John Hanson to handle the family's affairs. There would be no more painful attempts to straighten Byron's club foot. Instead, Byron was fitted with a special shoe. Hanson arranged for the management and restoration of Newstead Abbey, which Byron inherited. He also arranged for Byron's education. Byron went to Harrow and then on to Cambridge University.

At Cambridge, Byron's behavior was anything but methodical. He loved to shock people by parading around with a pet bear, by losing an immense amount of weight on a diet of soda and crackers, and by publishing his first poetical endeavor, *Fugitive Pieces,* which included very explicit sexual descriptions.

After Byron completed Cambridge, he went on a continental tour with his closest friend, John Cam Hobhouse. It was Greece that particularly captivated Byron's heart. In 1810-1811, during Byron's first visit, Greece was under the control of the Ottoman Empire. When Byron returned home he carried with him the completed manuscript of a long poem, *Childe Harold,* which was a poetical rendition of his travels.

The first few months of 1812 were packed with exciting events that changed his destiny. Byron did not like the industrialization that was sweeping England. On 27 February 1812 he made his maiden speech before the House of Lords, a passionate plea for the plight of the Frameworkers of Nottingham. He decried how industrialization threw superfluous laborers out of work. Byron became involved with the political circle of Lord and Lady Holland, who were a major force in the Whig party. But it was not Byron's political finesse that captivated the Hollands or the English people – it was his poetry.

When *Childe Harold* was published by John Murray on 10 March, Byron awoke the next day to find himself famous. Although Byron's poetry appealed to people of all social classes, it was not just his poetry that captivated people but his personality and tumultuous life style. Byron arrived on the historical scene just at the right moment.

At the beginning of the nineteenth century, England was involved in the Napoleonic wars; Englishmen fought and won famous battles in Spain and at Waterloo. When the soldiers returned home victoriously, they found that industrialization had spread. People migrated from the countryside to the cities to make their fortunes. The flowing descriptions of the English Lake District in Wordsworth's poetry were for many city dwellers a nostalgic memory, but Byron's passionate poetry describing the lure of foreign places struck a familiar chord to many people. He became a symbol of an England that was expanding its influence throughout the world. Whereas his passion was the liberation of foreign people, the passion for others was the profit to be made in foreign places.

During the last week in March, Ada's parents met for the first time at a morning party. Just two weeks after *Childe Harold* was published, Byron's fame was already established. He was surrounded by adoring women and received many sexual overtures, some of which he fulfilled. His most ardent admirer was Caroline Lamb, who was married to Annabella's cousin William. William was Lady Melbourne's son and a future prime minister. According to Annabella's observation, Caroline draped herself all over Lord Byron. Caroline wrote in her journal that Byron was "mad – bad – and dangerous to know" and proceeded to become emotionally entangled, making a spectacle of herself.

Annabella did the opposite. She wrote that she did not worship at the shrine of *Childe Harold*, but demurely stayed in the distance. That strategy worked, for Byron was intrigued. He was finding Caroline too hot to handle and characterized her as having "lava running through her veins." After meeting Annabella for the second time, Byron approached his good friend, Lady Melbourne, Annabella's aunt, to write to Annabella on his behalf about his interest in this "amiable Mathematician."

Lady Melbourne was anxious to see the relationship between her daughter-in-law Caroline and Byron end because Caroline was indiscreet – to Lady Melbourne that was inexcusable. She was not particularly fond of her brother's spoiled daughter, but she agreed to be Byron's proxy. She wrote Annabella asking her what she required in a suitor and Annabella replied with a carefully thought out treatise. Lady Melbourne continued to be the liaison and forwarded Byron's proposal, but she was annoyed with her niece and described Annabella as walking on stilts. Annabella's analytical mind dissected and disapproved of Byron, yet she was intrigued by him and did not want to lose his friendship. She rejected his proposal because of a "defect in her feelings."

We do not know whether Byron could understand the details of mathematics, but he certainly knew how to use mathematical terms and concepts, with the aid of vivid metaphors, to evaluate Annabella and their relationship. When his first proposal of marriage was rejected, it evoked a good-natured response on his part. He dubbed her "The Princess of Parallelograms." He recognized that they viewed the world differently, and Byron wrote on 18 October 1812: "Her proceedings are quite rectangular, or rather we are two parallel lines prolonged to infinity side by side but never to meet."[3]

Byron turned to other interests. From 1812 to 1814 Annabella wrote to Byron, usually initiating the sermonizing correspondence. During this period Byron became close to his half-sister Augusta, who was married with three children. Augusta gave birth to her fourth child, Elizabeth Medora, in April 1814. Byron wrote an enigmatic letter to Lady Melbourne stating that

Elizabeth Medora was not an "ape," a reference to a child of incest. It was not known whether he was jesting or implying that suspicions about his relationship with Augusta were unfounded. Caroline continued to hound him and entered his apartments, uninvited. According to Caroline's statement two years later, Byron "showed me letters & told me things I cannot repeat & all my attachment went."[4]

Augusta became increasingly concerned that her relationship with Byron was the source of continual gossip. She suggested Byron marry and settle down. When he received a letter from Annabella, he replied, asking whether her initial objections to marrying him were insuperable or whether any change on his part could remove them. She replied that she rejected him at first because she was involved with someone else. This time she accepted his proposal. She could see her mission: to reform Byron.

He went to visit her several months later and noted how she analyzed everything ad nauseam: "the least word – or alteration of tone – has some inference drawn from it . . . this comes of a *system* – & squaring her notions to the Devil knows what."[5] When Annabella worried about being inconsistent, Byron worried about her consistency.

Despite these observations, the marriage proceeded on 2 January 1815. Ada was conceived the beginning of March, about the time that they went to visit Augusta, a visit that Lady Byron would remember and replay for the rest of her life. During the visit Lady Byron analyzed every move, watched every interaction of Augusta and Byron, and determined that she would be their guardian and save them from the evil, real or imagined, that was between them. Byron did not not recall that anything extraordinary happened on the visit. He was drunk some of the time, and was beginning to have very serious financial worries. Lady Byron's family had not given him the money promised in the marriage settlement agreement, and living in London was expensive.

During the first year of marriage, Lady Judith Milbanke's brother, Lord Wentworth, died. Though he had lived with Helen

Vanloo and fathered two illegitimate children, he never married her because Lady Judith Milbanke insisted that he should not. As a result, Lady Milbanke inherited the bulk of the estate, and the Milbankes became Sir Ralph and Lady Noel in 1815.

Byron thought that Lord Wentworth's estate would help to ease his financial burdens, which were overwhelming since he was unable to sell Newstead Abbey, but Lord Wentworth's estate was a financial mess. Tormented by creditors, Byron continued to drink, had an affair, and spent hours pacing the floor in their rented London home followed by his menagerie of dogs and birds, barking and squawking. In desperation Annabella invited Augusta to help her control Byron, but Augusta was not successful in taming him either. Hobhouse came to visit a week before Ada was born and noted that things were not going at all well.

Augusta Ada Byron was born on Sunday afternoon, 10 December 1815 at 13 Piccadilly Terrace in London. Her father wrote in a poem that she was "the child of love – though born in bitterness, and nurtured in convulsion." When Ada was just a month old, Annabella took her to visit her grandparents. Annabella wrote Byron a famous letter in which she cautioned him not to "versify" – strange admonishment to make to a poet!

Several weeks later Byron was informed by his father-in-law that Annabella wanted a separation. Byron admitted there were problems but he protested. Annabella left Ada in the care of her parents and went to London to meet with her attorney, Stephen Lushington. She voiced her suspicions about Byron's incestuous relationship with Augusta, but Lushington said he needed more proof. In addition, there were rumors that Annabella was not the virtuous and caring mother she proclaimed herself to be. Lushington advised her to write letters of concern about Ada. She did. It was feared that the case, including the issue of Ada's custody, would go to court.

It was very difficult for a woman at that time to obtain a separation. Accusing a husband of sins like adultery, though enough reason for a man to gain separation, was not enough for a woman. Even though Byron's behavior was never considered exemplary, more serious sins had to be found. Ada's custody was an issue as well, since children did not automatically go to the mother. There were rumors that Byron wanted Ada to be in the custody of his sister Augusta. Lady Byron was worried. She had given extensive testimony after the separation to Lushington about the visit to Augusta the previous March. She gave Lushington more details in order to build a successful case, but Lushington needed corroborating evidence. It may be imagined how relieved Annabella was to receive a letter from Caroline Lamb in March 1816: "I will tell you that which if you merely menace him with the knowledge shall make him tremble."[6] After meeting with Caroline, Lady Byron had the evidence she needed.

Byron knew about various allegations against him but was furious when he received a paper from Lady Byron's attorneys that stated: "Lady B. positively affirms that she has not at any time spread reports injurious to Lord Byrons [sic] character." Hobhouse and Byron, reading this document, considered it clearly "the *bribe* for separation." Hobhouse described: "Byron was indignant . . . I said the disavowal was in itself not sufficient. Lady Byron must not only disavow the rumours having been spread but that the specific charges – that is incest and . . . made no part of her charges."[7]

Byron agreed to the separation, left England on 25 April 1816, and dubbed Lady Byron the "Mathematical Medea." Augusta Ada, from that time on, was called Ada. Ada's custody was not solved as simply. She was made a Ward of Chancery and put in Lady Byron's sole custody. Byron was afraid Lady Byron might take Ada to a foreign country where the law would allow him no parental control. In January 1817 he wrote Augusta and she forwarded the letter to Lady Byron. He wrote: "I require an explicit answer that Ada shall not be taken out of the country on any pretext whatever. . . I repeat that I have no desire to take the child from her, while she remains in England, but I demand that the infant shall not be removed. . ." Byron won that battle.

Ada's heritage consisted of two diametrically opposed points of view: her mother, the archetype of the new industrial age who could use analysis, facts, and objectivity to gain her clearly defined goals, and her father, the romantic poet, who took life as it came without predetermined goals and used imagination to view the world through a subjective lens. He died fighting for the independence and liberation of a foreign nation. This conflict was especially difficult for Ada since her parents separated when she was only five weeks old. Yet, throughout her life her father's heritage could not be ignored. In frustration, Ada verbalized this struggle when she wrote in an undated fragment to Lady Byron: "You will not concede me philosophical poetry. Invert the order! Will you give me poetical philosophy, poetical science?" Lady Byron never saw the connection.

A Brief Summary of Ada's Life

Lord Byron went off to the continent, sending back a collection of gifts for Augusta's children and a crystal specifically for Ada. He spent the summer of 1816 in Switzerland with Percy and Mary Shelley. The movie *Gothic* described the events that summer on the shores of Lake Geneva when Mary Shelley conceived the story *Frankenstein*, now considered the first story about artificial intelligence, and Byron wrote the poem *Darkness,* describing the end of the world. During this period he fathered a daughter, Allegra, with Mary Shelley's step-sister Claire Clairmont. He then moved to Italy, where he established the longest relationship he had with any woman – with Countess Teresa Guiccioli, whose family was very active in the Italian liberation movement. Byron had custody of Allegra, who lived in a convent. Though he would often take Allegra about, one observer remarked how it was Ada's birthday, Ada's picture, and all the information he garnered about Ada from his sister Augusta that Byron doted on. Allegra died when she was five years old in 1822. Byron hoped that Ada would be a comfort to him in his old age, but accepted that she was better off with her mother at this time.

When Ada was two years old, Lady Byron decided that she would write her autobiography to protect Ada from "the poetical colouring of circumstance." Lord Byron retaliated in his epic poem *Don Juan* by drawing a thinly veiled characterization of Lady Byron in his description of Donna Inez, whose "favourite science was . . . mathematical . . . her thoughts were theorems, her words a problem . . . she was a walking calculation . . . in short . . . a prodigy." And that was precisely what Lady Bryon expected Ada to be – a mathematical prodigy. Lady Byron was determined that Ada would be a mathematician and a scientist, not a poet like her father.

Though both Dr Frend (Lady Byron's tutor) and Augusta cautioned Lady Byron about putting pressure on five-year-old Ada to learn from dawn to dusk, Lady Byron proceeded with her "system" of education. When Ada remarked that she wished that she could get to the end of arithmetic, she was reprimanded. Ada recognized her error and wrote in her journal for Lady Bryon's inspection, "I was rather foolish in saying that I did not like arithmetic and to learn figures, when I did – I was not thinking quite what I was about. The sums can be done better, if I tried, than they are."

It was on Sundays, when Ada did not have formal classes, that the theories of the Swiss educator Pestalozzi were integrated into Ada's educational program. Pestalozzi was one of the first educators to gear instruction to the level of the child by using concrete objects. Working with blocks, Ada had to form a design. Ada's governess, Miss Lamont, was pleased with how animated Ada became and how she took more pleasure "in imagining for herself as she proceeded" than in being guided by a model. This was a very astute observation because Ada followed that pattern throughout her life.

Ada's health was often precarious. At age seven she complained of severe headaches. At thirteen she contracted the measles and was bedridden for three years with serious side effects of the disease. Lady Byron made sure that Ada received a rigorous education in mathematics despite her physical impediments. In addition, Ada was introduced to the fruits of the Industrial Revolution: machines and factories. To round off Ada's education, Lady Byron encouraged her to know those people who were at the forefront of scientific and technological developments.

In 1833 when Ada was seventeen, she met Charles Babbage,

a forty-two-year-old widower and one of the most famous geniuses of the nineteenth century. Ada was captivated by him and his first calculating engine, the Difference Engine. In 1834 Babbage started to visualize and then make plans for another calculating engine, the Analytical Engine, which is now heralded as the first computer. Ada was witness to those speculations and was impressed by the universality of Babbage's ideas.

In 1835 Ada married William, Lord King. In 1838 he became the Earl of Lovelace, and Ada, the Countess of Lovelace. By their fourth anniversary, Ada, at the age of twenty-four, had three children: Byron, Annabella and Ralph. Ada observed and vividly described her children's personalities and their development, but she was no model of Victorian motherhood, or motherhood of any age. Her reactions to her children varied, and like most parents she had moments of adoring her children and other moments of wanting to destroy them. Even with the help of maids and servants, it was difficult for her to find enough time for her intellectual interests.

Like many aristocratic ladies, Ada had the responsibility of running three homes as well as the social duties demanded of a countess. She often balked about both. Ada wanted a "profession," whether in music or mathematics, she was not quite sure. In November 1839 she approached Babbage to help her find a mathematics teacher and by the summer of 1840, after a break of four years, she resumed the study of mathematics, primarily by correspondence.

Meanwhile, from 1834 to 1840, Babbage had toiled on his ideas and his many plans for the Analytical Engine. He tried to perfect each part of the proposed Analytical Engine, and as a result kept changing his designs. He could think about nothing else. William and Ada saw Babbage intermittently during this period and were very concerned that he was overworking himself. Though they believed in Babbage's goal to make the Analytical Engine a reality, they were frustrated that Babbage had little support in England. They were delighted when they heard that Babbage accepted an invitation to go to Turin, Italy to a meeting of philosophers to describe his plans for the

Analytical Engine.

When Babbage told Ada about the meeting in Turin, she was beginning to make progress in her mathematical studies and wondered how she might be of service to Babbage. Just a few months after Ada had this thought, Lady Byron explicitly stated what Ada had implicitly felt for many years: her father had broken the traditional bounds of the mores of society. Ada was disturbed by the revelation and referred to it as "her most <u>strange</u> and <u>dreadful</u> history." She tried to handle her emotions by drowning herself in calculus, but did not succeed. She then turned to music to express the "scorn and fury" she felt. Neither her mother nor her husband was pleased at this development and suggested that her mathematical studies would be a better path for her to follow. Once again Ada resumed, most likely in the summer of 1842, the study of mathematics.

In October 1842 Babbage's presentations at the meeting in Turin were published in French in a Swiss journal. One of the participants, an Italian soldier-engineer named L. F. Menabrea, wrote an article that summarized the technical aspects of the Analytical Engine. Ada read the article and translated it into English. When Babbage came to visit her in early 1843, she showed him the translation and he was puzzled. He wondered why she had not written an original piece. She replied that she had not considered it. Babbage then suggested she should add Notes to the article. Her Notes turned out to be longer than the original article.

Ada's Notes are remarkable because of her conceptual understanding of the Analytical Engine and her ability to express that understanding by using apt metaphors and visual examples. Her descriptions of the Analytical Engine can also be used to describe the modern computer. She put the Analytical Engine in the appropriate context, defining its limits and its potential. By understanding the significance of the Analytical Engine in the development of science and technology, she expressed a vision for it that still has meaning today. This pattern, fitting her conceptual understanding into an appropriate context and then visualizing the future, is one that Ada applied to many aspects of her life.

After she wrote the Notes, Ada's desire for a profession was inhibited by her chronic ill health, yet her own descriptions of her life between 1843 and her tragic death in 1852, at age 36, reveal her gift for describing, synthesizing, and speculating about various issues, from the nervous system to the trivia of daily life. Ada's letters are more than intellectual discussions, metaphysical speculations, and technological predictions. They reveal a fascinating human story. Dealing with trivia as well as major events, they are beautifully written, imaginative, skeptical, demanding, mocking, flirtatious, and passionate. Though Ada's work was not the foundation for other scientific and technological advances, her speculations today, almost 150 years after her death, are not as wild as they might have appeared at the time.

Ada's Letters

The format of this book is a perfect fit for the era of Internet communication. Many of us have heard Marshall McLuhan's famous quote: "The medium is the message," but it is as much a statement of fact as it is a warning. Today the medium – the way information comes to us – is so seductive that it is especially important to separate out point of view, the story teller, and the medium from the actual content. This format of part biography and part original sources, the email of the nineteenth century, allows the reader to have a more intimate, interactive relationship with the information and come to his or her own conclusions – that is the promise and the power of the 21st century. Since literary remains are a skewed sample, the narrative informs the reader about what the selections represent. The reader may choose to read just the biographical narrative, or skip parts of the book, just as one cruises the Internet; however, in so doing, the reader might miss the significance of what Ada did and why her struggle to integrate her heritage is of critical importance to all of us today.

Just as Ada in her Notes describing Babbage's Analytical Engine selected enough information to give the reader an understanding of that innovative idea, I have tried to use the same strategy to enable the reader to meet, through her letters, a remarkable woman. The strategy and dating procedure that I used are clearly presented in the original version of *Ada, The Enchantress of Numbers*. Although this revised book contains formal acknowledgments, footnotes, and bibliography, I would like to acknowledge Ada's letters; Babbage's fascinating books; the many Byron scholars such as Leslie Marchand, the late Malcolm Elwin, the late Doris Langley Moore, and Lady Longford; and George Lakoff's marvelous book, *The Metaphors We Live By*. These sources provided invaluable insights into the importance of Ada's intellectual and personal struggle.

Since *Ada, The Enchantress of Numbers* came out in 1992, excerpts are now on over twenty Web sites, from Yale University to universities in New Zealand. Most of the sites I have found have properly credited those excerpts. People who copy excerpts from this book should be mindful of the copyright statement at the beginning of this book.

Ada as a Modern Myth: A Pathway to the 21st Century

Ada was not only an unusual woman of the nineteenth century – she is a symbol and a myth for many people today. Myths can be based on fantasy and used as fantasy, but they can also be used to convey a deep understanding of the needs of a civilization. They can be used as a bridge to a new conceptual framework – a pathway to the 21st century.

More people know Ada's name through her association with the birth of the computer revolution than as Byron's daughter. Yet, being Byron's daughter gives her letters a passion that is critical to understanding her, her letters, and her description of the first computer. Many educators today use information about Ada in their schoolrooms. A presentation I did for the National Council of Teachers of Mathematics, called "Poetical Science," highlights Ada's skills and is now part of a mathematics textbook being used by over 243 school districts in the United States. Much information and misinformation about Ada is found in the popular press, and as I write this, an excellent and original work, a virtual reality movie, *Conceiving Ada,* is being released. I hope that *Ada, The Enchantress of Numbers, Prophet of the Computer Age: A Pathway to the 21st Century* will help to put Ada and her accomplishments in perspective by providing Ada's actual words, "the real stuff."

Ada could not have imagined that one day a computer software language would be named after her, and that she would become a symbol to people who use *Ada*. I have chosen Colonel Rick Gross, U.S. Air Force, intimately familiar with *Ada*, the software language, to help me annotate Ada's Notes and relate those Notes to the software language. Colonel Gross's views expressed herein are his own and are not to be construed as an official policy or position of the U.S. Department of Defense.

Throughout Ada's life it was drummed into her that she had a destiny, a mission to accomplish. As Byron's daughter she accepted that destiny, trying to shape it to fit with her own character. She was always questioning and trying to discover the reason for her own existence, a path she termed <u>Poetical Science</u>.

I hope this selection of Ada's letters, and my biographical narrative, will provide an understanding of who Ada was, what she symbolically represents today, and how her pattern of thinking might be a bridge to the future.

Some predictions are based on conceptual understanding and some are just chance, but in the last year of Ada's life she wrote what she thought was her destiny:

> . . . I think when you <u>do</u> bye and bye, see certain productions, you will not even despair of my being <u>in time</u> an Autocrat, in my own way; before whose <u>marshalled regiments</u> some of the iron rulers of the earth may even have to give way! –
>
> But of <u>what</u> <u>materials</u> my <u>regiments</u> are to consist, I do not at present divulge. I have however the hope that they will be most <u>harmoniously</u> disciplined troops; – consisting of vast <u>numbers</u> & marching in irresistible power to the sound of <u>Music</u>. Is this not very mysterious? Certainly <u>my</u> troops must consist of <u>numbers,</u> or they can have no existence at all, & would cease to be the particular sort of

troops in question. – But then <u>what</u> are these <u>numbers</u>? There is a riddle.

In light of the interaction between the computer and nuclear power, *Ada* is an appropriate trademark or "symbol" of the U.S. Department of Defense. The critical connections that Ada made between poetry and science and analysis and metaphysics are the same connections needed in the 21st century to enhance conceptual understanding. Without these connections, computer science could lead to the vision her father had in 1816 of the dark end of things:

> I had a dream, which was not all a dream
> The bright sun was extinguish'd, and the stars
> Did wander darkling in the eternal space,
> Rayless, and pathless, and the icy earth
> Swung blind and blackening in the moonless air;
> Morn came and went – and came, and brought no day.

Ada did not want what he described in his poem *Darkness* – she wanted light. She wrote to her mother:

> I have now gone thro' the <u>night</u> of my life, I believe. I consider that my <u>being</u> began at midnight, and that I am now approaching the <u>Dawn</u>.
> My sun is rising with a <u>clear,</u> <u>steady,</u> & <u>full</u>, rather than <u>dazzlingly brilliant</u> light, and is illuminating all around me. He will I expect gradually run his course, to his zenith, with the same full, steady, even, light; and <u>then,</u> <u>maybe,</u> he will eventually set amidst rosy, golden, dazzling clouds, that may show to <u>me</u> something of the Spirit Land to which with <u>his</u> last rays <u>I</u> must gently depart, & he will tell me to leave for mankind in my footsteps a little of that brightness from <u>Beyond</u>, which he has reflected on <u>my</u> head, an earnest, an indication, a glimpse of that which the great Future will unroll!–
> Now all this is highly figurative. Perhaps it is <u>too</u> figurative for you, or for anyone. Perhaps it is too glowing, too imaginative, too enthusiastic.

But it was none of these for Charles Babbage, the pioneer of the first computer, who suggested:

"Forget this world and all its troubles and if possible its multitudinous Charlatans – every thing in short but the Enchantress of Numbers."

1.
Cats and Flying Machines
[1824-1828]

ADA WAS BROUGHT UP in the sole custody of her mother, Lady Byron, who tried to protect Ada from the notoriety of being Lord Byron's daughter by keeping her out of the limelight. If there were a *People* magazine at that time, Byron would no doubt have been on the cover and his family tormented by the paparazzi.

Ada spent the first seven years of her life in several rented homes far from London. When her Mother went off for health cures, Ada was left with her grandparents or Lady Byron's spinster friends, Louisa Chaloner, Mary Montgomery, and Selina Doyle.

Lady Byron decided that Ada was a most precocious child, especially in the field of mathematics, and supervised her rigorous education from the time she was four years old. Ada was taught by a variety of governesses who never lasted very long. When Lady Byron could not find a suitable governess, she taught Ada herself. Discipline was strict. Lady Byron set up a system of reward and punishment. Ada was given paper "tickets" when she performed well, and the "tickets" were confiscated when she did not meet her mother's expectations. When "tickets" did not motivate Ada to do her lessons, she was put in a closet until she realized the error of her ways.

When Lord and Lady Byron separated in 1816, Byron left England for the continent, where he kept in contact with Ada through his sister Augusta. During his time in Italy he produced volumes of epic poetry and prose. A picture of Ada was always on his desk. In his letters to Augusta he expressed his interest in the direction of Ada's education: he wanted her to learn music and Italian. When Lady Byron reported that Ada was interested in mechanical things, Lord Byron was not disappointed. "One poet in the family was enough," he remarked. Lady Byron was relieved. She was anxious to see that Ada's imagination was bounded by mechanical and mathematical facts.

Ada could not help but wonder who her father was. When she asked her mother whether a father and a grandfather were the same, she was so severely rebuffed by her mother (as Ada recounted almost thirty years later to her attorney, Woronzow Greig) that she "acquired a feeling of dread toward her mother that continued till the day of her death."

Ada's correspondence reveals that although she tried to please her mother, her feelings for her parents were complex. Conflicting emotional and intellectual seeds were planted in her childhood. In the foreground was the factual, scientific, technological world of her omnipresent mother, and in the background was the amorphous image of the romantic absent father.

When Ada was seven and a half years old, she became very ill with a mysterious disease that affected her eyesight and gave her headaches. Her education was halted on doctor's orders. Lord Byron heard about the illness in 1823, soon after he arrived in Greece to help liberate Greece from the Ottoman Empire and was so disturbed that he could not even write in his journal. He was relieved to receive a letter from Lady Byron in early 1824 detailing Ada's improvement.

Ada was never to know her father. In April 1824 Lord Byron became ill with the flu and died in Missolonghi, Greece at the age of thirty-six. According to the account of his valet Fletcher, the last words Lord Byron spoke were: "Oh, my poor dear child! – my dear Ada! my God, could I have seen her! Give her my blessing . . ."

When Lady Byron informed Ada of her father's death, Ada cried. Lady Byron concluded that it was for her, not her father, for how could the child feel sadness for a father she had not known.

Lord Byron's body was carried back to England on the ship, the *Florida*, and huge crowds watched the funeral entourage of forty-seven carriages pass through the streets of London. Several of his friends urged that Byron be buried at Westminster Abbey, but perhaps because of the notoriety of the separation and Byron's reputation as being "mad and bad," he was buried instead near his ancestral home, Newstead Abbey, in a small village church at Hucknall Torkard.

His cousin George Anson Byron, a naval officer, became the seventh Lord Byron. The new Lord Byron was a close friend of Lady Byron's, and he went with his family, including his son George (who was eighteen months younger than Ada) to visit Lady Byron and Ada. Ada pleaded with her mother to have George come to live with her as she did not have many companions or siblings, but Lady Byron did not agree to Ada's request. The first letter is edged in black in memory of the death of her father.

To Lady Byron

Tuesday, 7 September [1824]

My dear Mama. I got my fryed fish yesterday. Frank goes today, but he is still Gobblebook for he is reading Captain Hall. I have got a good deal of cold. . . I hope she liked the needle-book. I should wish that whatever good conduct you hear of on my part of that you do not give me a reward because I think the reward of your being pleased with me sufficient besides when you do that I don't do the good thing because I know I ought to do it but because I want to obtain the reward, and not because I know it to be right, and if I was encouraged in this, when I was grown up I should be a very disagreeable creature, and I should never do any good without I had a reward. Puff is on the sofa in the drawing room. I am neting a purse. Good bye Yours affectionately

Ada

SINCE GEORGE DID NOT GO to live with Ada, she turned for comfort to her cat, Mrs. Puff. Animals were to play a great part in Ada's life, especially since Lady Byron was often absent on health cures or busy being a "good Samaritan."

By 1825 the Wentworth estate had been settled, and Lady Noel had passed away. Lady Byron was a very wealthy woman, even by the standards at the time. In addition to estates in Leicestershire that she rented out, she also owned coal mines. Throughout her life she was an astute investor and managed to increase her holdings.

Politically, she was a Whig as Lord Byron had been; however, she did not decry industrialization but attempted to help farmers make the transition to an industrial society. Lady Byron was involved in many educational endeavors. She sponsored industrial and agricultural schools at a time when only one out of eleven children received a formal education. The first school she established was based on the school begun in Scotland by Mrs. Henry Siddons, a member of a prominent acting family.

Lady Byron was interested in the ideas of Emanuel DeFellenberg, who had established a school in Switzerland where aristocratic young men learned practical as well as intellectual skills. Cooperative groups were set up throughout England and America to foster moral, social, industrial and agricultural development.

In June 1826, two years after Lord Byron's death, Lady Byron went to London to make final preparations for taking Ada on a trip to the continent. Ada was left in the care of Louisa Chaloner and Miss Briggs, Ada's attendant. Louisa Chaloner told Ada she was not pretty. Although Ada was quite upset, she used the comment to explore her feelings and concluded that vanity was "the cause of all people's foibles, and unhappiness. . ." Seventeen years later Ada continued the discussion and wrote to Charles Babbage about her opinion of vanity. Ada spent her time developing mathematical skills with Hugh Montgomery, the nephew of Mary Montgomery.

To Lady Byron

Thursday, 1 June 1826   Library House, Hastings

My dearest Mammy... Today I have been doing some Italian,
and I have written about Arrowroot, and ... I have been puz-
zling hard at a sum on the rule of three which I could not do.
The question is "If 750 men are allowed 22500 rations of bread
per month how many rations will a garrison of 1200 men
require?" I think by the time you come back I may have learnt
something about decimals, I attempted the double rule of three
but I could not understand it, however I will not give it up yet,
the book does not teach as well as you do ...

Have you got me a governess yet? ... Hugo is in ecstasies
that he is soon to have the kitten... I have written you a long
letter in revenge for it write me a much longer one. I must now
conclude, If you have too much to do, pray don't write to me at
all, I am dying to ride over on horseback to Battle to meet you
on Wednesday. Good bye, Yours affectionately

A. Ada Byron

ADA EMBARKED WITH HER MOTHER and her new governess,
Miss Stamp, for the continent in late June 1826. They trav-
eled with an entourage of friends and one of Lady Byron's
cousins, Robert Noel, who remained Ada's friend and correspon-
dent for the rest of her life.

Robert was one of four sons of the Reverend Thomas Noel,
Lord Wentworth's illegitimate son. If Lady Byron's mother had
not prevented the marriage of her brother, Lord Wentworth, the
Noels would have inherited the Wentworth fortune, estimated as
varying from about £3000 to £6000 a year (approximately ten to
twenty times the annual teacher's salary of £300 at the time).
Lady Byron felt herself under a financial obligation to her
cousins and paid for their education. Robert received a stipend
of £100 per year. Lady Byron encouraged him to drop out of
medical school and pursue a career in writing about science,
and he began to spend a great deal of time in Germany circulat-

ing in scientific and aristocratic circles.

Ada enjoyed the company of her new governess and touring on the continent for fifteen months. She wrote to Mrs. Joanna Baillie about the beautiful views of the Alps from every street in Turin and how she enjoyed watching the punch and tumblers parading through the streets. Turin was later to be an important city in the life of Charles Babbage.

Ada drew chalk sketches of the exquisite scenery in Switzerland. She was impressed by the steamboats on Lake Lucerne and inspired by the organ music she heard in the churches. At this time, Ada wrote that her future vocation (she termed it her destiny) might be in the field of vocal music.

When Ada and her mother returned to England, Lady Byron rented a home, Bifrons, near Canterbury. In early 1828 Lady Byron went away for a health cure for many months. Even though Ada continued to observe every antic of her cat Puff, she was very lonely and her imagination began to soar. She played with the idea of flying, an ancient myth since the Greek Daedalus attempted to escape a Cretan prison by fashioning wax and feather wings. Ada's imaginative approach was scientifically sound. Many of her ideas about flying in 1828 predate Henson's design for an aerial steam carriage in 1842.

Ada started on her unique path to understanding science and technology, a combination of imagination and experimentation.

To Lady Byron

Thursday, 3 February 1828   Bifrons, near Canterbury

My dearest Mammy. Though your nice little letter which I received this morning consisted of only three lines yet the words "much better" made it most welcome to me . . .

I am going to begin my paper wings tomorrow and the more I think about it, the more I feel almost convinced that with a year or so's experience & practise I shall be able to bring the art of flying to very great perfection. I think of writing a book of <u>Flyology</u> illustrated with plates, if ever I really invent a method of flying. With respect to my present new idea on the subject I have but one doubt about its complete success but I am inclined to think that overcoming the difficulty I speak of (if it exists) depends only upon trick and rack in which case continual and persevering practise alone would completely surmount it, but by means of paper wings I shall explain all to you when I see you, & listen to your opinion and advice on the subject. – Your very affectionate <u>Carrier</u> <u>Pigeon</u>

A.<u>A. Byron</u>

To Lady Byron

Wednesday, 2 April 1828   Bifrons near Canterbury

My dear Mammy. Since last night I have been thinking more about the flying, & I can find no difficulty in the motion or dis-tention of the wings, I have already thought of a way of fixing them on to the shoulders and I think that they might perhaps be made of oil silk and if that does not answer I must try what I can do with feathers.

I know you will laugh at what I am going to say but I am going to take the exact patterns of a bird's wing in proportion to the size of its body and then I am immediately going to set about making a pair of paper wings of exactly the same size as the birds in proportion to my size. I shall make my paper wings stiff with wire and, though I do not intend to begin making any experiment with such wings, yet I shall when we next meet fix them on to my shoulders and show you what my plan for flying is, which I do not think that I could well make you understand by any other means. Should you think, (which however I do not think you will), my plan not likely to answer I have two other new ones in store which might also do.

I ought not to forget to tell you that in my new flying plan if it answers I shall be able to guide myself in the air by a method I have lately thought of. – I have now a great favour to ask of you which is to try and procure me some book which will make me thoroughly understand the anatomy of a bird and if you can get one with plates to illustrate the descriptions I should be very glad because as I have no inclination whatever to dissect even a bird. I do not think that without plates, I could be made thoroughly to understand the anatomy of a bird. – . . .

Miss Stamp desires me to say that at present she is not particularly pleased with me on account of some very foolish conduct yesterday about a simple thing, and which she said was not only foolish but showed a spirit of inattention, and though today she has not had reason to be dissatisfied with me on the whole yet she says that she can not directly efface the recollection of the past. Goodbye, Your affectionate <u>Pigeon</u>

A. A. <u>Byron</u>

To Lady Byron

Monday, 7 April 1828

Bifrons near Canterbury

My dear Mammy. Today I have been flying particularly well and I think you will really say I have much improved in that exercise. My wings are going on prosperously but do not expect to see a pair of <u>well</u> proportioned wings though they are quite sufficiently so for me to explain to you all my ideas on the subject of <u>flying</u>.

As soon as I have brought <u>flying</u> to perfection, I have got a scheme about a . . . steamengine which, if ever I effect it, will be more wonderful than either steampackets or steamcarriages, it is to make a thing in the form of a horse with a steamengine in the inside so contrived as to move an immense pair of wings, fixed on the outside of the horse, in such a manner as to carry it up into the air while a person sits on its back. This last scheme probably has infinitely more difficulties and obstacles in its way than my scheme for flying, but still I should think that it was possible and if I succeed in the flying it will be an encouragement <u>to me</u> to try the horse. – . . .

Your very affectionate <u>Carrier Pigeon</u>

A. <u>Ada</u> <u>Byron</u>

LADY BYRON SCOLDED Ada for spending too much of her time on flying. She believed it diverted Ada from her studies. That suggestion did not please Ada, who was very lonely and searched for new interests. In the following excerpt from a gossipy five-page letter, she carefully laid the groundwork for her mother to accept her new passion.

To Lady Byron

Sunday, 12 October 1828   Bifrons

To the Right Honourable
Immortal Grand <u>Crockery</u> Panjandrum
                              Lady Noel Byron
from the little Panjandrum of <u>Clay</u>. – Oh Alas!

My dearest Mammy. Here we are at Bifrons and strange to say I have just been riding on horseback: a fact to which Miss Stamp herself stands a witness. Here is the explanation of this mystery. When Lady Athlone came here – Mary Cole, very wisely had the ropes in the flying room taken down and all your harness and saddles placed there to avoid all confusion in the stables with Sir William's harness and things. Now this morning I took a fancy to go and look at your harness in the flying room, and had no sooner gone in than I discovered an excellent side-saddle belonging to you, and placed on a wooden frame called a horse which happens to be just the height that you would like for a little pony to trot about upon in the park. I immediately put my foot in the stirrup and jumped up; and may therefore truly say that I have been riding on a horse. If this sort of riding satisfied me, I could easily ride at all times, and in all places. I have been thinking this morning of the real riding; and to speak truly, if you were to stay here this winter, I should be quite satisfied in point of riding if I had a pony not bigger than a donkey. We think that you must have forgotten the little shaggy pony you have here, not Robert's of course, but the other which though its walk is probably not smooth enough for you or Fanny, yet seems in every respect calculated for me to ride. It looks very gentle, and is just a little pottering thing about the same size as the one you tried at Epsom.

It probably does not canter, but that would not be of much consequence to me, as I should not certainly want to scour the country. –

You have a side-saddle and plenty of bridles quite ready, and I really think that when you came back, an arrangement might be made without any trouble or inconvenience to any one for me to ride little Shag, as I call him . . .

Yours most affectionately

A. Ada Byron

THE FOLLOWING MONTH Ada began her formal studies in geometry, attacking the theorems with gusto. She used logic to dispute her mother's claim that she was a "flawed stone." Ada wrote: " . . . if you choose to call _me_ a jewel of _any_ class, even of the _last_, it is very inconsistent of you, afterwards to call yourself a flawed stone. . ."

To Lady Byron

Friday, 22 November 1828   Bifrons

My Dearest Mammy. Hugo's Geometry went yesterday by Creswell. I am much delighted with the entertaining pamphlet you left me on that subject. I possessed myself this morning of the preliminary part, which I found very amusing indeed. I am a little afraid of the Theorems, however I must attack them boldly & do my best. . . Now then. Good bye Ever Your Affectionate Corngiver

A. Ada Byron

2.
Conversational Litigation,
<u>*I Am an Altered Person,*</u>
Ada Meets Babbage,
The Rainbow
[1829-1834]

ADA'S LIFE CHANGED DRAMATICALLY at the end of 1828. Not only did she have to cope with being thirteen and the on-set of puberty, but Miss Stamp left to get married. Rather than hire another governess, Lady Byron enlisted the help of various friends, Sophia Frend (Dr William Frend's daughter), Dr King, and Miss Arabella Lawrence, to guide Ada's studies. Sophia Frend was not iconoclastic like her father but very prim, proper, and critical. Dr King was head of the Brighton Cooperative Society, and his wife Mary was an Evangelical Christian. Miss Arabella Lawrence, a Liverpool educator, was also involved in the Cooperative movement.

Just as Lady Byron was making plans for Ada's education, Ada contracted the measles in early 1829. Instead of designing flying machines and riding horses, she was bedridden until mid-1832. Lady Byron believed Ada's illness was an opportunity for her to concentrate on her studies. She hired Miss Lawrence to supervise those studies, primarily by correspondence. Miss Lawrence made visits every few weeks to the bedridden girl.

Ada's letters to Miss Lawrence were scrutinized by Lady Byron, who added her own postscripts. She warned Miss Lawrence that Ada had a propensity to "conversational litigation" and asked Miss Lawrence to help curb this trait since it was "very necessary for this habit to be checked, both as disagreeable and inconsistent with the feeling of respect."

The following letters contrast sharply with the previous ones, which were light-hearted and fun-loving. Ada's snide comments might have been not only a reflection of a thirteen-year-old's adolescent rebellion but also the mirroring of her mother's behavior. Just at this time Lady Byron was involved in her own "conversational litigation," enlisting a wide range of people to join in her fight to prevent Thomas Moore (a close friend of Lord Byron's) from publishing his biography explaining Lord Byron's perception of the separation.

Ada walked a precarious line. She tried to set the boundaries of her own identity and at the same time please her mother.

To Sophia Frend

11 February 1829

My dear Miss Frend. I have finished my Planetarium all but the part which relates to the Ephermeris which I have not yet got. I am extremely obliged to you and your father for the excellent descriptions you sent me.

Mama has been very unwell since she came here and has been obliged to be cupped. She must for a few days avoid writing which has prevented her from communicating with Mr Frend. Yours sincerely   A. A. Byron

To Arabella Lawrence

[No date, Summer 1830]

My Dear Miss Lawrence. . . I really am so happy at the thoughts of your return; I hope, indeed I think you will perceive improvement in me in some points; but I am afraid there is one thing that you won't like much, viz: my arguments. Perhaps I have not disputed quite so often during this week; but when I do take up any point, I speak with as much anxiety and vehemence as if the fates of the nation depended on my words. I perceive that whatever good effects may have resulted from my illness, it has nevertheless had one very bad effect upon me; for, from the quiet & unvaried life I have necessarily led for the last year and a half, the smallest incidents have become to me matters of as much importance as the French revolution to Charles the tenth; this may seem incomprehensible to you who really have important objects affecting the happiness of others; to argue about; but I certainly believe that I feel as much weight of care upon me about the issue of an argument upon the merest trifle, as Charles the 10th could do on the subject of the loss of his kingdom. And I am sure that in order to correct myself of my disputation habits, the only thing for me to be occupied during some part of every day, about the happiness of other people; thus giving me subjects of real importance to think about, which would set common every day trifles before me in their true light. . .

Ever your most grateful   A. A. Byron

I N 1832 ADA AND HER MOTHER moved to Fordhook, a mansion that had been the home of the writer Henry Fielding. By the end of 1832 Ada's health had improved, but she was overweight from being bedridden. In letters not included here, Ada continued to voice her passion for horses and music. Miss Lawrence had been replaced by a series of tutors for chemistry, Latin, shorthand (William Turner), and music. Ada was watched carefully by her mother's spinster friends, whom Ada dubbed "the three Furies." Sometimes they were not watching too closely.

According to Ada's confidences to Woronzow Greig more than fifteen years later, despite being constantly watched, she had an affair with her tutor, most likely in late February or early March 1833. Although the date of her fall from grace is uncertain, Greig's account of the event, whenever it occurred, was vivid. He always saw Ada in the context of being Lord Byron's daughter, and in turn Ada loved shocking Greig. In recollecting the event, Ada told him that she and her lover went about as far as they could go without "connection."

Inevitably, Ada was caught. When Selina Doyle observed

her being a little too familiar with the tutor, she alerted Lady
Byron. The tutor was fired. Furious and distraught, Ada ran off
to his home but was promptly returned to Fordhook. After the
escapade, Ada received sermons from Miss Briggs, Dr King, Mrs
King, and others. Turner was paid a partial salary for the year
on April 6, and although Ada's other tutors are listed as having
being paid after that date, Mr Turner's name never appeared in
the bank books again.

After some soul searching, Ada saw the error of her ways, according to her letters, and began to ride her horses, Dubby and
Sylph, with a wild passion. She also began to lose her baby fat.

Ada had many other things on her mind in addition to sex.
She was presented at Court on 10 May 1833. Lady Byron described this event on 13 May in a letter to Mrs King: "Ada wore
White Satin & Tulle. She was amused by seeing for the first time
– the Duke of Wellington – Talleyrand – and the Duke of Orleans.
– She liked the straightforwardness of the first – the second gave
her the idea of an 'old monkey' – the third she thought very
pleasing." In a letter started on 19 May, but written over several
days, Ada defined her relationship with her mother.

To Fanny Smith

5 Aug. 1832   Brighton, Albion House Preston St

My dear Fanny. Will you tell Miss Doyle that Sylph and I both
improve very much, but I have not yet commenced riding her;
Mama is quite satisfied with her progress & mine, and desired
me to say that for the first time in her life she saw me canter up
to the Hotel door circling round a corner, holding my reins
entirely to her satisfaction, a few days ago. My studs are of
every colour; black, grey, chestnut . . . & my riding master keeps
me in good order. . .

I have a guitar master, a Spaniard of high rank, Count
Urraea, but who has been reduced to poverty & expelled from
his country along with many other unfortunate refugees; he is a
very beautiful player indeed, and whoever calls the Guitar a
paltry instrument . . . ought to hear him play; I have heard him

produce the effect of a full band or orchestra at a little distance, of the harp, the castagnettes; in fact he does anything with the instrument. – Give my love to Miss Doyle. –

Ever Affectionately Yours   A Ada Byron

To Lady Byron

[Postmarked 8 March 1833]   Fordhook

My dear Mama. I must now thank you for your last very kind letter. Though deeply impressed by the ceremony I attended on Sunday for the first & I hope not the last time, certainly I had no inclination to weep. – The more I see & the more I think & reflect, the more convinced do I feel that no person can ever be happy who has not deep religious feeling & who does not let that feeling be his guide in all the circumstances of life. Had I entertained my present sentiments two years ago, I should have been now a very different person from what I am. But I am yet quite in the spring of life & hardly indeed full blown. I trust I may be spared many years longer, & may thus be allowed the opportunity of showing that I am an altered person. –

We went to the Concert yesterday, and there was much that was worth hearing. We dined afterwards at Mrs Montgomery's. I am sorry this is my last Dubby day, & I do not particularly enjoy the thoughts of the dinner tomorrow. – I am sure your house will be clean when you come back, never was such scrubbing & scouring! – It is just Sylph time, so Good Bye. Your very affectionate   A Ada Byron

To Lady Byron

Sunday, 19 May 1833   Fordhook

The principle point on which I differ from you is "your being constituted my guardian by God forever." "Honour thy father & thy mother," is an injunction I never have considered to apply to an age beyond childhood or the first years of youth, in the sense at least of obeying them. Every year of a child's life, I consider that the claim of the parent to that child's obedience, diminishes. After a child grows up, I conceive the parent who has brought up that child to the best of their ability, to have a claim to his or her gratitude. The child should serve the parent & next himself to make him or her comfortable, the same as a friend to whom he was under an obligation. But I cannot consider that the parent has any right to direct the child or to expect obedience in such things as concern <u>the</u> <u>child</u> <u>only</u>. I will give a practical illustration of my meaning. If you said to me, "do not open the window in my room," I am bound to obey you whether I be 5 or 50. But if you said to me, "don't open your room window. I don't choose you should have your window open," I consider your only claim to my obedience to be that given <u>by law,</u> and that you have no <u>natural</u> right to expect it after childhood. The one case concerns <u>you & your</u> comfort, the other concerns <u>me</u> <u>only</u> and cannot affect or signify to you. Do you see the line of distinction that I draw? I have given the most familiar possible illustration, because I wish to be as clear as possible. Till 21, the law gives you a power of enforcing obedience on <u>all points;</u> but at that time I consider your power and your claim to cease on all such points as concern <u>me</u> <u>alone,</u> though I conceive your claim to my attention, and consideration of <u>your</u> convenience and comfort, rather to increase than diminish with years . . .

CHARLES BABBAGE, 1833

> Sir Alphabet Function, a knight much renowned,
> Who had gained little credit on classical ground,
> Set out through the world his fortune to try,
> With nought in his pate but his x, v, and y.
>
> Charles Babbage

O N 5 JUNE 1833, Ada attended a party where she met Charles Babbage. Babbage, who later dubbed himself Sir Alphabet Function, was a 42-year-old mathematician and widower, who, like Ada's father, had gone to Cambridge University. He was regarded as one of the greatest minds of the nineteenth century. His interests ranged from mechanical dolls to mechanical machines, from the probability of games of chance to the moves in a chess game. Compared to most of the adults Ada knew who were so very proper, Babbage was an iconoclast. He viewed politics, science, technology and mathematics in an unusual way.

When Babbage was a student at Cambridge, he founded the Analytical Society with his friends John Herschel and George Peacock. They wanted the university to adopt Leibnitz's notation of calculus rather than Newton's method. The three men were determined to do their best to leave the world wiser than they found it.

Herschel became a noted astronomer. George Peacock, later to become the Dean of Ely, was responsible for major educational reform at Cambridge. Babbage left us with the conceptual building blocks for the birth of the computer revolution. It all began, according to Babbage's autobiography, *Passages in the Life of a Philosopher* (see Appendix I), when Herschel encouraged Babbage's idea to build an engine that could calculate numbers by steam. Babbage thus became part of the history of brilliant mathematicians who turned their attention to the mechanical and technological manipulation of numbers.

One of the first mechanical calculating machines was invented in 1642 by the French mathematician Blaise Pascal, who was nineteen years old. Bored by working on his father's accounts, Pascal invented a machine that was capable of addition.

In 1671 the German mathematician Leibnitz designed a machine capable of multiplication by means of repeated additions using a stepped reckoner. Babbage adapted the stepped reckoner in the design of his first calculating engine, the Difference Engine.

Ada, in this series of letters, made only remote references to Charles Babbage, but it is evident even from these remarks that someone very special had come into her life. The bulk of her correspondence with him, which Babbage preserved, took place during the summer of 1843, when Ada was writing the Notes describing his Analytical Engine. For the years 1833-1835 we must rely on other sources to gain an idea of Ada's relationship with Babbage and the Difference Engine. The following information comes primarily from Lady Byron's diaries and letters found in the Lovelace-Byron Collection; Babbage's marvelous autobiography, *Passages*; Anthony Hyman's *Charles Babbage, Pioneer of the Computer*; and other sources listed in Appendix I.

In the Notes describing Babbage's Analytical Engine, which Ada wrote in 1843, one of her greatest strengths was her ability to distinguish between Babbage's calculating engines. Also, Ada's passionate support and belief that Babbage's engines were not only of practical advantage, but would lead to a deeper understanding of mathematics and science, most likely stemmed from her first encounter with the Difference Engine. It is important, therefore, to understand the history of the Difference Engine and highlight it as Ada first saw it and as Babbage described it in June 1833.

In 1823 Babbage received what can be considered the first government grant to support technological development to build his first calculating engine, the Difference Engine. The government supplied part of the cost, but by the time Babbage met Ada in June 1833, funding of the engine was in jeopardy. A part of the engine was built. It had a feedback mechanism and when completed would be able to print out logarithm tables that could be used for navigation. It worked on the theory of calculating differences.

Babbage had supervised construction of the engine in a fireproof building with a glass roof behind his house in Dorset Street. The machine was 29 inches tall, 27 inches wide and 36 inches deep, which is about the size of a small modern business computer.

Babbage was famous for Saturday night soirées at his home that attracted hundreds of the most prominent people of the time: the Duke of Wellington, Charles Darwin, Charles Dickens, Michael Faraday, Andrew Crosse (an experimenter in electricity), and Harriet Martineau (a popular science writer). The star attraction of these soirées was the Difference Engine.

Babbage was delighted to show the Difference Engine to his guests. When he showed it to the Duke of Wellington for the first time, he left pieces of music lying near it. He knew the Duke loved country dance music, and Babbage wanted him to associate the engine with music. Instead, the Duke remarked how the engine might be a help in handling all the variables a general might need in conducting a military campaign.

When one woman saw the Difference Engine, as Babbage recollected in *Passages*, she asked him: "If you put in the wrong figures, will the right answers come out?" Today, we refer to such statements as GIGO, or Garbage In Garbage Out. Harriet Martineau described Babbage's response to such questions: ". . . I always thought he appeared to great advantage as a host. His patience in explaining the machine in those days was really exemplary. I felt it so, the first time I saw the miracle, as it appeared to me."

Babbage invited Ada to see the miraculous Difference Engine a few weeks after they met. Ada's impression of the Difference Engine was recalled by Sophia Frend more than fifty years later: "Miss Byron, young as she was, understood its working, and saw the great beauty of the invention." An excerpt from Lady Byron's letter to Dr King on 21 June gives us more information about the first time she went with Ada to see the Difference Engine:

> We both went to see the <u>thinking</u> machine (for so it seems) last Monday. It raised several Nos. to the 2nd & 3rd powers, and extracted the root of a Quadratic equation. I had but faint

glimpses of the principles by which it worked. – Babbage said it had given him notions with respect to general laws which were never before presented to his mind – For instance, the Machine could go on counting regularly, 1, 2, 3, 4, &c – to 10,000 – and then pursue its calculation according to a new ratio . . . He said, indeed, that the <u>exceptions</u> which took place in the operation of his Machine, & which could not be accounted for by any errors or derangement of structure, would follow a greater number of uniform experiences than the world has known of days & nights. – There was a sublimity in the views thus opened of the ultimate results of intellectual power.

Lady Byron's calling the Difference Engine a "thinking machine" was not an accurate description of its ability but a common name given to such machines at the time. It was a calculating engine. Numbers were put on successive carriages consisting of toothed wheels that had ten digits marked on the edge. Whenever any wheel, in performing addition, passed from nine to zero, the projecting tooth pushed over a certain lever. Babbage described how a calculation could be done in nine seconds, quickly and accurately.

Babbage's description, as Lady Byron recorded it, must have touched Ada, since it was more than just an explanation of the mechanical manipulation of numbers. To both Ada and Babbage the manipulation of numbers was not just a practical exercise but a path to mathematical and metaphysical understanding.

Metaphysics was not an area that interested Lady Byron. She regarded Babbage's metaphysical views as "the whim of the moment," and preferred for Ada to be grounded in what she considered the facts. She was always watching for signs of Lord Byron's influence – his passionate nature – in Ada's personality. Lady Byron enlisted the sober Dr King to help Ada not only with mathematics, but to insure that Ada's passions were directed along a proper path. Dr King wrote Ada sermons, and when she asked him concrete questions about mathematics, he replied that he was puzzled. He explained that as a student at Cambridge University he seldom read a book that was not assigned.

Despite Dr King's moralizing, when Ada met Babbage, learning more about mathematics, science and technology became not a duty to her but a joy. Ada stepped back from asking Dr King any more questions about mathematics and attempted to find solutions by using her own imagination, visualizing mathematical problems and solutions. She would not destroy her imagination but use it in her own way. She could not understand the rainbow and directed her questions not to Dr King but to her mother's old tutor, Dr Frend.

To Dr William King

Sunday, 9 March 1834   Fordhook

Dear Dr King. I must thank you for your kind & affectionate letter of encouragement & advice. How far I am really & permanently awaking to a sense of religious duty & religious obligations, time alone can prove. I cannot but feel very distrustful of myself. To you, as well as to Mrs King, do I consider myself to be deeply indebted – more so than I can express. You may remember perhaps that in more than one of our "pleasant walks," you said much on the subject of controlling our imaginations and our thoughts. I often think of this now, as I cannot but perceive that it is a paramount duty for one in my circumstances to exercise this sort of self-government, and indeed upon its' performance depends my future welfare. I must cease to think of living for pleasure or self gratification; and there is but one sort of excitement, if indeed it can be called by that name, which I think allowable for me at present, viz: that of study & intellectual improvement. I find that nothing but very close & intense application to subjects of a scientific nature now seems at all to keep my imagination from running wild, or to stop up the void which seems to be left in my mind from a want of excitement. I am most thankful that this strong source of interest does seem to be supplied to me now almost providentially, & think it is a duty vigorously to use the resources thus as it were pointed out to me. If you will do me so great a favour as to give me the benefit of your advice and suggestions as to the plan of study most advisable for me to follow, I shall be most grateful. – I may say that I have time at my command,

& that I am willing to take <u>any</u> trouble. It appears to me that the first thing is to go through a course of Mathematics – that is to say – Euclid, and Arithmetic & Algebra; and as I am not entirely a beginner in these subjects, I do not anticipate any serious difficulties, particularly if I may be allowed to apply to you in any extreme case. My wish is to make myself well acquainted with Astronomy, Optics &c; but I find that I cannot study these satisfactorily for want of a thorough acquaintance with the elementary parts of Mathematics... In short, here I am, ready to be directed! I really want some hard work for a certain number of hours every day... Yours most gratefully & affectionately

A.A. Byron

To Dr William Frend

15 March 1834   Fordhook

Dear Mr Frend. You have always been very goodnatured to me, & have seemed exceedingly willing to answer any ignorant questions. I shall be very grateful if you will be kind enough the first time you have a few spare moments, to write me a letter about rainbows. I am very much interested on the subject just now, but I cannot make out one thing at all, viz: why a rainbow always appears to the spectator to be an arc of a circle. Why is it a curve at all, and why a circle rather than any other curve? I believe I clearly understand <u>how</u> it is that the colours are separated, and the different angles which the different colours must make with the original incident ray. I am not sure that I entirely understand the <u>secondary</u> rainbow. –

Is the spectator's eye supposed to be in the centre of the circle of which the arc of the rainbow forms a portion? –

Have you read Mrs Somerville's new book, and what do you think of it? – I hope I am not boring you with my ignorance. Pray remember me most kindly to your daughter Sophia, believe me, Yours sincerely obliged

A Ada Byron

3.

Make It Part of Your Mind,
Solving Unsolvable Equations,
The Royal Road to Mathematics
[1834-1835]

EVEN THOUGH DR FREND was helpful in trying to answer Ada's questions, he was growing old. He encouraged her to become friendly with Mrs Somerville, a prominent scientist, whose *Connection of the Physical Sciences* had just been published. Today there is a college named in her honor at Oxford University.

Mary Somerville was essentially self-taught. Her interest in mathematics was sparked by reading mathematical puzzles in a sewing magazine. After the death of her first husband, she studied mathematics on her own, reading Newton's works in Latin. George Peacock (Babbage's friend) used her translation from French of LaPlace's work as a textbook at Cambridge University. In addition to respecting her as a scientist, everyone regarded Mrs Somerville as a gentle, humble, and kind human being.

From Mrs Somerville's letters to Ada, it is apparent that she was anxious not only to help Ada with her mathematics but also to put that passion in a proper perspective. As a result Mrs Somerville encouraged Ada in all pursuits from knitting caps to riding on the downs. Ada became a frequent visitor (sometimes at her own request) to the Somerville home at the Royal Hospital in the Chelsea section of London, where Dr Somerville (Mrs Somerville's second husband) was a physician.

This was Ada's first involvement with a traditional family. She became close friends with the whole family: Martha and Mary, Mrs Somerville's daughters, and Woronzow Greig, her son from her first marriage. Greig became Ada's friend, confidant, and attorney. She spent many happy moments playing music, riding horses, and going to Babbage's home with members of the Somerville family.

Ada refers in her letters to Dionysius Lardner, who was a friend of Babbage's. Lardner was a popular scientific personality who gave lectures about the Difference Engine at the Mechanics Institute, which Ada attended. She used the mathematics textbooks he wrote and was particularly impressed by his article about the Difference Engine published in the *Edinburgh Review*. By June 1834 Lady Byron wrote that Ada regarded "the Difference Engine as a friend."

Ada continued to attend Babbage's Saturday night soirées. He sent her an invitation enticing her to come to see the "Silver Lady," one of the two automatic dolls he had. In *Passages* he described one of the dolls, "whose eyes were filled with imagination . . ."; however, from Ada's letters to Mrs Somerville, it appears that she was more captivated by the Difference Engine than by the "Silver Lady."

During the summer of 1834 Ada had a chance to see the Industrial Revolution in action. She went with her mother on a trip to the north of England and visited many of the new factories blossoming throughout England. They visited printers and ribbon factories in Coventry. Lady Byron drew a picture of a punched card used to instruct the loom. After several weeks of factory tours in the Midlands, they settled down with one of Lady Byron's friends, Lady Gosford, and her two daughters Annabella (named after Lady Byron) and Olivia (Livy) Acheson. While the mothers were busy with a health cure, Ada decided to make good use of her time and teach Annabella and Livy mathematics.

As a teacher Ada revealed how she approached a subject that normally does not evoke passion, especially in young women. She used both reason and imagination to get her mathematical message across. Like her mother, she insisted on excellent performance, but her method was not "tickets." Instead, she tried to build an esprit de corps by involving her students in a mission. She defined mathematical terms verbally and visually. Ada's letters were written on Cambridge quire paper, a parchment paper about four times the size of regular paper. She used color and what were then considered vulgar instruments – compasses and protractors. She scolded her students for using indirect proofs when a direct proof should be used. As did her father, she believed that mathematical explanations and allusions are reinforced by the apt use of metaphor. Of particular interest is Ada's letter about the inflected line, a topic in topology, where she approached her subject by integrating what today we refer to as analog and digital skills.

Even though Ada was busy with mathematics and Babbage's Difference Engine, she did not forget her music. She was still playing the guitar and at this time started harp lessons.

Varying moods and language emerged in Ada's growing correspondence. She began to show different aspects of her personality depending on whom she was writing to. She continued to write to Dr King, explaining her method of understanding mathematics; to his wife, explaining the state of her moral development (perhaps more to please than to give the true state of her thoughts); and to Mrs Somerville, explaining more truthfully, without fear of a sermon, what she was doing, thinking, and feeling.

To Mary Somerville

Thursday 19 [March 1834]   Fordhook

Dear Mrs Somerville. I hope I may have the pleasure of meeting you on Saturday Evening at Mr Babbage's. I am going with Miss Montgomery to dine at Mrs Murchison's, & we shall be at Mr B [Babbage]'s for a short time in the evening. I have not seen him yet, but he sent a very respectful message through Mrs Murchison, inviting Miss Montgomery & me to his Saturday parties. I am afraid this may be my only chance of seeing you for the next three weeks.

Hoping therefore to see you, believe me, Most Sincerely Yours   A. Ada Byron

To Dr William King
24 March 1834   Fordhook

Dear Dr King... I do not consider that I know a proposition,
until I can imagine to myself a figure in the air, and go through
the construction & demonstration without any book or assistance whatever...
Yours affectly   A. Ada Byron

To Dr William King
13 April 1834   Fountain Cottage Tunbridge Wells

Dear Dr King... Euclid is going on very well. Lardner's Euclid
is like going through 3 others – there are so many propositions
& so much matter in the notes. I am in the 2nd book, & shall be
very glad when I am fairly master of it. The deductions from it
are so numerous & so similar, that it requires a good deal of
repetition to retain them all distinctly. – Will you answer me
the following question? Can it be proved by means of propositions & deductions from the 1st book only, that equilateral
triangles being constructed on the sides of a right angled triangle, and also on the hypotenuse, the sum of the triangles on the
sides is equal to the triangle on the hypotenuse? I think I have
heard that this is capable of proof by the 1st book, but that the
proof is a difficult one. It strikes me that it ought to be as
demonstrable as when the figures are four-sided &
equilateral...
Ever Yours Affectly & obliged   A.A.Byron

To Mary Somerville
Tuesday Evening, 8 July [1834]

My dear Mrs Somerville. I am only afraid I must have seemed
to you very presuming for venturing to suggest such an arrangement as I proposed, and I assure you I had little difficulty in
making up my mind to be so impudent. Nothing but my great
anxiety about the machine, [Babbage's Engine] could have

made me so I believe. But I think you must be fond enough of those things, to sympathize with my eagerness about them. I am afraid that when a machine, or a lecture, or anything of the kind, comes in my way, I have no regard for time, space, or any ordinary obstacles. This is the only excuse I can offer, and you must always tell me whenever I encroach on your very great kindness. . .

Believe me ever, Your sincerely obliged

A Ada Byron

To Dr William King

1 September [1834]   Buxton

Dear Dr King. We are now at Buxton in Derbyshire. We came to see our friend Lady Gosford, who is here for her health. She is one of those who certainly make religion the rule of life. Her daughters too are doing me great good I believe, though in a very different way. They are amiable young women, with good natural abilities, but of rather indolent habits. I am trying to excite & rouse them to various objects of study & interest, and as much as possible to make my little talents, such as they are, of use to my young friends, whom I would gladly serve, were it only for their Mother's sake. I teach during three fourths of the day at least, and find that I myself gain more perhaps than they do. I am endeavouring to induce one of them to take up Mathematics, but I have rather a difficult task there; however I do not despair. . . hope I have gained somewhat from the many new & beautiful specimens of nature (both human & inanimate) that have been presented to my eyes & ears. A tour of friends and of natural beauties too, is the very perfection of a tour, so far as enjoyment is concerned, except perhaps that I could wish to add that it was also a tour of manufactures and machinery. . . This Machinery reminds me of Babbage and his gem of all mechanism. At the beginning of the last Edinburgh Review, there is a very clever article on this Machine, which you should read. I can hardly judge whether it will be perfectly intelligible to one who has never seen the original, or models; but I

should think it would to you. At all events a great part would.
Pray get it. . . Yours most gratefully   A Ada Byron

To Mary Somerville

Monday Morning, 8 November [1834]   Fordhook

My dear Mrs Somerville. . . May I trouble you the first time you
see either Mr Babbage, or his son, to say how exceedingly
obliged I am to the latter for his unexpected kindness in sending me the plates & account of the Machine, which is exactly
what I was in want of; & is a very great help to me. I am very
busy copying the Steam Engine paper I carried off from Mr
Babbage's the other day. I have finished two & expect to complete the 3rd in a few days. I hope he is not in want of them, &
would have no scruples in claiming them immediately! Believe
me with kind regards to your daughters. Yours most sincerely
                                                         A Ada Byron

To Annabella and Olivia Acheson

10 November 1834

[To Annabella]. . . I have written out for you the proof of the
little Proposition mentioned in the last paragraph of Note to
Prop 1st; and if you have not already made it out for yourself, I
think you will find this perfectly clear & easy. It is a very
pretty little Theorem – so neat & tidy – the various parts dove-
tail so nicely! I wish to know if I have made myself perfectly
intelligible. . . Do not be alarmed at the apparent length of the
proof, for you must remember that it would look much shorter
in print. –

    With respect to Lardner, I am much more anxious that you
should become thoroughly familiar with book the 1st up to the
point I told you in the Division Chapter, than desirous to push
you on; so do not be in a hurry, but make all you read of it as it
were, part of your mind!

    Remember you are to apply to me in every difficulty – how-
ever small, however great – without scruple, and I shall be

much disappointed, if you do not, my dear little Friend. How much time per day do you generally spend on Mathematics? I wish to know.

So this you see, is the commencement of "A Sentimental Mathematical Correspondence carried on for years between two young ladies of rank," to be hereafter published no doubt for the edification of mankind, or womankind. –

My own Mathematical Studies are prospering! – . . . Ever yours mathematically . . .

For Livy

My dear Livy. A few lines I must write you to thank you for your nice letter. Early rising is more in force than ever, and Trifles diminish both in number & magnitude – or to speak in mathematical language both in an Arithmetical & a Geometrical sense. I believe I may say with <u>truth</u> that there has been no apparent trifle since you left.

Your guitar is in progress, but I certainly shall not keep it a day even. It would be wicked to do so. Believe me, Yours ever musically

To Annabella Acheson

19 November 1834

My dear Annabella. I was much gratified by your letter & very intelligent questions & remarks. You are going on as well as possible. But I will now reply in order to your observations.

The note on the <u>inflected</u> line is only difficult to you, <u>because it is so easy</u>. There is in fact nothing in it, but you think there must be some grand mystery hidden under that word <u>inflected</u>! I will make it clear to you immediately.

Whenever from any point <u>without </u>a given line, you draw a line to any point <u>in </u>the given line, you have <u>inflected</u> a line <u>upon</u> a <u>given</u> line:

ADA'S DIAGRAM OF INFLECTED LINES

Let AB be the given line, & C any point <u>without</u> it, D any point <u>in</u> it; then, in all these diagrams, CD is a line <u>inflected</u> on AB. . . The word <u>inflected</u> means literally <u>to throw upon</u> or to <u>turn upon</u>, & is derived from two Latin words, <u>in</u> and <u>flecto</u> – to turn. . .

Remember above all things, that you are not to hurry over anything. There is plenty of time, and if you lay a good & solid foundation, the superstructure will be easy, & delightful to build!

Do not become afraid of my becoming too learned to teach you. The more I know myself, the more pleasure I shall take in going over with you the ground I have myself successfully trans-versed; I get so eager when I write Mathematics to you, that I forget all about handwriting and everything else. – Your progress is the only thing I desire. Believe me, Your affection-ate & untenable Instructress   A. Ada Byron . . .

T HE PREVIOUS LETTERS to Mrs Somerville, Annabella, and Livy Acheson were written during an exciting period in Charles Babbage's life that Ada was witness to – the birth of an idea that has changed all our lives. Ada did not write letters about this exciting period; however, she did leave an account of several evenings during which the fate of the Difference Engine was discussed and Babbage revealed his conception for a new calculating engine. What Ada heard at this time no doubt formed the foundation of her understanding of the Analytical Engine, which is now regarded by many as the conceptual birth of the computer revolution.

Ada's impressions are found in Lady Byron's diaries. Lady Byron accompanied Ada on a few occasions to the dinner parties, but when she was ill, Ada went on her own to dine with Mrs Somerville and Babbage. When she returned home she recounted to her mother what had been discussed during the evening. These discussions give us a glimpse of Babbage's creative mind. During this time he discussed the importance of color and how he had experimented with the printing of logarithm tables using different inks and colored paper. This information might have prompted Ada in her next letter to instruct Annabella in using color in drawing a geometric figure.

The major issue discussed was the Difference Engine. On the evening of 15 November, Babbage was concerned about the future of the Difference Engine since the British government was not going to financially support the completion of the engine. According to the *Times*, the week of 15 November was filled with stormy weather and political turmoil. On the 15th there were rumors that Lord Melbourne (Lady Byron's first cousin) had resigned as prime minister and that Lord Wellington would head a caretaker government. A few days later, on the 18th, those rumors were confirmed. Since the duke was impressed with the Difference Engine, Babbage hoped that this change in government would mean that he could get the necessary funds to complete the Difference Engine.

Ada went with Mrs Somerville to see Babbage on 28 November, and the discussion that evening was lively. According to Lady Byron's diaries, Ada listened as Babbage and Mrs Somerville argued about the reasons for the lack of continued support of Babbage's plans. Mrs Somerville suggested that perhaps the world was not ready for such an engine. Babbage replied that if he did not develop it, someone else would. It appeared that Sir Robert Peel, no friend of the Difference Engine, would become the new prime minister.

The discussion then turned to miracles and mathematics. Babbage alleged that the engine could show that miracles were not only possible but probable. Ada listened to his ideas and was captivated by the thought of where mathematics might lead. She continued to teach Annabella. From the tone of her letters, Ada was becoming overbearing. She looked forward to her next evening with Babbage and Mrs Somerville.

To Mary Somerville

Wednesday Morning [postmarked 26 November 1834] Fordhook

My dear Mrs Somerville. I am very much obliged to you for your kindness, & shall be most happy to spend a few hours so delightfully on Friday. I shall be at No 10 Wimpole St by 1/2 past 11 o'clock, & as this is not out of the way from Chelsea to Mr Babbage's I should be obliged to you if you would be so good as to call at the door as you pass, & then our carriages can go together, as I should wish to arrive with you. I shall therefore wait in Wimpole St till I am summoned.

Mama has never yet ventured out of the house, but she continues on the whole better, & hopes soon to have the pleasure of calling on you.

With my kind regards to your daughters, believe me, Yours most sincerely obliged   A. Ada Byron

ON 15 DECEMBER Ada once again spent the evening with Babbage and Mrs Somerville. This time Babbage explained his theory of the process of discovery. He said: ". . . the difference of opinion amongst mankind could be traced to the different degrees of power to individualize." Babbage continued by explaining that a person would have a general idea of an objective and then would proceed, for example, in designing a machine, to the particular part of the mechanism that could achieve that objective. He concluded that between these two types of minds there are various grades: ". . . the rarest mind is that which unites both powers in considerable degree." In order to understand anything we ought first, said Babbage, to place ourselves at a distance from it and then approach gradually to investigate the details. Astronomy, therefore, was the most per-

fect science since we were forced to view it at a distance.

Babbage then described the strange sensation that the first glimpse of his discovery aroused in his mind, ". . . when the possibility of throwing a bridge from the known to the unknown was first apprehended." Babbage used an example to clarify his point. A man was standing on a mountain with mountains surrounding him on all sides. The man felt closed in by the mountains. As the man watched, the mist in the valley below began to disperse and he caught a glimpse of a river whose course he could not follow, yet he felt sure that there must be an egress.

Babbage recalled in *Passages* how he conceived the idea of the Analytical Engine: ". . . it occurred to me that it might be possible to teach mechanism to accomplish another mental process, namely – to foresee. The idea occurred to me in October, 1834. It cost me much thought, but the principle was arrived at in a short time. As soon as that was attained, the next step was to teach the mechanism which could foresee to act on that foresight."

Lady Byron wrote in her journal the evening of 15 December that Babbage reported he had made a discovery ". . . in the highest department of mathematics. – I understand it to include the means of solving equations that hitherto had been considered insolvable." Lady Byron discounted Babbage's views as "unsound and paradoxical." Ada, on the other hand, stated to her mother that she was touched by the "universality" of Babbage's ideas: to Ada it was the threshold of a new world.

4.

Love and Marriage, Establishing Three Households, The Birth of Byron
[1835-1836]

THOUGH ADA CONTINUED TO CORRESPOND with Annabella and Livy in 1835, her social life centered on the Somerville family and London activities. It took several hours to go by carriage from Fordhook to London, and Ada often spent the night at the Somerville home in Chelsea.

Woronzow Greig wrote a short biography of Ada after her death, about twenty handwritten pages, which is found in the Somerville collection. He recalled that when he first met Ada, she still suffered lingering side effects from her bout with the measles – giddiness while riding horses and moments of nervousness and fatigue. However, Ada's busy schedule – her continued interest in mathematics as well as her harp, riding, and active social life – filled every moment. In the first letter in this series it appears that Mrs Somerville was concerned that Ada was overdoing all these activities, but there was no stopping her.

In the spring of 1835 the nineteen-year-old Ada, on a visit to Sir George Phillips's home in Warwickshire, was introduced to William, Lord King, who was thirty years old. He was from an illustrious family whose social, political, intellectual, and religious background was similar to Ada's; he was considered a conscientious, quiet, intelligent young man. He had been a classmate and close friend of Woronzow Greig's at Cambridge University.

William had just returned from the Ionian Islands, where he was secretary to his cousin, Lord Nugent, governor of the Islands. A portrait of him in his Ionian dress evokes memories of

Lord Byron's famous portrait in Albanian dress. But the comparison stops there because William was a very precise man. His interests were scientific and technological.

Their courtship was short and sweet, which was not unusual at the time. The following "courtship letters" contain thoughts and language that one would expect; yet Ada's individuality comes through clearly. Ada was concerned that because she was Lord Byron's daughter, she was the object of fascination. She was cautious about information of her forthcoming marriage being published before she was ready to announce the news. She shared the "news" with Mrs Somerville on 21 June but did not tell Woronzow Greig, Mary, or Martha. Woronzow Greig recalled how he found out about the coming marriage at a luncheon with William. Greig then teased Ada about her summer plans, but she still refused to divulge or even hint at the impending marriage.

The adults surrounding Ada at this time included Miss Carr, the spinster sister-in-law of Dr Stephen Lushington's (Lady Byron's attorney), Miss Mary Montgomery, and Miss Selina Doyle. Ada dubbed these three spinsters "the three Furies." They were, according to Ada, always interfering in her life, though she did not criticize them to her mother. At the other end of the spectrum was Mrs Somerville, who was deeply concerned about Ada's happiness and replied to one of Ada's mathematical letters: "Riding on the downs, & even in the riding school conduces more to health than reading mathematics."

To Mary Somerville

Friday, 20 February [1835]   Fordhook

My dear Mrs Somerville. I cannot help laughing at the idea of Mama's being "angry" because I chose to tire myself at your house. I assure you that in the first place, she says she is too happy to allow me to profit by your kindness, & in the next place she is too much used to my tiring myself at home, & in short I could bring forward half a dozen reasons at least to prove, (excuse my presumption) that your proposition is an absurd one, & quite unworthy of Mrs Somerville.

But I am beginning to be alarmed, for I am afraid you mean to keep me in desperate tight order, & do you know I dare not disobey you for the world? I cannot deny that I was shattered when I left you, but then I am for some unaccountable reason in a weak state, altogether now, & at this moment can hardly hold my pen from the shaking of my hand, though I cannot complain of being what people call ill. –

In a few weeks I dare say I shall be quite strong, (particularly if I see a good deal of you). When I am weak, I am always so exceedingly terrified, at <u>nobody knows what</u>, that I can hardly help having an agitated look & manner, & this was the case when I left you. – I do not know how I can ever repay or acknowledge all your kindness; unless by trying to be a very good little girl & showing that I profit by your excellent advice. I feel that you are indeed a very sincere friend, & this makes me very happy I assure you.

Pray give your daughters my best & kindest wishes <u>for their early rising</u>. – Mama desires her kind regards; & if you hear of any invention for <u>starching</u> young ladies fingers, pray let me know, for mine really are like old rags. Hoping to see you again very soon. I am ever, Yours most sincerely obliged

Augusta Ada Byron

To Mary Somerville

4 April 1835   Brunswick Hotel, Brighton

My dear Mrs Somerville. We have been here now ten days, having arrived as proposed on Wednesday last week. Perhaps you will hardly believe that Miss Carr & I were sadly fatigued with having travelled fifty miles in an easy carriage in the course of two days, but such was undeniably the fact. I travelled the greater part of the way outside, which much lessens the disagreeableness of a journey to me, & our carriage has fortunately a box both behind & before. You see I begin by being circumstantial, which your daughters were kind enough to wish I should be. We are all very glad that we are here...

As for myself, I am much stronger. I have been taking what has always been to me the finest of all medicines – horse exercise; & if I am to believe your daughters' own account of their feelings on this tender subject, I am afraid I shall excite in them hatred, & malice, & envy, & all manner of bad passions, when I say that I generally ride in the riding school everyday, and – best of all – leap to my heart's content. I assure you I think there is no pleasure in way of exercise equal to that of feeling one's horse flying under one. It is even better than waltzing. I recommend it too as a nervous medicine for weak patients. –

I am very well able now to read Mathematics, provided I do not go on too long at a time; & as I have made up my mind not to care at present about making much progress, but to take it very quietly & and as much as possible merely for the sake of improvement to my own mind at the time, I think I am less likely to be immoderate. . .

I wonder why it did not occur to any of our bright understandings, that you & your daughters might have come to Brighton too. It is not too late either now, & so pray take it into consideration. . . Most Sincerely Yours   A. Ada Byron

To William, Lord King

Monday, 8 June [1835]   Fordhook, Acton

Your letter has been an unexpected happiness to me this morning; but I cannot allow you even to mention such a thing as my "repenting" of anything that has passed between us. I do not know when I have been in so calm and peaceful, & I hope I may add with truth, so grateful a state of mind, as since Thursday last . . .

I am going this evening to my friend Mrs Somerville's to stay the night. She has kindly offered to take me to a Concert, which my love of music cannot resist. Sir George Philips and I intend having a tête-a-tête ride tomorrow before my return. By the bye, it will be just one week since our ride from Chelsea, and of which it is possible you may have some recollection.

Four more "<u>long days</u>" must pass before Friday Morning will arrive, & so both until then and for ever afterwards, you

must believe me, with the most sincere Attachment & Gratitude, Yours   A. Ada Byron

WILLIAM AND HIS SISTERS, Hester and Charlotte, all
moved in the same social circles as Ada did and attended
Babbage's parties. Ada started to call Hester and Charlotte "her
sisters" even before the wedding; however, her relationship was
cautious with the rest of the family since William did not get
along with them. He had a cool relationship with his mother,
and argued with his sister Emily and his brother Locke.

With the wedding only a few weeks away, Lady Byron felt it
was her duty to inform William of Ada's escapade with her tutor.
Ada very subtly refers to it in a letter to William by stating her
gratitude to him for marrying her.

Before the wedding Ada received letters from Mrs King and
many of Lady Byron's spinster friends. They wrote her that she
should be thankful that William was marrying her and instructed her about how to be a proper wife. It must have been a
relief to receive a letter from the Reverend Samuel Gamlen, a
Yorkshire minister, who poked fun at the impending marriage.
He wondered whether there was a "Royal Road to Love," since
he thought there certainly was not one to mathematics.

Ada and William were married by the Reverend Gamlen at a
small ceremony held at Fordhook. Ada chose Livy Acheson as
her maid of honor. In the marriage settlement William was
given one-half of Ada's legacy (£3000 annual income), which he
would receive upon the death of her mother. In exchange, Ada
was to receive annually from William a £300 discretionary income, about the annual salary of a tutor at the time.

To William, Lord King

Sunday Afternoon, 28 June [1835]   Fordhook
I think I had better begin writing to you today, as I may not
perhaps have much time after I get your letter tomorrow, par-

ticularly as my harp mistress is coming to me. Sir George
Philips & Mr. Philips & <u>our</u> uncle have just been here. We were
<u>all</u> of us very shy, except Sir George; so you may imagine that
we were rather a foolish party. However I like Lord Ebrington
very much, & I am sure his manners to me were very cordial
through his shyness, which was fortunately transparent. . . Sir
George was at Mr Babbage's last night, & says we (that is you
& I) were well talked over by the philosophers &c; but I was
happy to hear from a friend who was in Town yesterday that
many persons had not yet heard of our engagement. They may
probably know it by this time, but we are in none of the papers,
not even the Court Journal. . .

What a happiness it is to feel towards any one what I do
towards you, & to feel too that it is reciprocal! – I do not think
there can be any earthly pleasure equal to that of reposing
perfect trust & confidence in another, more, especially when
that other is to be one's husband.

I hope, my dear William, that I shall make you a very affectionate & a very conscientious wife, & shall fulfil all my duties
towards you & towards your family in such a manner as to make
you the only return I can make for all I owe you, & of which I
am so sure that I shall never be reminded by you, that I must
take care to keep the remembrance of it in my head. Now do
not be angry with me, because I have only just spoken the truth
– neither more nor less. – . . .

I have but a quarter of an hour to write to you, my dear, –
as I expected. Many thanks for your letter this morning, which
was brought to me in the middle of my harp lesson, & a very
welcome interruption it was too. . . We are in the Morning Post
& Morning Herald this morning – only a <u>slight notice</u> – nothing
that need annoy us. – Their Majesties have sent their congratu-
lations to Mama. The King particularly says "<u>he is very glad,
for that he has never heard anything but good of Lord King</u>." –
So that I do not think you are out of favour at Court, though
this is of very little consequence to us. –

My love to your Sister, if still with you, & tell her I have
been seeing about <u>Duets</u> for Harp & Piano-forte. –

And now, my Dearest, Good Bye. How <u>annoyed</u> you must be at having so much time taken up in reading my stupid letter! – Very Affectly Yours   A. Ada Byron

To William, Lord King

Sunday Afternoon, 5 July [1835]   Fordhook

My Dearest. – What a wet drive you must have had this morning; & what is more, I am afraid it is going to rain all this week, which would be rather tiresome... Mr Gamlen drove me to Brentford Church this morning in our phaeton. I suppose next Sunday I shall go to Ockham Church with you, in a character very interesting to your neighbours at all events – that of your Bride. May she be deemed worthy of her Lord, & what is more to the purpose, may she prove herself so in reality! ... but, have I the requisite perseverance & self denial? – For, properly to fulfil the duties of a wife, it requires both these qualities ... Monday Afternoon. – What a nice letter, my dear, you have sent me, & how politely & distinctly it is written too. I scarcely dare hope to see you this evening, for fear I should be disappointed ... I knew your drive would be wretched yesterday morning. How well I understand your state of spirits- sometimes too high – sometimes too low. Happily I think we shall be ballast to one another! ...

Most Affectionately & Devotedly Yours,   Ada

A FTER THEIR MARRIAGE on 8 July, William and Ada started their honeymoon at Ockham, the family estate in Surrey. They then proceeded to Ashley Combe, Porlock, near Minehead in Somerset, another family property overlooking the Bristol Channel. William had a passion for architecture and was transforming a charcoal burner's cottage into a suitable home. They also retained a London residence at 10 St James's Square, where in 1993 English Heritage placed a blue plaque in honor of Ada, "a pioneer of computing."

During their honeymoon William and Ada walked the Ash-water path, which ran through their property at Ashley Combe. It was a famous path because Coleridge and Wordsworth had also walked on the same wooded trail. She most likely read Coleridge's poetry at Dr Frend's suggestion because Coleridge organized the student defense of Dr Frend at Cambridge University. If Ada did read Coleridge, it was most likely his understanding of the nature of imagination and the creative act as it applied to poetry that would have intrigued her.

Ada had just witnessed a very imaginative description by Babbage in December 1834 of what it felt like to discover a totally new approach to the technological manipulation of numbers, and in 1841 Ada would write an essay that connected the role of imagination to the creative act in science. In the summer of 1835, just getting to know William and wandering along these peaceful paths in privacy, on foot and on horseback, was all she wanted. That did not last long.

In September Lady Byron and the wife of Dr William King visited the newlyweds at Ashley Combe. Mrs King took Ada aside and warned her that her mother was very ill. Whatever Lady Byron's illness was, she quickly improved after being with William and Ada, especially since William was very anxious to please his mother-in-law. By the end of September they referred to one another with pet ornithological names: Ada became Bird, Thrush, Avis; William became ou, Crow, Cock; and Lady Byron became the Hen.

In October after William and Ada returned to Ockham, Surrey, they were separated for the first time. William went off on practice maneuvers with the Surrey militia, and Ada went to join her mother at Fordhook. Ada realized that soon there would be another major change in her life. She was pregnant. In December William went away again, this time to their home at Ashley Combe, to do work on the estate there. Love letters flew back and forth.

Ada was busy with chores as well. In addition to running the Ockham home, she supervised the servants, took harp lessons, had her portrait painted by Margaret Carpenter, and continued to study mathematics on her own. She often turned to Mrs Somerville for help.

Ada had misgivings about the portrait painted by Mrs Carpenter. This portrait can be found on the Web site, adapicture gallery, http://www.cs.kuleuven.ac.be. Ada was very sensitive about the size of her jaw, which, from some paintings of Lord Byron, appears to be a characteristic she inherited from her father. She had never seen a painting of her father until her late teens when the Phillips painting, which had been hidden behind a curtain and turned to the wall, was finally displayed. Her description of her jaw was vivid but she never mentioned, at this time, her physical similarity to her father or her Byron heritage. Her world was confined to walking and riding through the countryside, playing her harp, and discussions of mathematics and science with her many intellectual friends.

William and Ada celebrated their first Christmas together with both the Somervilles and Charles Babbage. Babbage brought a special gift, and Ada's thank you note is the first letter we have of her correspondence with him. Ada's correspondence with Mrs Somerville was not just about mathematics, but continued to be filled with light-hearted banter.

I have deleted all mathematical formulae from Ada's letters to Mrs Somerville and Augustus DeMorgan. The literary remains of Ada's mathematical correspondence are a skewed sample since they reflect what she did not understand. She was not paying her tutors and was very sensitive to their taking their time to help her. However, it is clear that Ada always questioned, as her teacher Augustus De Morgan later pointed out, first principles or basic assumptions. Computers today can substitute a variable in a functional equation, but questioning first principles, or assumptions, is still a critical skill that we all need.

To William, Lord King

Thursday Eve, 8 October 1835   Southampton

My Dearest. The Birdie was very happy, poor little thing,

when it got its dear Master's letter. It was in bed this
morning...

I have got a very nice horse – just the thing. He is safe &
strong, & quiet to so extreme a degree that I think he will quite
break my associations of fear with riding. I rode for an hour &
a half this afternoon, & I have also had a little walk. I have
been a naughty Bird, for I contrived during my walk to gamble,
& to cheat also. – My gambling adventure is hardly worth detailing on paper. Suffice it to say that any lurking propensity
that might have existed in my mind for the chances, must have
been nipped in the bud by the timely loss of four shillings
today in exchange for a most vile basket not worth four pence.
My cheating exploit is an affair of twopence. I was not aware
that each person has to pay that sum for walking on the pier, &
nobody claimed it as it happened which was strange...

The Hen won't let me read her letter to you. I am afraid
she must have said I am a <u>bad bird</u>. I assure you I am kept
somewhat in order – poor little thing that I am! . .

My dearest husband, Your most affectionate. Birdie

A.A.King

To Lady Byron

[29 October 1835]

My dear Hen. You are not a good Hen today & I shall peck at
you... I think Mrs Carpenter mistaken in her taste about my
hair. She insists on its being either quite plain, or in curls & to
my fancy much too short, I think scarcely reaching as low as my
ear, so that I should be like a crop-cared dog. I conclude she is
bent on displaying the whole expanse of my capacious jaw
bone, upon which I think the word Mathematics should be written...

Your very affectionate Little Bird

A.A.K.

To Mary Somerville

1 November [1835]   Ockham Park

My Dear Mrs Somerville. You must not think that I have forgotten you, although it is so long since I have written to you. – I am ashamed to think <u>how</u> <u>long</u>. We only came home last week . . .

I now write, partly to <u>ask</u> news, partly to <u>give</u> news, principally &, <u>to remind you of your promises to visit us</u>. Will you name your own time, & I can only say the sooner the better, & if your stay is long it will be <u>best</u> <u>of</u> <u>all</u>. . .

I now read Mathematics every day, & am occupied on Trigonometry & in preliminaries to Cubic & Biquadratic Equations. So you see that matrimony has by no means lessened my taste for those pursuits, nor my determination to carry them on, although it has necessarily diminished the time I have at command. But I suspect it is no bad thing to be limited in that respect. . .

I have troubled you with a very long letter, & though I could add much more, yet I think it would not be <u>justifiable</u> to occupy another minute of your time. –

Believe me, Yours Affectionately   A A King

To Mary Somerville

18 November 1835

My Dear Mrs Somerville. I have another trigonometrical question to ask you, & am encouraged by your kindness to trouble you with these things, which is almost a shame too, when you are so busy. . .

Mr Greig comes on Saturday next, I am happy to say; and I think it very probable that Mr Babbage will be here next week. I wish you were at present a <u>plus</u> instead of a <u>minus</u> quantity.

The head of my picture is now completed, but I would rather not give my opinion of it, that your judgment may be unbiased. Mrs Carpenter would be very glad of your opinion & so should we. The picture is going to Town this week. Would it be asking too great a favour of you, to call at Mrs Carpenter's

some time next month to look at it?. . .Yours Affectly &
Gratefully   A.A.King

To Charles Babbage

18 January 1836   Ockham

Dear Mr Babbage. I will not any longer delay thanking you for
the Minerals, which I received a few days ago from St James's
Square. I hope I shall also find courage enough to take to
pieces one of the wooden crosses, though even with the other
before me, I doubt if I have ingenuity to put it together again. –

I have got on delightfully with Lardner's Trigonometry,
which so far as I have yet gone I think <u>excellent</u>. His road
seems at all events to be the one most suited to my mind. I
have had quantities of formulae to work out myself, & have
destroyed a great deal of paper. –

Lord King desires to be remembered to you, & we both
hope to see you here again before long. Believe me, Yours
truly   A.A. King

ADA'S INTEREST IN MATHEMATICS was not just the solving of
formulas; the visual and tactile approach to mathematics
was very important to her. Ada wanted models of geometric figures to help her understand and enlisted Babbage and Mrs
Somerville to help her find suitable ones. Models are still a wonderful way to illustrate mathematical and scientific concepts;
for example, the models of Watson and Crick explain in a simple
way the structure of RNA and DNA molecules. Today, computer
simulations of models are an invaluable tool in understanding
science.

At the end of April, Ada moved to her London home at St
James's Square to await the birth of her first child. Byron,
named after his illustrious grandfather, was born on 16 May
1836. William informed Babbage that the happy event caused
Ada to miss seeing an eclipse.

Ada was in a good mood in late August when she went with Byron, Hester, and the servants to visit Lady Byron in Brighton. When she returned to Ockham her duties as a wife and a mother began to fall into place and she tried her best to continue her musical, mathematical, scientific, and equestrian interests. William had set up an Agricultural and Industrial School at Ockham based on one Lady Byron had set up at Ealing, and Ada tried to help him by designing the curriculum.

Life was not free of worries. Throughout Ada's life she always feared her mother was on the brink of death. At this time Lady Byron described and analyzed every ache and pain, yet the doctors never found anything specifically wrong with her. Ada blamed the doctors.

To Mary Somerville

25 March 1836   Ockham Park

My Dear Mrs Somerville. Can you tell me if any solid models have ever been made for illustrating some of the Propositions of Spherical Geometry, and if so where such things are best to be had. Next to this, some extremely good plates on the subject would be a great help. The kind of propositions I refer to are those on the intersections of Circles of the Sphere; for instance the following, which I take from Spherical Geometry which precedes Lardner's Spherical Trigonometry . . . These are enough to put me in despair and I have been in danger of turning crazy in trying to imagine the circles in my mind's eye. . .
Ever yours Affectionately   A.A.King

To Mary Somerville

Sunday, 10 April [1836]   Ockham

My Dear Mrs Somerville. I was very glad to receive your letter this morning, though I had not imagined I was forgotten, Mr Babbage having mentioned in a letter to Lord King that he was making enquiries by your desire. – I only hope the person you mention may be forthcoming, and should of course be too happy to remunerate him. – Does it appear to you that Dr Ritchie, as a teacher might know of any models or very good plates? I should not wish <u>my</u> <u>name</u> to be mentioned to him, if the enquiry was made. – . . .

How much I should like to have a mathematical child, and only think what pleasure I should have in teaching it, and how capable I might hope to be too by the time it was old enough (for I should not begin I think the <u>1st year</u>). . . My love to your daughters. – Ever Yours Affectly   A.A.K.

To Lady Byron

Tuesday [Undated, postmarked 27 August 1836]

Dearest Mama. . . I am just going out riding & were there a possibility of my being in any sort of time, I would go to see you. But I could not be back till much too late. –

I <u>played</u> last night to the company, with really <u>brilliant</u> success. I never was so applauded & admired, & poor Self-Esteem is so much astonished that he can scarcely hope ever to be so successful again. Lady George was quite surprised at the performance.

> Damm the Doctors!
> Damm the Doctors!
> Damm the Doctors!
> Damm the Doctors!
> That is my only observation upon your health. –

5.

Two More Children, Ada Becomes a Countess, Gift of Tongues
[1836-1839]

M ANY PARENTS TODAY who are sharing responsibility for household chores and child-rearing tasks know how such tasks divert them from developing their professional careers. From 1836 to 1839 Ada was much too busy with motherhood, marriage, and participating in the ceremonies that marked the beginning of the Victorian era to concentrate on her career. The advantage for Ada in delaying her formal studies was that the many demands upon her forced her to develop creative and critical thinking skills.

The development of mathematical and scientific understanding can no longer be measured by the ability to add a column of numbers (a calculator can do that) or to substitute a variable in a functional equation (computers can do that), but by the ability to use and integrate a variety of skills including digital skills such as objectivity, observation, and experimentation, and analog skills such as imagination, visualization, and metaphor. These were just the skills that Ada was developing during this period. She became an observer, carefully noting her son's motor activities. She continued her search for geometric models to help her visualize spherical trigonometry and received, for her twenty-first birthday, a telescope to view the stars. Her interest in the latest happenings in mathematics and science continued unabated.

In 1837 she was pleased to receive Babbage's book, *The Ninth Bridgewater Treatise*, published by John Murray, who also published her father's poetry. The treatise explored the connection between science and religion. Babbage had expressed some of these ideas to Ada in 1833 and 1834, and Ada questioned some of his views.

All of these activities and interests marked the beginning of an era. In 1837 Princess Victoria became Queen, and Ada wondered what her reign would be like. William became the archetype of the perfect Victorian: doing his duty, outwardly unemotional, industrious, a conscientious landlord taking a patriarchal interest in his tenants. He was parsimonious, except when it came to building, which was William's passion. He was constantly enlarging his estates and would later become even more ambitious architecturally.

Ada tried to play her role as wife. She tended to the daily accounts and decorating their homes. Once again she found she was pregnant. If there was to be another child, Ada had strong opinions about what sex she preferred and shared those sentiments with Mrs Somerville, who kindly watched Byron to give Ada some rest. In June of 1837 Woronzow Greig, Mrs Somerville's son, married Agnes Graham, and they both remained Ada's close friends.

Ada's letter of 21 July might be of special interest to readers of Stephen Hawking's *A Brief History of Time* since it discusses the controversy between Flamsteed and Newton. Newton wanted data Flamsteed collected and was going to have it printed, attributing it to Edmond Halley. Flamsteed went to court and got an injunction to stop Newton from using his data. In this letter Ada mentions Sir David Brewster, a Scottish scientist who was a pioneer in the field of optics, a science writer, and the developer of the kaleidoscope.

To Mary Somerville

Friday Afternoon, [most likely early 1837]

My Dear Mrs Somerville. I am longing to hear something from you or your daughters about your little visitor ... Are you not surprised at the child's taking the weaning so quietly? Will you tell Green that I am quite strong & well, & have not a drop of milk left. – I was glad of her note. –

I think of going to Chelsea Weddy or Thursdy (we intend moving to Fordhook Tuesdy) partly to see you of course, but I must confess principally to carry away the little treasure. The house is quite different without him, & I shall hardly spare him longer. – I hope he makes himself very amiable, & displays all new accomplishments, especially that of <u>crawling</u> on all fours. I am so exceedingly well that I can hardly think there is to be a second yet. I am sure if there is, it must be a <u>boy,</u> for a <u>girl,</u> never would leave me in peace. You see I <u>cannot</u> help being spiteful about the nasty girls, and suppose I never shall until I have something in the feminine gender. – Pray read your daughters the last half- page, because it will annoy them. But I will thank you not to let anyone know my suspicions. – Whatever it is that is coming, whether boy, girl, or neuter, it has certainly put me into uncommonly good spirits . . .
Yours ever Affectionately.   A.A.King

To Mary Somerville

22 June [1837]   Ashley Combe

My Dear Mrs Somerville. . . I am so glad there is prospect of Mr Greig's marriage taking place this autumn, and I am sure I can sympathize with your ardent wish to be in the country. I am only rather sorry that you will according to your present plans, be away at the time of my confinement, as I reckoned much on the enjoyment I should have in seeing a great deal of you all in that quiet London month of September, & 2 or 3 weeks previous to the event.

I am longing to see Mr B [Babbage]'s book. . . I have gathered it is a pity it was written in much haste & is so fragmentary and underdevelopped in its' character. It seems to resemble one of the curious (<u>multum</u> in <u>parvo</u>) algebraical expressions of which you know infinitely more than I do, which under a few simple symbols involve & indicate to the initiated quantities endless in their complication & variety of mutual relations. But <u>what</u> a pity that such a mind has not in some degree filled up the crude outlines, for the benefit of those who

could not! – I fear the work will be underrated, and the circumstances you mention of the extreme haste fully accounts for
this, though it in <u>fact</u> enhances its merit & indicates the more
what might be. – However, I am criticizing what I have not
read. I think when <u>I have</u> read it, after our return to Surrey . . .
I shall probably give my opinion about it to Mr B himself.
    Would this be presumptuous do you think?
    I am doing a little here at a very snail's pace, in Mathemat-
ics. I should be devoting some hours to it now, but that I am at
present a condemned slave to <u>my</u> <u>harp</u>, no easy Task master
either. I sent it down here, determining during our stay to
devote as many hours as I had strength for, to practise every
day, & to make great progress. I play 4 or 5 hours generally, &
<u>never</u> less than 3. I am not tired at the end of it, & from habit
the position is quite natural to me & perfectly agrees with the
young master. In fact I think the exercise rather beneficial. . .
My love to the two M's. Yours ever affectionately   A.A. King . . .

To Lady Byron

21 July [1837]   Ockham

Dearest Hen. We were very glad of your letters this morning, it
being now near a week since we heard. . .
    People tell me that I seem so very little encumbered. I
wish I felt so, but I certainly show very little in front, which is
like last time. I feel <u>monstrous</u>, like a giant cask. . .
    I must now tell you about the Newton M.S. They are in Sir
David Brewster's hands and a large selection is making of
highly interesting correspondence. – The vol will, I am afraid,
be in the quarto form. It is likely to come out next year. It is
thought that the evidence from correspondence is such as to
entirely explain Newton's conduct about Flamsteed. Mr Henry
Fellows surprised me much by saying that "of theological
papers, only such will be published as are sufficient to <u>prove</u>
<u>that</u> <u>Newton</u> <u>believed</u> <u>strictly</u> in the Trinity, so as completely to
answer the <u>Unitarians</u> <u>and</u> <u>Deists,</u> who had hitherto gloried in
his authority, & appropriated him to themselves." – . . .

I suppose he must have inferred our opinions though we did not allude directly to our individual feelings.

My love to your friends. –   Avis

AFTER THE BIRTH OF Annabella (named after her grand-mother) on 22 September 1837, Ada developed cholera. According to a report at the time, it was very unusual for a member of the aristocracy to contract cholera, which was rampant in London that year because of unpurified drinking water from the Thames. Ada experimented with various cures and as a result became very thin, much to Lady Byron's dislike and William's delight. He detested anyone who was fat.

Lady Byron was a faithful believer in the latest rage, mesmerism. Ada questioned that belief and whether or not it could be considered scientific. She replicated an experiment her mother had performed: the mystery of the oscillating shilling.

Her duties as a wife continued to occupy her time. William set up an agricultural school similar to the one Lady Byron had established at Ealing, and Ada designed the curriculum. She suggested various people could help: Frederick Knight, a Somerset neighbor and publisher; Sophia DeMorgan, Dr Frend's daughter; and Harriet Martineau, a popular writer at the time. Ada suggested using Cobbett or his work. Cobbett was a radical, and his paper *Rural Rides* chronicled the daily life of ordinary people.

Still ill in 1838, she went to London to get the house at St James's Square in order. While she was there, she was criticized for not "going out into society" and performing the social commitments of an English "lady." Ada voiced her own views on the matter. She also expressed her own views on interior decoration, which was William's expertise, and they started to argue. Just at this time they received important news.

In June 1838 William was made the Earl of Lovelace, and Ada became a countess. As much as Ada wanted to keep out of the social whirl, she could not. She left vivid accounts of that exciting period: dressing for the many balls, meeting Queen Victoria, attending concerts, and seeing the opera *Norma,* by Bellini, performed with Giulia Grisi playing the part of the high priestess (Ada later uses this term to describe her relationship to Babbage's plans for the Analytical Engine). She also went to see exhibitions of the latest developments in technology such as Charles Wheatstone's telegraph, and most likely attended Michael Faraday's (the discoverer of electric magnetism) popular lectures at the Royal Institution.

Ada's portrait by Châlon, on the cover of this book, was done at this time; no doubt sittings occurred amidst a hectic schedule, discussing the latest findings of Andrew Combe, a famous phrenologist (who was quite the rage at the time), as well as helping William with his school and participating in a very active London social life. Ada spent time reading Babbage's book, the second edition of *The Ninth Bridgewater Treatise.*

Once the social season of 1838 was over, Ada settled down into domesticity and became pregnant once again. William's sisters, Hester and Charlotte, went off to Holland for a vacation, and Mrs Somerville moved to Italy. Lady Byron, now living at Acton, took the children for short periods of time; however, Ada and her mother had different views about how to discipline children. Given the strains of motherhood, Ada wondered about the intellectual contributions that women could make to the history of civilization.

To Lady Byron

[Undated, late 1837 or early 1838]

Dearest Hen. I am dismayed at hearing no tidings from you. . .

I think that on my recovery from the attack of Cholera, I considerably erred in <u>overeating</u> the quantity of food that would assist in re-establishing my strength. And that some starvation has become subsequently necessary, as a balance to my having over-loaded my system . . .

And what might be bad as a system in general, might be good as a remedy for a few weeks; & I think <u>has</u> been very useful. –

To William, the Lord King

Sunday 5 o'clock [January or February 1838]

Sweetest William. . . I had an interesting post this morning, – a curious letter from the Hen about the shilling experiment. I send it to you, but take care of it pray. Also a letter from Dr Locock, expressing the greatest interest & curiousity about the divining rod, & seeming inclined to join in investigating the subject; in consequence of which I am going to send him in a parcel . . . with some remarks & suggestions of my own, together with an account of the shilling experiment. – I have made up my mind not to let this matter rest, & shall endeavour to turn Faraday's attention to the subject. If he, Mrs Somerville, Babbage & Dr Locock, would unite in investigating it, which I think I can manage to effect, probably something would in course of time be made of it.

Am I not a fine stirrabout meddlesome avis? I have so much to write to the Hen, that I must end. Ou loving little Birdie

Ada

To Lady Byron

[January or February 1838]

Dearest Mama. The experiment has just been tried on Hester, Green & me . . . With me it is <u>very</u> marked indeed, & equally so with Green. –

The first time I tried it after holding the shilling a few minutes I felt a tingling & throbbing in the thumb & finger, & the shilling began to oscillate, at first gently, then with violence swinging all around the glass & striking the sides, then gradually subsiding to almost stillness, and beginning the same rotation of movements again. After waiting a few minutes I tried it again, & the effect was then <u>immediate,</u> & not as at first after some minutes. I repeated it in the same way three or four times, with less effect however the last time. This is about half an hour ago, & on trying it again just now, it had no perceptible effect, as if the power whatever it is were worn out. –

I should add that when the oscillations were at their
height, I had a sensation at the top of my head like a gentle
current flowing, & with which I am rather too familiar, since it
has accompanied some of my worst derangements of circulation. –

We have been trying with Hewitt, with whom there is no
effect. – When W comes in, he shall try, without our telling him
anything about it . . .

To Lady Byron

Wednesday [Circa 1838]

Dearest Mama. . . I am going to enquire of Mr Knight, who
William says is the best person for publishing these kinds of
books . . . & we could then decide on what would be a proper
offer to make Mrs De Morgan. I think that the expense &
bother of publication should be saved her, & that she should
perhaps have the profits; or half the profits . . . Miss Martineau
could write the book for parents, if she would avoid any of her
queer theories. –

To Charles Babbage

2 March [1838]   Ockham

Dear Mr Babbage. I have just received amongst a number of
packages from Town, the new edition of your work which you
have so kindly sent me; & I will not delay another day thanking
you for it, as I am much gratified by the kind recollection it
shows. –

You may possibly have heard of the very tedious & suffering illness which has occupied so many months, since a Miss
<u>King</u> has been added to our family. Though I am now to all
<u>appearance</u> perfectly well again, & am in fact most wonderfully
improved, yet I am still far from being really strong. – But for
these untoward circumstances, Lord King or I myself should
probably have written to you long ago, & have strongly urged a
visit or visits to Ockham. –

With Lord K's very kind remembrances, & hoping soon to renew my acquaintance with you. Believe me, Yours sincerely

Augusta Ada King

To William, Lord King

Tuesday, 5 o'clock, 13 March [1838]   Ockham

Dearest Mate. I am very much better today, & quite coming around again. I think you will like to see Locock's letter to me. From it as well as from something he said in London, he seems rather to think it would be a good thing for me soon to increase the family. He has I believe no doubt that it would operate as an <u>immediate</u> cure, & from his experience of my constitution & weak points, hopes he might prevent all ill consequences after-wards . . . though I do not think he is sanguine to my <u>nursing</u> again . . .

I am sure you will approve the avis' views as soon as she comes fully to explain them, & <u>ou</u> will probably be glad that she makes up her mind as to what she likes, as <u>ou</u> has some-times grumbled a little at her referring everything to you. . .

To Mary Somerville

Sunday 12 o'clock [Before June 1838]   St James' Square

My Dear Mrs Somerville. . . We have just parted with our sis-ters. Lord K & I deposited them an hour ago on the Antwerp steam-boat. We half felt inclined to go with them when it came actually to the parting moment. <u>I</u> feel as if I had lost two <u>daughters;</u> – I scarcely know why, since they are both <u>older</u> than I am. But it is rather a <u>sad</u> separation to us, & I envy them the <u>excitement</u> of travelling. –

By the bye, since I profess to <u>hate</u> <u>daughters,</u> I have done ill thus to compare my feelings about my sisters, since this would argue that I <u>rejoiced to</u> <u>get</u> <u>rid</u> of such nasty appendages. I hear that my own <u>nasty</u> daughter is very well, & Byron is at Acton again. Dear little creature, he talks charmingly! – Yours Affectly.   A.A. King

To Lady Byron

Saturday Morning, 21 July [1838]   St James' Square

Dearest Mama. I am going this morning to the Horticultural Show at the Common House, which is within the Horticultural establishment, so I have very little time to write. . .

You will like to hear about the Ball on Thursday. I had the black dwarf dreadfully; – worse than ever, & there was nothing to be done but to resign myself to my misfortune as quietly as possible. However I very nearly got into a scrape through it, for when we passed the Queen to make our bow & curtsey (there was <u>not</u> to be a presentation Lord B [Byron] had ascertained), she made a kind of motion implying that she wished me to go up to her. W luckily understood this & said to me "Go up to the Queen," otherwise I should never have dreamt of such a thing, as being much to presuming & obtrusive. She looked very kind & gracious & immediately held out her hand, which of course I had sense enough to take. – But I thought it very goodnatured in her to notice such an <u>ugly</u> <u>nasty</u> little bird at all. –

It is quite curious how diffident & almost ashamed of myself I felt this whole evening, & how good natured I felt it to be of everybody who was kind enough to speak to me. Putting aside the <u>monster,</u> I was very much amused & am very glad I went. I saw the Queen dance with Lord Villiers. Her dancing is most graceful & ladylike, & really worth seeing. We met Lord Falkland again there, & I like him extremely. He talked to me a good deal about the life of English <u>girls</u>, which he thinks <u>shocking,</u> & says nothing could induce him to permit a daughter of his to engage in the usual routine of <u>husband seeking</u>. . . Yours most affectly.   A.A. Lovelace

THE FOLLOWING LETTER was one of the most difficult to transcribe: the ink was muddy, the paper was thin, and Ada cross-hatched a good deal of the letter. It took me a week to transcribe it. Ada's selection of a corn headdress had political significance since the Corn Laws were being discussed in Parliament. According to the *Times,* Ada attended a performance of *Lucia* at the Majesty Theater, with an all-star cast. *Lucia* was sung by Madame Persiani, who had sung the premier performance in London on 5 April 1838. The first act of *Norma* was performed with Madame Giulia Grisi as *Norma.* After this marathon performance, Ada still had energy to visit the exhibit of Wheatstone's electric telegraph, and that turned out to be an unusual event.

The last letter in this series was written about the time that Charles Dickens's *Oliver Twist* was being serialized in the newspapers. Charterhouse was one of the "public schools" that was the basis of this satirization.

To Lady Byron

Thursday Evening [26 July 1838]   St James' Square

Dearest Mama. This is the night of the ball, where I am to appear as a pale yellow avis, of the maize tint, decorated with a silver fringe, & corn flowers (I am sure you know not what that means) mixed with silver corn. The attempt above at a diagram may give you an idea of the style of hair I think I mentioned to you, brought down plain even with the chin, & a wreath round the head with a little branch from it coming down on each side over the front hair. In the back hair there are to be marabou feathers mixed with silver corn. The wreath is of corn flowers and silver corn. . .

30th July Monday . . . The ball did very well on the whole. I was discomposed a little on observing that many persons looked at me, & then spoke to their companions, who upon that also looked. I did not notice that there was any peculiar expression of ridicule on their faces, otherwise I was inclined to calculate that there must be some very remarkable deformity to account for this since I really could not suppose that people (<u>many</u> of whom I am sure did not know who I was), should notice me one way or another when there were so many <u>real</u> beauties, Lady Seymour & others, to look at. –

On Satdy evg we went to the Opera, & were extremely pleased. We took two stalls which we found very tolerably comfortable & excellent for seeing & hearing. We had the whole of Lucia di Lammermoor, a beautiful new opera by Donizetti & in which the Persiani was the heroine Lucia. The first act of Bellini's Norma & Grisi was Norma & a most stately and magnificent high priestess does she make. We did not stay for the Ballet...

Last week I went to see a model of the Electrical Telegraph at Exeter Hall. It was one morning & the only other person was a middle-aged gentleman who chose to behave as if <u>I</u> were the show which of course I thought was the most impudent & unpardonable. – I am sure he took me for a very young (& I suppose he thought rather handsome) governess, as the room being one of the inner halls he could not know I came in a carriage, & being in the morning my dress happened to be very plain though nice. I took care not to appear the least curious of his impetuousness, but at the same time to behave so that it should be impossible for him to speak or take any real liberty. He seemed to have been there some time, but he stopped as long as I did, & then followed me out. – I took care to look as aristocratic & <u>as like a Countess</u> as possible. Lady Athleton is an admirable model on such an occasion. I am not in the habit of meeting with such impertinence anywhere, though I have of late been about a good deal alone, so I think he must be a very blackguard kind of man. W – thought he certainly supposed me unmarried & I must try & add a little age to my appearance, – but I think I get younger looking every month of my life. I was pleased with the Telegraph so I did not care for the impertinence of the other spectator...

I have been also to the Coliseum & to the Exhibition & to
the Surrey Zoological Garden. I wish I had to make my stay in
town over again, with my present strength which is sufficient. I
would go & see something everyday & I am sure London would
never be exhausted.

Tomorrow we go to Ockham. I shall be delighted to have
Byron again. He cut his thumb when W [William] was last
there with a razor. I hope after this lesson he will never touch
anything sharp again. Annabella <u>stands</u> <u>very</u> <u>well</u> alone & I
believe walks alone a little. How forward! B goes & knocks her
down like a minniken when she stands up. –

To Lady Byron

Sunday Morning [Circa October or November 1839]

Dearest Mama. How I do wish I had your gift of tongues, &
persuasiveness. Mr Gamlen came into the room on Friday &
found me delivering to Mr Frederick Knight a religious & moral
discourse. He caught only a tail of it, but it met his approval
for he interposed "very right, very good sound doctrine, that's
<u>orthodox</u>!"

But how I had been wishing in that very conversation for
the gifts of eloquence; how <u>ineffectively</u> I felt I spoke on a very
interesting & important subject! Surely to sow a single seed of
truth in the mind of another is the noblest of deeds. We <u>may</u>
never know its' results <u>here</u>, but how inestimable they <u>may</u> be!
This is my idea of the <u>real</u> use & object of all graces & all
accomplishments in woman. Let her be as attractive as she can
in all the <u>externals</u>, & she will find powerful <u>auxiliaries</u> to her
more important influence. A woman of <u>principle</u> will never
suffer these attractions to become snares to others, but they
will give her just that influence, particularly with <u>men</u>, which
she may turn to precious account, and which wicked, vain,
unprincipled women <u>have</u> turned to <u>infinite</u> <u>evil</u>.

If I thought that the mere <u>passing</u> agreeable impressions
produced on others, & admiration engendered, by distinguished
perfection & grace in musical performance, – the <u>harp</u> for

example, – were the <u>only</u> good & delightful results . . . I should
have little interest in working so hard at my harp as I do. – But
I take another view. I think it adds a very important means of
attraction, & very particularly for that age when the <u>personal</u>
attractions of youth diminish at all events, even if they do not
go off entirely. – But above all, the power of expressing oneself
with <u>force, clearness,</u> & <u>persuasion,</u> is to be desired. This I fear
never will be mine. No language from <u>my</u> lips will have that
winning awakening influence I could desire. How dead & powerless are my words compared with the thoughts within. . .

Mr Gamlen gave us a very interesting account of his introduction of some very pretty impressive singing in his church at
Bossall . . . & What a good, excellent delightful man he is! –
With all my fondness for Mr Babbage (by no means inconsider-
able), how superior is Mr Gamlen! . . . Yours most affectionately
                                                            A. A. Lovelace

6.

A Peculiar Way of Learning, Immeasurable Vista, Solitaire, The Great Unknown
[1839-1841]

WHEN ADA WAS not quite twenty-four years old, after four years of marriage and only four months after the birth of her third child, Ralph, she decided to return to the study of mathematics. She turned to her old friend Charles Babbage for help in finding a mathematics tutor, whom she dubbed "the great Unknown." Ada described her way of learning as "peculiar."

Even before she found a proper teacher, she suggested that the language of mathematics might be extended to games. This idea was not surprising since Ada and Babbage delighted in all sorts of mathematical games, from backgammon to chess. She started a process for writing a winning strategy for a game in mathematical terms that predates Boole's first published work in 1847, a pamphlet entitled *The Mathematical Analysis of Logic*, which, with his other works, is the foundation of our ability to program games on our modern computers.

Ada's mother, William, and certain ladies continued their criticism of Ada's performance of her social duties, but Ada stood by her own views. As for her relationship with Charles Babbage, it was certainly not based on social obligation. We have very few letters from Ada to Babbage before this time, but from this period on Ada's letters to him are a marvelous mixture of determination and teasing. She mentions Babbage's friend, Fortunato Prandi, a radical Italian politician living in England. Ada refers to the Eglintoun Tournament, a fascinating event that occurred in 1839. The Earl of Eglinton held a tournament at Eglintoun Castle that was carried out in ancient and grand style. All the participants dressed as knights. Lady Seymour, later the Duchess of Somerset, and a friend of Babbage's, was selected the Queen of Beauty. The cost of the occasion, which was not expected to exceed £2000, amounted to £40,000. It rained, and the event turned out to be a wet and messy disaster.

To Charles Babbage

[November 1839]

[Dear Mr. Babbage] [I have] quite made up my mind to have some instruction next year in Town, but the difficulty is to find the <u>man</u>. I have a peculiar <u>way</u> of <u>learning,</u> & I think it must be a peculiar man to teach me successfully. –

Do not reckon me conceited, for I am sure I am the very last person to think over-highly of <u>myself</u>; but I believe I have the <u>power</u> of going just as far as I like in such pursuits, & where there is so very decided a taste, I should almost say a <u>passion</u>, as I have for them, I question if there is not always some portion of natural genius even. – At any rate the taste is such that it <u>must</u> be gratified. – I mention all this to you because I think you are or may be in the way of meeting with the right sort of person, & I am sure you have at any rate the <u>will</u> to give me any assistance in your power. –

Lord L [Lovelace] desires all sorts of reminiscences, & that I am to take care & remind you about coming to Ockham. –
Yours most sincerely   Augusta Ada Lovelace

To Charles Babbage

16 February 1840

My Dear Mr Babbage. Have you ever seen a game, or rather puzzle, called Solitaire? – There is an Octagonal Board, like the enclosed drawing, with 37 little holes upon it in the position I have drawn them, & 37 little pegs to fill the little holes. <u>One</u> peg is abstracted to begin with, and then the remaining ones

hop <u>over</u> & <u>take</u> each other. For instance if peg No 19, the center one is taken out to begin, then peg 6 may hop over peg 12
into the empty hole 19, & peg 12 is taken off the board; or, peg
21 might hop over peg 20 into 19, & then peg 20 goes off the
board. The pegs are only allowed to hop over each other at
right angles, not diagonally. – The puzzle is to leave <u>only</u> <u>one</u> on
the board. People may try thousands of times, and not succeed
in this, leaving three, four, five, or many more even which have
no neighbours to give them a lift off the board. <u>I</u> <u>have</u> done it
by trying & observation & can now do it at any time, but I want
to know if the problem admits of being put into a mathematical
Formula, & solved in this manner. I am convinced myself that it
does, though I cannot do it. There must be a definite principle,
a compound I imagine of numerical & geometrical properties,
on which the solution depends, & which can be put into symbolic language. – I believe that much depends, to begin with,
on the particular peg first abstracted, & am inclined to think
there is but <u>one</u> which will admit of subsequent success. – I
will not name which – I believe these boards are to be had at
every toy-shop. –

I have numbered the holes in my drawing for the sake of
convenience of reference. The real boards are not numbered. –

Do not forget that I am to have the "Stratagems of Chess."

I hope you are bearing me in mind, I mean my mathematical interests. You know this is the greatest favour any one can
do me. – Perhaps, none of us can estimate <u>how</u> great. Who can
calculate to <u>what</u> it <u>might</u> lead; if we look on beyond this present condition especially? –

You know I am by nature a bit of a philosopher, & a very
great speculator, – so that I look on through a very immeasur-
able vista, and though I see nothing but vague & cloudy uncer-
tainty in the foreground of our being, yet I fancy I discern a
very bright light a good way further on, and this makes me care
much less about the cloudiness & indistinctness which is near.
– Am I too imaginative for you? I think not. – . . .

To Charles Babbage

Saturday, 14 March [1840]   Ockham

My Dear Mr Babbage. Can you be so kind as to tell us your friend Prandi's address? – We want to ask him here for Satdy next, & cannot you <u>add</u> <u>yourself</u>? – Or if not that day, is the following Tuesday, the 17th, quite out of the question? –

I fear not withstanding the Eglintoun Tournament, that the real days of Chivalry are gone bye, or you would never resist a lady's entreaties as you do. –

We shall not I think be in Town quite in time for your party the 21st; – probably a day or two later.

I am reading a book which is really well & lucidly explained, & to me very interesting; – Mosely's Mechanics applied to the Arts, &c. Do you know anything of him? – If I can judge from a man's writing, he is no common person. –

Should there seem no chance after I go to Town, of the much desired <u>great</u> <u>Unknown</u> being found for me, I have some idea of having instead for this season some German lessons. I know a little of it already, & have always intended to know more. Indirectly I think it would bear on some of my objects...

Yours most sincerely   A.A. Lovelace

To Charles Babbage

24 March [1839?]

Dear Mr Babbage. Satdy next will suit us perfectly, but we hope you will stay on as far into the following week, as possible. Surely the machine allows you a holiday sometimes. –

Lady N. Byron <u>will</u> be here. – Believe me, Yours sincerely

Augusta Ada Lovelace

AUGUSTUS DE MORGAN became Ada's teacher. He was a friend of Charles Babbage's, but a much closer friend (because of his wife Sophia Frend De Morgan) of Lady Byron's. He was considered one of the greatest logicians of the nineteenth

century and taught at the University of London. De Morgan assigned work for Ada to do from textbooks, and he met with her about every fortnight, sometimes only once a month. Email would certainly have been a great advantage since her instruction was primarily by correspondence.

The language of their mathematical correspondence was full of poetical allusions and metaphor. He talked of algebraic functions "sowing their wild oats"; such allusions were a perfect fit for Ada's peculiar way of learning. Despite a very flimsy background of what today would be considered a minimum high school mathematics program, Ada quickly moved into differential and integral calculus.

Any conclusion about Ada's mathematical expertise based on the remains of their correspondence is unwarranted. De Morgan was not paid a fee and as a result Ada most likely did not bother him unless she had a serious problem. Thus, these letters reflect what Ada did not understand, not what she did understand. They are, in statistical terms, a skewed sample – not the whole story. De Morgan knew the whole story and later assessed Ada's expertise.

The importance of these letters is that they give us a glimpse of the kind of material she was studying and the questions and problems she had. Her questions very often came down to basic principles, as she stated in a letter written in 1842: "what does it mean, & how was it got?"

To Augustus De Morgan

Sunday, 13 September [1840]   Ashley [Combe]

Dear Mr De Morgan. I am very much obliged by your remarks & additions. I believe I understand as much of the points in question as I am intended to understand at <u>present</u>. . . I expect to gain a good deal of new light & to get a good lift in studying from page 52 to 58, though probably I shall be a long time about this. I could wish I went on quicker. . . I should like much at some future period, (when I have got rid of common algebra & Trigonometry which at present detain me), to attend particularly to this subject. – At present you will observe, I have four distinct things to carry on at the same time: – the Algebra; – Trigonometry; – Chapter 2nd of the Differential Calculus; – & mere practice In Differentiation...

With many thanks, Yours very truly   A.A. Lovelace

LADY BYRON WENT OFF TO France in the summer of 1840 to visit her cousin Edward Noel, who was married to Ada's childhood friend Fanny Smith. They had just had a baby girl. Their permanent home was on the island of Euboea in Greece, where Edward acted as Lady Byron's land agent. Land was cheap, 30 shillings an acre, and Lady Byron invested £1000. In addition, Edward, who had been trained at DeFellenberg's school, instructed the local population about cooperation and agricultural techniques.

The focus of Lady Byron's time in France turned to Ada's cousin Elizabeth Medora Leigh, who lived in Tours. Medora, the daughter of Augusta Leigh, Lord Byron's half sister, had fallen on bad times. She had gone to France to join her sister Georgiana (who had been Lord Byron's favorite niece) and her husband, Henry Trevanion. Sixteen-year-old Medora, who was soon pregnant by her brother-in-law, was abandoned and sought help from her mother.

In 1838 Lady Byron had written that she was bored; now faced with Medora's problems, she had found a situation that interested her. She gave Medora financial aid and invited Medora to join her in Paris. Lady Byron wrote Ada how she was helping Medora, and Ada was impressed by her mother's noble actions. Since Medora was Augusta's daughter, Ada had seen very little of her. In the following correspondence, Ada expresses some concern over Medora, but Ada was fully occupied with her own concerns.

This period of Ada's life was happy – her letters were enthusiastic and hopeful. She continued to ride her horses, to ice skate, and to socialize with her many scientific friends. Even with all these activities, her mathematical studies proceeded full speed ahead. When her mother expressed concern that Ada was not paying attention to her studies, Ada replied that "Calculus was King." She was interested in developing skills for a profession. De Morgan cautioned her to slow down, and Ada stepped back and continued to question basic mathematical assumptions, or first principles.

To Lady Byron

21 November [1840]   Ashley Combe

Dearest Mama. Oh No! There is I think little danger of Mathematics being "eclipsed". I have quite recovered the simultaneous departure of my Sisters & the Sun, partly I imagine by the aid of Mathematics, which is an excellent resource on such occasions. I work on very slowly. This Mr De Morgan does not wish otherwise. On the contrary he cautioned me against a wish I had at one time to proceed rather too rapidly . . .   Avis

To Lady Byron

Thursday, 26 November [1840]   Ashley Combe

Dearest Mama. Your letter of the 22nd, just received, is a budget of news. – I am very glad about Fanny Noel, & I suppose another girl is quite as welcome there as a boy. The Queen doing excellently, (not in my way xcellently), & it's a good deed well over. A Prince of Wales would have been more popular, but I dare say that will come by & bye, & meantime there is an heir all the same. Everyone has been taken by surprise, for the event was not anticipated before the 1st week in December. . .

We shall certainly go to Paris, if you remain there. Probably my sisters would go at the same time, as they have long indicated such an excursion. – I should perhaps remain longer than William could. At any rate you may depend on seeing us. – The loss of you however this winter at Ockham, would be very great to every member of the family. Still if health is likely to be benefited, we could not of course really regret it, as we should hope to enjoy more of you in the end in consequence of the present privation. But have I grown philosophical enough yet to do without the merry old Hen for so long? I allow that Mr De Morgan & the Mathematics are a wonderful ballast, but still now & then Concentrativeness takes some queer whim; and the excess of that organ is so great, that while the whim lasts, it is a <u>very</u> <u>serious</u> matter indeed, whatever it may chance to be.

The Professor & I certainly pull well together. Never was a better hit than that. – It will be a <u>slow</u> business, but a very <u>certain</u> one I imagine. . .

B [Byron] has shown a bit of the Devil today. That will happen sometimes of course. – There is always a mixture of waggery in <u>his</u> Devil, who is evidently a funny fellow. –

William has had a dreadful lumbago. One day he would not move at all, & kept his bed. I never saw any one so bad, or so <u>patient</u> either.   Avis

ADA WAS DOING HER BEST to bring up her children, but handling three children under the age of four was a difficult task. She relied on William's sister Hester to help her. Lady Byron complained that the children were undisciplined and suggested that Ada consult her friend Mrs Barwell to help find suitable supervision. Taking her mother's advice, Ada wrote to Mrs Barwell and received more criticism. Mrs Barwell suggested that Ada was "secretive" about how she handled her children.

In 1885, Annabella, later Lady Anne Blunt, recalled what life was like at St James's Square. She described how they played steeplechase over their beds when the nursemaid thought they were asleep, and how she was constantly hungry. If Byron were eating a mutton chop, she would eye it until he relented and gave it to her. She recalled how she felt no guilt over their raucous behavior.

Ada wrote once again to Mrs Barwell and stated how she intended to handle her own children. She focused on her studies and made great progress. She began to feel confident and to think about ways that she might help Charles Babbage. It had been a long time since she had seen him, and she invited him for a visit.

To Augustus De Morgan

Friday, 17 December [1840]   Ockham Park, Ripley, Surrey

Dear Mr De Morgan. This is very <u>mathematical</u> <u>weather</u>. When one cannot exercise one's muscles <u>out</u> of doors, one is peculiarly inclined to exercise one's brains in-doors. – Accordingly I have been setting vigorously to work again, with much satisfaction. . .

But I am sorry to say I am sadly obstinate about the Term at which Convergence begins for the Series (A) page 231 of Algebra, and which we thought had been made clear by you on Monday Evening. . . I have enclosed my Demonstration of <u>my</u> view of the case . . .

I have thought much about my agreeable evening on Monday, – mathematical & educational. Your most truly

A.A. Lovelace

To Augustus De Morgan

Tuesday, 22 December [1840]   Ockham

Dear Mr De Morgan. I now see exactly my mistake. I had overlooked that the Series in question is not one in <u>successive</u> Powers of x, like that on page 185, but only in <u>successive</u> <u>even</u> powers of x. . .

But I have materially altered my mind on this subject. I often gain more from the discovery of a mistake of this sort, than from 10 acquisitions made at <u>once</u> without any kind of difficulty. . .

I can only end by repeating what I have often said before that I am very troublesome, & only wish I could do you any such service as you are doing me. Yours most truly

A.A.L.

To Lady Byron

Saturday, 2 January 1841   Ockham

Dearest Mama. I have neglected you sadly this week, & especially after your pretty compliment about "my most agreeable
letters", which actually made the Bird blush. The fact is that
we have had company; – & between this, much Skating practice
(until the thaw on Thursday, which turned our world green
again & injured our ice) . . .

I shall be curious to see Medora's little present. I am wonderfully interested about her. . .

The Hen is a little out of favor owing to her observation
about the plaguing children. "Now that is one of the Hen's
crotchets," says the Bird . . .

The Greigs have been here. . . Then we have had Sir Gardner Wilkinson upwards of a week. He & I are great allies. I like
him more & more. . . We expect Mr Babbage about the 10th. We
shall have quite a week now. . .

7.

In Due Time I Shall Be a <u>Poet</u>, A Scientific Trinity, A Most <u>Strange</u> and <u>Dreadful</u> History
[1841]

ADA BEGAN THE YEAR 1841 with high hopes for the future. On 5 January 1841 she wrote at least seventeen pages ranging in content from the personal to the practical to the metaphysical.

She replied to Mrs Barwell's persistent criticisms about the children by defending them and then wrote to Charles Babbage inviting him to come and tell her all about the latest developments with his Analytical Engine. Since 1834 when he first shared his vision for the Analytical Engine with Ada, he had toiled away on the designs and plans. He believed that no one in England, especially the English government, was interested in his idea, but Ada was interested, and several other people as well.

In the autumn of 1840 Babbage was invited to go to Turin to explain his idea for the Analytical Engine before a gathering of Italian philosophers. He took with him examples of how the engine would handle calculations. Today these iterations would be called "programs." An engineer soldier in the audience, L. F. Menabrea, was particularly interested. He listened attentively and examined Babbage's drawings and sample "programs." The presentation was well received, and King Charles Albert gave Babbage a gold medal.

Babbage, pleased with everything that had transpired in Turin, left by mail coach for England. He recounted the day vividly, years later in his autobiography, and it is striking to compare the following account to the one he described to Ada in

1834, when he foreshadowed his pathway to a new discovery.

Before Babbage and an aide reached Annecy, they crossed a famous suspension bridge named in the King's honor, the Pont Charles Albert. A third of a mile from the bridge, Babbage descended from the carriage, instructing the postillions to drive slowly across and wait on the far side. The gorge was deep and the bridge itself partly covered in clouds:

> We were singularly favoured by circumstances. We saw the carriage which had left us apparently crossing the bridge, then penetrating into the clouds, and finally becoming lost to our view. At the same time the dissolving mist in our own immediate neighbourhood began to allow us to perceive the depth of the valley beneath and at last even the little wandering brook, which looked like a thread of silver at the bottom.
>
> The sun now burst from behind a range of clouds, which had obscured it. Its warm rays speedily dissipated the mist, illuminated the dark gulf at our own side, and discovered to us the mail on terra firma on the opposite side of the chasm waiting to convey us to our destination.[1]

Ada was as interested in the process of scientific discovery as she was in the result of the discovery. To Lady Byron and to many people, science meant and still means "the facts," or digital, quantitative skills and analysis, based on observation and experimentation. Yet to Ada science meant much more, for it involved the integration of digital skills with what today we refer to as analog skills such as imagination and metaphor. She was her father's, as well as her mother's, daughter: the role of imagination was critical to her understanding of science. The romantic poets had discussed the role of imagination in the creation of poetry, and she pondered its connection to science and the process of scientific discovery.

Shelley, her father's close friend, wrote in the *Defense of Poetry* that "imaginative language marks the before unapprehended relation of things." Coleridge's view of metaphysical poetry was that it was both intelligible and mysterious or imaginative. In her essay of 5 January Ada used what was almost a cliché about imagination to define mathematical language, only to fold this back on itself and claim that the two are indeed, if not identical, necessary for each other. Ada juxtaposed opposites, imagination and science, and saw their necessary connection just as her father did in his description: "I stood in Venice, on the Bridge of Sighs: A palace and a prison on each hand . . ."[2]

Like Holmes's description of Coleridge, ". . . fascinated by anything that promised poetical marvels or metaphysical peculiarities,"[3] Ada saw in Babbage's designs the opportunity for scientific miracles and metaphysical speculations. And then, there was no stopping her.

To Charles Babbage

Tuesday, 5 January [1841]   Ockham

My Dear Mr Babbage. You have put me into a Dilemma, because I should naturally say – Come on Friday, & come <u>again</u> rather later.

If you come this week, you will I <u>believe</u> find us quite alone; if later, suppose about the 15th, there will probably be company. Now we like so much to have you in <u>either</u> circumstances; when alone the pleasure of <u>monopolizing</u> you is so great; when in company, you make the company so tenfold agreeable, that <u>I</u> cannot choose between them. I can only say we wish to see you at <u>all</u> times, & as much as possible . . .

I much wish to have you here, & talk with you over some of my own doings &c. Today, I have been working much at Mathematics. It has been bad for <u>outdoors,</u> & therefore I have got a <u>lift</u> at <u>in-doors</u> pursuits. –

I must show you a certain book called my Mathematical Scrap-Book. . .

But pray do not think of coming for so <u>very short</u> a time as only 3 nights. It would be shameful! –

Some day or other, you will have to put me in possession of the main points relating to your engine. – I have more reasons than one for desiring this. – Yours most sincerely

A.A. Lovelace

Part of an essay Ada wrote

Tuesday, 5 January 1841

. . .What is Imagination? We talk much of Imagination. We talk of the Imagination of Poets, the Imagination of Artists &c; I am inclined to think that in general we don't know very exactly what we are talking about. Imagination I think especially two fold.

First: it is the Combining Faculty. It brings together things, facts, ideas, conceptions, in new, original, endless, ever varying, Combinations. It seizes points in common, between subjects having no very apparent connexion, & hence seldom or never brought into juxtaposition.

Secondly: it conceives & brings into mental presence that which is far away, or invisible, or which in short does not exist within our physical & conscious cognizance. Hence is it especially the religious faculty; the ground-work of Faith. It is a God-like, a noble faculty. It renders Earth tolerable (at least should do so); it teaches us to live, in the tone of the eternal.

Imagination is the Discovering Faculty, pre-eminently. It is that which penetrates into the unseen worlds around us, the worlds of Science. It is that which feels & discovers what is, the real which we see not, which exists not for our senses. Those who have learned to walk on the threshold of the unknown worlds, by means of what are commonly termed par excellence the exact sciences, may then with the fair white wings of Imagination hope to soar further into the unexplored amidst which we live.

Mathematical Science shows what is. It is the language of unseen relations between things. But to use & apply that language we must be able fully to appreciate, to feel, to seize, the unseen, the unconscious. Imagination too shows what is, the is that is beyond the senses. Hence she is or should be especially cultivated by the truly Scientific, – those who wish to enter into the worlds around us!

🐾

O N 10 JANUARY Ada sent De Morgan a fourteen-page letter (not included in this series) filled with differential calculus equations. She concluded that "I am much pleased to find how very well I stand <u>work</u>, & how my powers of attention & continued effort <u>increase</u>. I am never so happy as when I am really engaged in good earnest; & it makes me most wonderfully cheerful & merry at <u>other</u> times which is curious & very satisfactory."

She wrote her mother she had a "mathematical week," which she associated with the immense development of her imagination. She speculated that though it might seem strange "I shall in due time be a <u>Poet</u>."

Despite her defense of her children, she characterized Ralph, her youngest, as a "troublesome virago." Years later Ada's future son-in-law, Wilfrid Scawen Blunt, would have delighted in Ada's description of Ralph. In his diaries that were not opened until fifty years after his death, and in his private correspondence that I consulted, Wilfrid described Ralph exactly as Ada did. In his diaries Blunt suggested that Ralph should be put in a laundry bag and thrown in the Thames for having made known the dirty family laundry in *Astarte*, his privately printed memoir of the family letters.

Ada had great hopes for her future and shared her enthusiasm with Greig, who, knowing Ada's personality, cautioned her to go slowly, like a mountaineer, taking it step by step. Ada repeated Greig's criticism of her to De Morgan by stating that she would try to keep her metaphysical head in order.

To Lady Byron

Monday night, 11 January [1841]   Ockham

Dearest Mama. How interesting your last letter is! Will you thank Medora for her pin-cushion, & tell her it is now by me, ready for use as soon as I want a fresh pin, & that I not only admire the taste & neatness of the workmanship, but am glad to be reminded by its bright black & red still more frequently than I might otherwise be, of the interest with which the donor is regarded by me. – . . .

And when are we to go to Paris? – You have never answered me that, & it depends much upon your wishes of course. – We propose it should be about the 1st April, when the Easter vacation will be beginning, & there will be no Parliament or business in Town. If however you have any strong urgent wish to see me sooner, I will go over the beginning of next month . . .

I have had a mathematical week since I last wrote. On Friday we again expect company. This alteration of company & mathematics suits me astonishingly. It is wonderful how I enjoy company (which I never did in my life before) in consequence of the Mathematics. – The latter is now become in good earnest a very serious pursuit. I work well, & with a facility strange to myself! I have gained a strength of head & attention which I never expected; and I have made some curious observations as to the effects of the study. The principals are as follows: immense development of imagination; so much so, that I feel no doubt if I continue my studies I shall in due time be a Poet. This effect may seem strange but it is not strange, to me. I believe I see its causes & connection clearly. – Secondly, a wonderful cheerfulness & exhilaration of spirits, this very obvious indeed; thirdly, a very increased Self Confidence, in the best sense of that term; fourthly, the determination & hope, (gaining in distinctness), to add my mite to the accumulated & accumulating knowledge of the world especially in some way more particularly tending to illustrate the wisdom & ways of God! – This is the remote & ultimate goal, not to be attained for many many years; – never to be attained for my own glory, which should be a most subordinate consideration.

I cannot but reflect on the vast change 6 months have made in me; – a change perhaps not the least evident to any one else, but most deeply felt by myself. I see ground for any degree of hope for the future. Those sorts of changes & improvements continue (the same Causes operating) in an increasing Ratio. –

I go on most delightfully with Mr De Morgan, – what can I do ever to repay him? I sometimes think with scruples on the subject. He is certainly most kind, & does what no one else I believe could do so well for me. – No two people ever suited better. I am not likely either to trouble him <u>less</u>, at present. I have some hard & dry work, & <u>much</u> of it, before me, but the greater the difficulty, & the less immediately inviting the subject, the more doggedly does that large Concentrativeness of mine, backed by Firmness, set about the matter. . .

I think altogether I have written you a very <u>flighty</u> letter. Pray do not think the Bird is going mad; which you know has often been my own horror. However I hope I shall never be madder than I <u>now</u> am. I think I <u>have</u> been madder sometimes on different former occasions; – some of them very trivial too. . .

To Charles Babbage

Tuesday, 12 January, [1841]   Ockham

My Dear Babbage. If you will come by the <u>Railway</u> on Friday, we will send the carriage to meet you at <u>Weybridge</u>, for the Train that leaves Town about 4 o'clock & arrives at Weybridge a few minutes before 5 o'clock.

Bring warm coats or cloaks, as the carriage will be probably an open one.

If you are a <u>Skater,</u> pray bring <u>Skates</u> to Ockham; that being the fashionable occupation here now, & one <u>I</u> have much taken to. –

I am very anxious to talk to you. I will give you a hint on <u>what</u>. It strikes me that at some future time, (it might be even within 3 or 4 years, or it might be <u>many</u> years hence), <u>my</u> <u>head</u> may be made by you subservient to some of <u>your</u> purposes & plans. If so, <u>if</u> ever I could be worthy or capable of being <u>used</u> by you, my head will be yours. And it is on this that I wish to speak most seriously to you. You have always been a kind and real & most invaluable friend to <u>me</u>; & I would that I could in any way repay it, though I scarcely dare so exalt myself as to hope however humbly, that I can ever be intellectually worthy to attempt serving <u>you.</u>

Yours most sincerely   A.A. Lovelace

You <u>must</u> stay some days with us. Now don't contradict me.

To Woronzow Greig

Friday [15 January 1841]   Ockham

My Dear Mr Greig. I am very much obliged by your letter
received yesterday morning, & anticipate with much pleasure
the rest of the promised Series. I have <u>so</u> much, on many subjects, that I should like to tell you, and <u>so</u> little time to tell any
of it, that I am puzzled. I have now had 10 days of good hard
mathematical work, & have at this moment beside me papers
from Mr De Morgan (in reply to some of mine) that require
both studying & answering. I am going on <u>most</u> <u>excellently</u>
with my studies; but this you know is but the beginning. . . I
consider it now as being, if I may so speak, my <u>Profession</u>. . .

　　<u>You</u> are <u>right</u>: I <u>ought</u> to do something; – to write
something. But <u>not</u> at <u>present</u>. It would be a thousand pities if
I were to attempt anything . . . for <u>long</u> <u>to</u> <u>come</u>.– You think I
have powers; and you are right. But I know <u>myself</u> <u>well</u>; and I
know that whatever powers I may have <u>now,</u> I shall have tenfold
those powers at 40, with the measures I am taking. Therefore
my maxim is – <u>Wait</u> <u>and</u> <u>Work</u>! –

　　I will confess to you, (for <u>you</u> will not attribute it to a vain,
empty self sufficient conceit), that I have on my mind most
strongly the impression that Heaven has allotted me some
peculiar <u>intellectual-moral</u> mission to perform. . . there <u>are</u>
missions for the <u>few</u>; these <u>are</u> missions to make better known
to the many laws & the glory of God; and blessed are those who
fulfil faithfully such missions, who fulfil them, not for <u>self</u> glory
& aggrandizement, but for the glory of Him who is so <u>darkly</u>
known as yet in the world, & for the love of those many whose
greatest blessing it is (tho' they may yet appreciate it not), to
know Him a little less imperfectly!

　　Now to such a possible mission, I will be true & faithful (to
the best of my ability) until the last pulse shall have closed for
me the <u>present</u> law of connection between the spiritual and the
physical . . .

　　Well! You will see, from the foregoing, that I have a great
& vast scheme! It becomes every year, every month, every
week, more definite & less vague in form; and <u>with</u> this

gradually increasing distinctness, grows the force of my will & determination. –

I am now happier than ever in my life before. I have never been happy, even in the ordinary earthly sense of that term, until just lately . . . What a long letter I have written! – Believe me ever, Yours most sincerely   A.A.L.

To Augustus De Morgan

Wednesday, 3 February [1841]   Ockham

Dear Mr De Morgan. . . And by the bye, I may remark that the curious <u>transformations</u> many formulae can undergo, the unsuspected & to a beginner apparently <u>impossible</u> <u>identity</u> of forms exceedingly <u>dissimilar</u> at first sight, is I think one of the chief difficulties in the early part of mathematical studies. I am often reminded of certain sprites & fairies one reads of, who are at one's elbows in <u>one</u> shape now, & the next minute in a form most dissimilar; and uncommonly deceptive, troublesome & tantalizing are the mathematical sprites & fairies sometimes; like the types I have found for them in the world of Fiction. . .

I had had the same objection to the Demonstration in <u>Bourdan</u> to which I have had the curiousity to refer. I am sometimes very much interested in see <u>how</u> the same conclusions are arrived at in <u>different</u> <u>ways</u> by different people; and I happen to be inclined to compare you & Bourdan in this case of developopping Exponential & Logarithmic Series; & very amusing has it been to me to see <u>him</u> <u>begin</u> exactly where <u>you</u> <u>end</u> &c. Your demonstration is much the best for practical purposes. . .

Yours most truly   A.A.L.

To Augustus De Morgan

6 February [1841]

Dear Mr De Morgan. . . You know I always have so many metaphysical enquires & speculations which intrude themselves, that I am never really satisfied that I understand <u>anything</u>, because, understand it as well as I may, my comprehension <u>can</u>

only be an infinitesimal fraction of all I want to understand about the many connections & relations which occur to me, <u>how</u> the matter in question was first thought of & arrived at, &c, &c, I am particularly curious about this wonderful theorem.

However I try to keep my metaphysical head in order. . .
Yours most truly   A.A. Lovelace

ADA ANALYZED her unique scientific skills, shaping them into a scientific Trinity. Her approach was and is for many people even today considered heretical. It moved effortlessly between science and imagination. She concentrated so much on her intuitive perceptions that she did not see the world of "facts," and Lady Byron would never let Ada forget those facts.

Lady Byron sent Ada letters from Paris detailing her latest illness and her involvement with Medora. Ada had received and commented on the pin cushion that Medora made, but most of Ada's responses to her mother's letters are filled with grand scientific dreams, the latest scientific developments, humor, and happiness. Then, like many people who walk confidently on a path, there is an unexpected and major diversion. Lady Byron revealed to Ada her "most <u>strange</u> and <u>dreadful</u> history."

To Lady Byron

Saturday, 6 February 1841   Ockham

Dearest Mama. By this time you have probably received my speculative letter. I have been reflecting since, that I much wish I could communicate to you the <u>whole</u> of my ideas & speculations, as they at present stand; more particularly about life & death. There are some so very extraordinary, & as I must firmly believe, so highly important, that I wish I could communicate a glimpse of them to any other mind capable of taking them in. And yours, dearest Mama, is more so than any. – At any rate it is my intention to make out notes of them by degrees, for my own future use, or in case anything should happen to me; and I will certainly endeavor during this year at any rate, to put you in possession of them. –

And now I must tell you <u>what</u> my opinion of my own mind & powers is exactly; – the result of a most accurate study of <u>myself</u> with a view to my future plans, during many months. I believe myself to possess a most singular combination of qualities exactly fitted to make me <u>pre-eminently</u> a discoverer of the <u>hidden</u> <u>realities</u> of nature. <u>You</u> will not mistake this assertion either for a wild enthusiasm, or for the result of any disposition to <u>self</u> <u>exaltation</u>. On the contrary, the belief has been <u>forced</u> upon me, & most slow have I been to admit it even. And now I will mention the three remarkable faculties in me, which united, ought (all in good time) to make me see <u>anything</u>, that a being not actually <u>dead</u>, can see & know, – (for it is what we are pleased to call <u>death</u>, that will <u>really</u> <u>reveal</u> things to us).–

Firstly: Owing to some peculiarity in my nervous system, I have <u>perceptions</u> of some things, which no one else has; or at least very few, if any. This faculty may be designated in me as a singular <u>tact</u>, or some might say an <u>intuitive</u> perception of hidden things; – that is of things hidden from eyes, ears & the ordinary senses. . . This <u>alone</u> would advantage me little, in the discovery line, but there is

Secondly; – my immense reasoning faculties;

Thirdly; my concentrative faculty, by which I mean the power not only of throwing my whole energy & existence into whatever I choose, but also bringing to bear on any one subject or idea, a vast apparatus from all sorts of apparently irrelevant & extraneous sources. I can throw <u>rays</u> from every quarter of the universe into <u>one</u> vast focus.

Now these three powers; (I cannot resist the wickedness of calling them my <u>discovering</u> or <u>scientific</u> <u>Trinity</u>), are a vast apparatus put into my power by Providence; & it rests with me by a proper course during the next 20 years to make the engine what I please. But haste; or a restless ambition, would quite ruin the whole.

My ambition, & I cannot say with any truth, that I feel

myself by any means able to <u>banish</u> ambition, must be of the most remote kind. And besides it is rather my belief that greatness of the very <u>highest</u> order, is never appreciated here, to the fullest extent, until after the great man (or woman's) death. <u>My</u> ambition should be rather to <u>be</u> great, than to be <u>thought</u> so. This however is a high philosophy, but I must believe perfectly attainable, as I say <u>all</u> <u>in</u> <u>good</u> <u>time</u>. Well, here I have written, what most people would call a remarkably <u>mad</u> letter, & yet certainly one of the most logical, sober minded, cool, pieces of composition, (<u>I</u> believe), that I ever penned; the result of much accurate, matter-of-fact, reflection & study. –

I could indeed tell you much that is curious. Meantime my course is so clear & obvious, that it is delightful to think how straight it is. And yet <u>what</u> a mountain I have to climb! It is enough to frighten anyone who had not all that most insatiable & restless energy, which from my babyhood has been the plague of your life & my own. However it has found food I believe at last. For 25 years have the feelers been out in every direction, trying all sorts of experiments.

Give me 30 more, & the feelers shall feel about to some purpose, & in a very different way from there hitherto <u>grovelling</u> <u>groping</u>. . .

It must, I think, be a comfort to you, to find that I have done on the whole, much better than might have been expected, without <u>you</u> this winter. Then to be sure, I have had your letters. You must manage if you die before me . . . to <u>vibrate</u> some little things now & then into my ear. Don't frighten me with a gawky, ugly ghost; but make some use of the little bit of an additional sense, which I affirm myself to have.

Or, if you <u>will</u> appear to my <u>eyes</u>, which I do not on the whole wish, pray be a very pretty comely-looking, & good-natured ghost.

To Lady Byron

[Undated, quoted in introduction, early 1841]

I have now gone thro' the <u>night</u> of my life, I believe. I consider that my being began at midnight, and that I am now approaching the <u>Dawn</u>.

My sun is rising with a <u>clear, steady,</u> & <u>full</u>, rather than <u>dazzlingly</u> <u>brilliant</u> light and is illuminating all around me. He will I expect gradually run his course, to his zenith, with the same full steady, even, light; and <u>then</u> <u>maybe</u> he will eventually set amidst rosy, golden, dazzling clouds, that may show to <u>me</u> something of the Spirit Land to which with <u>his</u> last rays <u>I</u> must gently depart, & he will tell me to leave for mankind in my footsteps a little of that brightness from <u>Beyond</u>, which has reflected on <u>my</u> head, an earnest, an indication, a glimpse of that which the Great Future will unroll! –

Now all this is highly figurative. Perhaps it is <u>too</u> figurative for you, or for anyone. Perhaps it is too glowing, too imaginative, too enthusiastic. . .

To Lady Byron

Sunday, 21 February [1841]   Ockham Park

Dearest Mama. It is a pleasure to be able to say now how much better William now is; & that he yesterday celebrated his <u>Birthday</u> by a little waltz with <u>me</u>; (we are quite alone except my sisters), at which I felt much pleased & honored. . .

So you say, "I am under the dominion of electricity;" which amused me so much, that instead of receiving the accompanying scold with a grave & contrite face, I was seized with fits of laughter. – But there is a little truth in your saying, I do really believe. The King of my mind is rather <u>electrical</u> in his attributes certainly right now. –

To Charles Babbage

Monday, 22 February [1841]   Ockham Park

My Dear Mr Babbage. We are to move to Town on Thursday; & I hope to see you as soon afterwards as you like, – the sooner the better. Remember that <u>one</u> o'clock is the best hour for a call. –

I believe I shall perhaps pass Sunday Evening with Mr &

Mrs De Morgan; but this is not yet quite fixed, & if it should not take place, will <u>you</u> come & spend it in St James' Sqre – You see I am determined to celebrate the Sabbath <u>Mathematically,</u> in one way or other. –

I have been at work very strenuously since I saw you, & quite as successfully as heretofore. I am now studying attentively the <u>Finite</u> <u>Differences</u> . . .And in this I have more particular interest, because I know it bears directly on some of <u>your</u> business. – Altogether I am going on well, & just as we might have anticipated. –

I think I am more determined than ever in my future plans; and I have quite made up my mind that nothing must be suffered to interfere with them. – I intend to make such arrangements in Town as will secure me a couple of hours daily (with very few exceptions), for my studies.

I think much of the possible (I believe I may say the <u>probable</u>) future connexion between <u>us</u>; and it is an anticipation I increasingly like to dwell on. I think great good may be the result to <u>both</u> of us; and I suspect that the idea, (which by the bye is one that I believe I have <u>long</u> entertained, in a vague and crude form), was one of those happy instincts which do occur to one sometimes so unaccountably & fortunately. At least, in my opinion, the results <u>may</u> ultimately prove it such. Believe me, Yours most sincerely   A.Ada Lovelace

To Lady Byron

Wednesday, 24 February [1841]   Ockham

Dearest Mama. I received this morning from Mrs De Morgan an account of Mr Frend's death, with interesting particulars. She had written me word two or three days ago of its probable occurrence . . .

Tomorrow the family & myself move to Town; I on the back of Tam O' Shanter. – William is to follow a day or two later . . .

Will you make all enquires for us about the best mode of getting to Paris from Rouen. I suppose the Steam-Boats will run to Havre & Rouen by the last days of March . . . We wish to

spend as little of this [time] on the road as we have both a very
limited period to be away altogether. In fact, we think we cannot extend our absence much if at all beyond the duration of
the Easter Holiday.

What is your advice about our route? –

William is quite himself again, & very gay, cheerful. It is a
great pleasure. –

All is prosperous. The Mathematics & Mr De Morgan going
on very well indeed. You would be much pleased to see the
<u>heap</u> of papers of my writing, which now accumulates into hon-
ourable & substantial evidence of my steady industry for some
months past & by the bye, it is a very strange thing, that so
disorderly as I generally am about papers & such things, there
is yet never any disorder in any part of my mathematical
papers,or proceedings. This is a curious phenomena! –

*Then a letter arrived, written most likely on 25 February. It
was most likely burned. Ada's response speaks for itself.*

To William, Lord Lovelace

Saturday, [Undated but most likely 26 February 1841]

St James' Square

Dearest William. I read the enclosed with <u>no surprise</u>. It is
exactly what I anticipated would some time be made; & shocking as it all is to reflect on. I have so long in my own mind felt
the conviction that such things, or something very similar, <u>had</u>
been, in my most miserable & unhappy family, that the proofs
of the <u>fact</u> come to me as no new or startling thing. –

It is tho' a most <u>strange</u> & <u>dreadful</u> history! And to think
that my Mother (then we may say a <u>young girl</u>) & purity & innocence itself, should have been suddenly plunged into the midst
of the greatest depths of depravity & crime, is almost more
dreadful than the crimes themselves. I only wonder she has a
<u>particle</u> of <u>confidence</u> in <u>anybody</u> whatever. I do indeed won-

der that she has! –

I rather wish you could have seen what I have written to my Mother. But it would lose time to send it to you, & I can repeat most of it when you come.

My different affairs go on well on the whole; but the weather is very gloomy, & I am rather dull than otherwise. –

I have many little things to tell you when you come, & I think you will approve of the arrangements I contemplate for the disposal of my various occupations & plans. –

Your Birdie . . .

8.

I Have a Duty to Perform, Avis-Phoenix, Will-o'-the-Wisps
[1841]

THE LETTER ADA RECEIVED from her mother no doubt accused Lord Byron of having had an incestuous relationship with his half-sister, Augusta Leigh, and of being Elizabeth Medora's father. Whether true or not, Lady Byron was successful in focusing attention on Byron's so-called "depravity," which colors people's perception of Byron even today. Whenever I mention to anyone that I am writing this book, the first question I am usually asked is: "Did Lord Byron commit incest with his sister Augusta (really his half-sister)? Was he Elizabeth Medora's father?" We do not know. Byron never gave any indication, other than the mocking letter to Lady Melbourne, that Medora was his child. When he sent gifts for Augusta's children, he did not specify Medora in any way. In contrast, he did seek custody of his illegitimate daughter, Allegra, and specified gifts for Ada. It is doubtful that he would not specify gifts for Medora if he believed he was her father.

Lady Byron's timing also evokes suspicion. She most likely was aware of the incest rumors circulating among the aristocracy before she married Lord Byron. However, when she was having trouble controlling Byron's obnoxious behavior during the month before Ada was born, she appealed to Augusta to come to London to help. If indeed she was suspicious of Byron's relationship with Augusta, it did not make sense for her to invite Augusta to help her.

A few months later when Lady Byron decided she wanted a separation, the evidence she used was based on remembered, or reconstructed, memories, memories that she fit into the perception that Lord Byron committed incest. She picked out data to support her view, and cast out as irrelevant what did not fit. Lady Byron was very eager to believe Caroline Lamb's allegations that Byron had committed incest with his half-sister. Like a computer, and many categorical thinkers, Lady Byron could not handle information that she could not fit into a category. Her goal was separation, and whatever helped her reach her goal she justified.

At the time of these letters, in 1841, everything was going well in Ada's life. Lady Byron knew Ada would be in Paris in six weeks, yet she could not wait to tell her daughter in privacy of Byron's sin, after keeping this "great secret" for twenty-five years. At the very least it appeared that Lady Byron's motive was to be on center stage. Whatever the motive, the effect was that she diverted Ada from her activities just as she diverted attention from Byron's accomplishments – his poetry – and turned the focus of attention to his vulnerability, his relationship to his half-sister.

Although Ada did not mention her mother's revelation to anyone (with the exception of William), that information affected all of her correspondence at this time. In the following letters Ada re-evaluated what it meant to be her father's daughter. How would she deal with her father's "misused genius," his "depravity," and her mother's innocence? Just as Ada looked into her past and her heritage, she also transformed and integrated the characteristics she had inherited from each of her parents and started to shape her destiny. At first she kept herself busy with all her activities, even enlisting Babbage's aid in a musical event. Then, in early April, Ada went to join her mother in Paris. William was supposed to go with her, but a bout of influenza delayed his passage.

Though Ada at this time did not question the validity of her mother's allegation that Medora was Lord Byron's daughter, William did. Many years later, after the deaths of Ada and Lady Byron, William stated that he never believed that Medora was Lord Byron's daughter. At this time, however, William was a very dutiful son-in-law, and it is highly unlikely that he shared that impression with Lady Byron.

To Lady Byron

Saturday, 27 February 1841   St James' Square

Dearest Mama. I have this moment received from Ockham your letter of the 23rd, with William's reply to it, which he desires me to enclose with my own. I am not in the least <u>astonished</u>. In fact you merely <u>confirm</u> what I have for <u>years</u> <u>&</u> <u>years</u> felt scarcely a doubt about, but should have considered it most improper in me to hint to you that I in any way suspected.

I told William last summer or autumn the <u>whole</u> of my ideas respecting the wickedness of Mrs L [Leigh], otherwise I scarcely think he would have seized the import of your present letter to him. In fact the very idea is so <u>monstrous</u> & <u>hideous</u> that I remember when I had communicated my own <u>more</u> than suspicions to William, I felt ashamed at having done so when I found how little definite & tangible <u>grounds</u> I could bring forward when he questioned me on what <u>could</u> have suggested so extraordinary a conviction to me. –

I trust that my most unhappy & unfortunate parent <u>is</u> now freed from some at least of his shocking & I must think <u>willful</u> defiance of law, nature, reason; & instinct. From all I can gather respecting him, I believe that his worst crimes even, originated more in <u>defiance</u>, than in <u>love</u> of the <u>crime</u>; – in short a <u>good</u> <u>principle</u> this <u>love</u> <u>of</u> <u>the</u> <u>exercise</u> <u>of</u> <u>free-will,</u> carried to a fearful & distorted extent. I trust it <u>has</u> been so; for I think it is a shade more easily retrievable than the absolute depravity which loves the crime for its <u>own</u> <u>sake</u>. When I reflect on my <u>own</u> natural <u>defiance</u> of <u>law,</u> of everything <u>imposed,</u> I sometimes tremble. But for my excellent understanding, (for which I thank heaven & you for your wise cultivation of it), I should not have been one whit better or happier than my unhappy parent. I might not have committed exactly the same crimes, but I should have been just as bad in some line or other. I may well tremble, when I think on all I might inherit. . .

If a questionable line of conduct occurs; the only way in which characters of the <u>Defying</u> & <u>determined</u> sort, can fully meet the consideration of it so as to decide wisely, is I conceive by remembering first that they have full <u>power</u> to carry it out (if such is the case; & it is well where it <u>is</u> the case, for then the defying principle is less actively excited). "But then. . . we must <u>foresee</u> a little. Carry it out thoroughly, in every principle & consequence. Carry it forward <u>ages</u>. And now let us see what are the various results that may probably follow. If you are satisfied then take your own line. <u>But</u> <u>remember,</u> <u>that</u> <u>the</u> <u>grand</u> <u>principle</u> <u>of</u> <u>free-will</u> <u>which</u> <u>you</u> <u>want</u> <u>to</u> <u>exercise</u> <u>to</u> <u>the</u> <u>very</u> <u>utmost</u>, is <u>equally</u> operating in a choice <u>either</u> way; that it is just as much a <u>volition</u> & an <u>activity</u> & a <u>choice</u> when you take a <u>negative</u> line as a <u>positive</u> line; & that Mr Free-Will must take care not to put himself within the domain & kingdom of certain laws which may come into operation necessarily when he passes certain boundaries, & which laws may then clip his wings before he is aware of it or can help it & in ways he does not anticipate." There is my lecture for Mr Defiance & Mr Free-Will! If they are wise men, they will avoid the sphere of action of certain <u>laws</u> which have no power over them as long as they keep clear of those gentlemen's territories. –

If my poor Father had but possessed a little of my real philosophical turn! Nothing else, depend upon it, can ever keep that sort of character in order. Neither circumstances, nor Conscience, nor impulses. They may all <u>help</u> materially; but <u>Philosophy</u> & the <u>Power</u> <u>of</u> <u>Foresight</u>, & a certain <u>principle</u> <u>of</u> <u>Hope</u>, are the real things. – And by the bye, you will be pleased to hear how my <u>Hope</u> flourishes! I mean in my character, & I dare say my Phrenology echoes it. – The cheerful principles have, in the long run very much the upper hand. I think this is my <u>natural</u> character, when properly occupied & in good health.

I will not now add more. But believe me, dearest Mama, your <u>Hopeful</u> <u>Bird</u>. Yes – I must hope well <u>even</u> for Mrs L; & I feel <u>she</u> is more <u>inherently</u> <u>wicked</u> than <u>he</u> ever was. I question if there is as much in <u>her</u> of the <u>defying</u> <u>principle</u> as the <u>Love</u> <u>of</u> <u>Crime</u>. . .

The "<u>one</u> <u>or</u> <u>two</u> <u>circumstances</u>" William alludes to as having caused a suspicion once to cross his mind, are the conversations I had with him last autumn. I then said that I could not

endure the idea of your suspecting that I had pierced so dreadful a secret, but of course the case is now altered. You will at
once see that while I had <u>no</u> <u>proof</u> whatever of my ideas being
<u>founded</u>, the merest suggestion to you of so horrible a thing, &
from <u>me</u> too, was frightful to think of; – convinced tho' I was in
my own mind that <u>you</u> too well knew much more than I could
suggest even. –

I N THE NEXT LETTER Ada discusses Dr Lamarck's evolution-
ary theories, which were at great variance to those of Babbage's friend, Charles Darwin, who at this time was busily
working on his *Origin of the Species.*

Another theory that is the subject of several letters is mesmerism. Elliotson, a mesmerist, expanded the theories of F. A.
Mesmer (1733-1815), who used animal magnetism to induce a
hypnotic effect. Elliotson founded the Phrenological Society of
London and established a journal in 1844, which ran to thirteen
volumes.

To Lady Byron

Wednesday, 3 March [1841]   St James' Square

Dearest Mama. I cannot recall the precise moment or circumstance which <u>first</u> suggested to me the idea of the miserable
events we have been writing about, although I can remember
<u>several</u> which have confirmed & strengthened the impression
already in my mind. I think however that it is some years at
least, perhaps, six, seven, or eight, if not more, since that
impression has been very distinctly teased (?) out. But it
appears to me very odd that I cannot remember its <u>origin</u>. Perhaps I may some day. –

I should tell you that I did not suspect the daughter as
being the <u>result</u> of it. – In fact the notion would not naturally
occur, because Mrs L [Augusta Leigh] being <u>married</u> at the
time, it might not have been easy to prove this, or even to feel

any degree of certainty about it. –

I should like some time to know how you ever came even to suspect anything so monstrous. The natural intimacy & familiarity of a Brother & Sister certainly could not suggest it, to any but a very depraved & vicious mind, which yours' decidedly was not. I cannot help fancying that he himself must have given you some very clear hint of it. He too well liked to taunt you with his crimes. – Alas!

Although it is impossible for me to think of my Father's memory with feelings of respect or veneration, still I am not wholly unable to contemplate him with some gratification. I believe I have derived from him the flower of his characteristics, & I cannot but think on this with pleasure; for his genius & superiority in certain ways were unquestionable. I ought to do greater things than ever he did, but there is less flash about me & much more depth, therefore I shall be a much longer time about it & also in all probability my reign (if ever I have one) over mankind will be chiefly after my death or at any rate a much more extensive & powerful one than at any period of my life. Whereas his reign is already less than it was – I once told you that I have an ambition to make a compensation to mankind for his misused genius. If he has transmitted to me any portion of that genius, I would use it to bring out great truths & principles. I think he has bequeathed this task to me! I have this feeling strongly; & there is a pleasure attending it. No – I cannot think on him without some associations that are pleasing, & also a feeling that I have a duty to perform towards him. –

. . . I am much interested in a book that Mr Babbage desired me to get – Lamarck's Philosophie Zoologique There are most curious things in it; & it seems to confirm some of my views. – I must manage to collect everything I can relating to the Nervous System . . .

Dr Elliotson is to show me by and bye his present most striking case. I hear that one theory of the mode of action of Mesmerism is that it is an abstraction of the Electricity of the body, electricity being the bond of union between mind & muscular action. . .

To Sophia De Morgan

6 o'clock Sunday Evening [Spring, 1841]   St James' Square

My Dear Mrs De Morgan. I am very sorry indeed at the extremely disappointing account you give of yourselves; & also I am much disappointed at losing the pleasure of spending this evening with you. – I was out when your note arrived...

Can I, (as far as you at present foresee), spend <u>next</u> Sunday Evening with you? I hope so, for I believe it will be my last Sunday previous to going to Paris.

Another of the little mathematical <u>epochs</u>, that are so interesting to me, has arrived; I mean another chapter of the Differential Calculus is just satisfactorily completed, & I have a whole bundle of papers to submit to Mr De Morgan upon it, & one or two questions to ask on some trifling points that are not perfectly clear. But as it is not of a nature that immediately presses, all this may I think wait till I can come to you. – Meantime I shall begin Chapter VI on Integration &c.

I have since I saw you had such a <u>wonderful</u> <u>quantity</u> of occupations of various sorts to get thro', that I feel a little surprised how I have managed to accomplish even this much Mathematics. – However I do not think anything will ever manage to oust the <u>latter</u>. Indeed the last fortnight is rather a convincing proof that nothing can. I have been out either to the Opera, German Opera, or somewhere or other, <u>every</u> night. I have had music lessons <u>every</u> morning, & practised my Harp too, for an hour or two; & I have been on horseback nearly every day also. I might add many <u>sundries</u> & <u>et-ceteras</u> to this list. –

I must however maintain that the Differential Calculus is king of the company;- & may it ever be so! – Believe me, Yours most sincerely   A.A. Lovelace

To Charles Babbage

[February, or March 1841]

   ... A Welsh Boy named John Thomas, who played the Welsh Harp with talent, & appeared to possess great musical powers,

was placed in Septr at the Royal Academy, by Lady Lovelace &
some friends, who contributed sufficient by private subscrip-
tion to keep him there a year. His parents are of the poorest
class, & unable to assist further than by <u>clothing</u> him. – To give
him anything of an education which could be permanently useful; he ought to remain at the Academy for at least 3 years, & it
is proposed to have a public Concert for his benefit in the
beginning of March, at the Opera-House Concert Rooms, under
the patronage of 8 ladies. . . It is proposed that each Lady
Patroness should endeavour to induce as many acquaintances
as possible to go to the Concert, & should have tickets in her
possession to dispose of. – The Concert is to be first-rate in
point of the performers, so that it may be really worth any one's
while to go for the sake of the <u>music</u>. . .

To Charles Babbage

Monday Night, 5 April 1841   St James' Square

My Dear Mr Babbage. Tomorrow morning sees me off in the
Boulogne Boat, long before you will receive this note. – All is
going on well here, & Lord L recovering now rapidly. I leave
him in charge of his Sisters, & expect him to follow me before
long. –

Now as to the Concert; it is <u>finally</u> arranged. I believe that
it will take place at Mrs David Barclay's house, 8 Belgrave
Square on Weddy the 12th May.

Costa to be the director; & in my absence Mrs D Barclay
acts as my proxy, & is to make all the arrangements which cannot remain till after my return. She asked me if I thought she
might venture to consult <u>you</u> on one or two points which may
occur; – as <u>intermediate</u> <u>to</u> <u>the</u> <u>Duchess</u> <u>of</u> <u>Somerset</u>, whom she
does not know. I replied that I felt sure you would not object.
Perhaps I should not thus have taken upon myself to answer for
you; but at any rate this may prepare you for some probable
communication from her. . .

It would perhaps be well to acquaint the Duchess of Somerset with the present state of affairs, & also that any reference

made to Mrs Barclay is the same as one to me, she having full powers in everything.

If you wish to write to me, Poste-Restante, Paris will do as my address. – I expect to return about the 25th. – Yours most sincerely,   Augusta Ada Lovelace

To William, Lord Lovelace

Saturday Morning, 8 April [1841]   Place Vendôme, Paris

Dearest William. I am very comfortably & happily established, here with the dear Hen, – who seems much pleased with Avis in all respects. I see a good deal of Medora; by my <u>own</u> <u>desire</u> <u>&</u> <u>choice</u> I mean, for so scrupulous is the Hen that she has placed her in an appartement quite in a separate wing of the house, in order that she may be in no way <u>forced</u> either on myself or any other of the Hen's visitors.

I therefore go there whenever I choose, & she does not come into the other apartments. I have formed a very favorable opinion of her. She impresses me with the idea of <u>principle</u> very strongly; & I find from the Hen, (who has now communicated to me everything) . . . I have heard altogether a history <u>most</u> <u>shocking</u>. The whole of it must be made known to you, but this can be done only in conversation.

As for the ruin of Medora, it was effected by the <u>united</u> <u>efforts</u> of the <u>Mother</u>; <u>the Sister Mr T [Trevanion]</u>; and Mr T himself; & by means of <u>drugging</u> the victim, who found herself ruined on coming to her senses.

Under these circumstances Medora herself (who always particularly <u>hated</u> Mr T) must be considered absolutely guiltless. She emancipated herself as soon as possible from Mr T; but owing to the evil conspiracy against her, she was in a manner <u>forced</u> to remain in his power during 2 or 3 years. The story is altogether a very horrible one, & yet Alas! it is <u>nothing</u> to what I have heard of circumstances now many years passed away! – So iniquitous & villainous a tale could never have entered into the imagination of any but the wretched actors themselves. –

How comes it that my Mother is not either dead, mad or depraved?. . . A <u>new</u> <u>language</u> is requisite to furnish terms strong enough to express my horror & amazement at the appalling facts! – That <u>viper</u> Mrs L [Augusta Leigh] – crowned all by suppressing letters of my Mother's to my Father when he was abroad after the separation, & <u>forging</u> <u>others</u> in their place! <u>She-monster!!</u>

As far as I can make out, my Mother will be in England this summer, but spend the winter abroad again. There is no doubt how very materially better in health she is out of England during the latter season.

I have never seen her so well; & she shines most brightly on the Avis. . .

I am very glad I have come here, & my journey has not in the least fatigued or troubled me . . .

The affectionate Avis

ADA DID NOT ALLOW HERSELF to be totally overwhelmed by Lady Byron's scenario and followed up Babbage's suggestion to visit his friend Arago, who was head of the observatory. Everyday concerns were also on her mind as she wrote that she needed a comb from her hairdresser, Isadore.

A reference in the next letter to past legal history needs clarification to understand the strange relationship between Lady Byron and Medora. As a result of Lord and Lady Byron's marriage settlement, part of what Lord Byron left to Augusta was tied up until Lady Byron died. Augusta did not get the money directly. Augusta wanted to help Medora, so she established a £3000 trust fund for Marie, Medora's illegitimate daughter, most likely from funds in the control of Lady Byron. My understanding is that Medora was trying to obtain the deed that was the legal acknowledgment of the trust fund so that she could borrow money against the deed.

When Ada and William returned to London in May, Ada was at first filled with hope that she could resume all her activities.

She encouraged William in his political career. Some of William's friends thought he did not live up to his political potential, even though he was the Lord Lieutenant of Surrey. Ada resumed her social activities and mathematical studies, but she also had bouts of illness. I have chosen not to speculate on the exact nature of Ada's illnesses. Some biographers have done that and have been wide of the mark. Physicians on the faculties of the University of California at San Francisco and Yale University have looked at these letters and stated that it is impossible to diagnose a patient you cannot examine who described an illness in terminology meaning one thing in the nineteenth century and another thing today. Whatever her illness was, in these letters she mentioned for the first time using laudanum, an opium derivative widely used at the time for various illnesses.

In June she met Dr James Phillips Kay, a physician and educational reformer. He is credited with establishing the British school system for which he was later knighted. He was totally captivated by Ada.

In August all the Lovelaces went off to Ashley Combe in Somerset. Ada took her mathematics papers with her and resumed her mathematical correspondence with De Morgan.

To William, Lord Lovelace

Tuesday Morning, 11 April [1841]   22 Place Vendôme, Paris

Dearest William. . . I am going this morning with Dr Mojon to the Observatory to meet Arago; & later in the day with Madame de Meulan to the Chamber of Deputies. I have not but very few moments that are idle. There is so much to be done. Last night Miss Montgomery & I went to the Theâtre Francais.

I believe I am to be presented at Court and the Hen intends giving the Bird plumage for the purpose; but we propose waiting for this till you come, as you should go too.

Will you tell Hester to be so kind as get me at Isadore's in Bentwich St, one of the little gum-brushes for putting gum on my hair. I am in great distress for one, mine having come to pieces; & I cannot find one here. – You can bring this. It is a very tiny thing. –

I continue from all I see & hear to have a favourable impression of Medora's character. But, there is at this moment a cruel conspiracy against her, – her Mother the instigator. I believe the affair <u>will</u> come into <u>Court</u>. <u>I</u> see no alternative.

Think of Mrs L [Leigh] sending word to Mr T [Trevanion] that her other daughter Emily is <u>ready</u> for him whenever he chooses to come to England for her; which, being outlawed, he luckily cannot do!

What a <u>monster</u> of iniquity! And how her wretched children, who are all her victims one way or other, are to be deeply pitied. –

I hope you burn these letters.

The affectionate Bird

To William, Lord Lovelace

Friday Afternoon [June 1841]

My Dearest Mate. I am <u>so</u> happy altogether, & so well & nice today, that I don't know how to put my <u>chirps</u> & gaiety on paper so as to convey the thrush's glee to her dear Mate. I have quantities to tell him – I have been making acquaintance with Sir William Molesworth. I <u>rode</u> with him two days ago, which was my first introduction to him, – arranged by Mr Duppa. We took to each other <u>much</u>, & I was most agreeably surprised & disappointed in his gentlemanlike respectful manners, & the <u>absence</u> of everything like self-sufficiency or conceit. He has just been with me today, & we have had a long & highly interesting conversation on science, mathematics, metaphysics &c.

I have invited him to Ockham (of which I hope you will not disapprove). He has a most extraordinary intellect, & I consider him a valuable addition to <u>my</u> flock. – . . .

This evening I go to the German opera with Dr Kay. –

I have been very much with the Hen since you went. She seems to like & approve me, & all my plans & intentions, as far as I have explained them; and especially my intended &

increasing intercourse & projects with Dr Kay. She has been further discussing <u>me</u> with him, & she tells me she is <u>aston-ished</u> at his knowledge, penetration, & judgement respecting me; & much <u>gratified</u> to see the honest & disinterested friend-ship he entertains for the <u>Avis</u>. –

Pray love the happy Bird, who never can be grateful enough for the relation & friends she is so singularly blessed with; from <u>ou</u> downwards.

I was disappointed to have no letter from you this morning . . .

Avis Phoenix . . .

To Charles Babbage

Tuesday night [Undated]   10 St James' Square

My Dear Mr Babbage. What say you to taking a Stall for the <u>Italian</u> Opera on Thursdy.

Miss King, Dr Kay, & I are going, & I want a fourth. If you agree, would <u>you</u> like to give away the two <u>German</u> Stalls for that night, to any friends of yours to whom it would be a treat. –

You never come & see me now, or take any notice of me. You see I am growing quite <u>huffy</u>. –

The reason I could not meet you on Thursdy <u>last</u>, was in consequence of a sudden arrangement about some <u>Mesmerism</u>, which it was important for me to attend to; & I could not with-out great inconvenience let you know. –

But you must dine here on Thursday. That I insist on. – And pray do not <u>quite</u> <u>forget</u> <u>me</u>, for I think there seems some dan-ger of it.

Yours most sincerely

A. Ada Lovelace

To William, Lord Lovelace

Monday 7 o'clock [June or July 1841]   Ockham

Dearest. You will like to hear that I am doing very well . . .

Dr Kay found it necessary to give me more laudanum &c before luncheon today; & it was not possible for me to think of going out even. But I have had a capital sleep this afternoon, & am much refreshed now, & mending fast. Dr Kay left, with the boots, about three. He is most kind, & leaving us <u>all</u> more than ever attached to him, particularly myself.

Indeed I will try & attend to everything he says to me, & I never can sufficiently be grateful & attached to him for all his kindness and friendship for me. . .

Dearest mate; forgive the poor naughty sick Bird. May it be Avis Phoenix?

To Augustus De Morgan

Saturday Morning [July 1841]   St James' Square

Dear Mr De Morgan. I hope you have not by this time come to the conclusion that I have drowned the Differential Calculus at least (if not myself with it also) in the Seine or the Channel.

I am setting about work again now in good earnest. To say the truth I find myself a little bit rusty & awkward. I have been some days getting my <u>head in</u> again & it is not yet even at all what it was. However this will soon mend, I doubt not. I very easily <u>lose</u> a habit, but then I very easily reform it. But I am a little vexed at this interruption. I was going on so nicely. . .

I think instead of plaguing <u>myself</u> more about the misty parts, I had better apply to you; for I am inclined to get a little worried about it, which is always to be avoided. – I should prefer <u>seeing</u> you to writing . . .

Pray believe me, Yours very truly

A.A. Lovelace

To Augustus De Morgan

Monday, 6 July [1841]   Ockham

Dear Mr De Morgan. . . Since dispatching my letter yesterday, I remember I have not even quite fully & <u>correctly</u> stated the whole points. . .

You must tell me if I presume <u>too</u> <u>much</u> on your kindness to me. I am so engrossed at present with my mathematical &

scientific plans & pursuits that I can think of little else; – &
perhaps may be a plague & bore to my friends about these
subjects; for after my <u>interruption</u> from Paris & London pursuits & occupations, my whole heart is with my renewed studies; & every minutia even is a matter of the greatest interest.
Believe me, Your most truly

A.A. Lovelace

To Charles Babbage

Thursday, 22 July [1841]   Ockham Park

My Dear Mr Babbage. I am exceedingly vexed, that the rain
yesterday disturbed my plans in Town, & prevented my going to
you as I intended. –

Will you come here Tuesday, by the Train which <u>leaves</u> at
five, & arrives at Weybridge Station a few minutes before six.

Another friend, Mr E Duppa, comes at that time; & our
carriage will be there. – Hoping to see you so soon (& that you
will <u>stay as long as possible</u>). I say no more. But I have much to
talk to you about. My studies &c, &c, &c. – Yours always, Most
sincerely   A.L.

To Charles Babbage

11 August [1842]   Ockham Park, Ripley, Surrey

My Dear Babbage. Will you come on Satdy the 20th, to visit us
for 3 or 4 days. We expect Fonblanque & others. In haste,
Yours most sincerely,   A.Ada Lovelace

To Charles Babbage

Sunday, 14 August [1842]   Ockham Park

My Dear Babbage. Will you come <u>Sunday</u> the 21st, instead of
Satdy. I find it will suit us better. And <u>pray</u> stay till Weddy
Morning. We have friends coming whom I am <u>very</u> desirous you
should remain for. In haste, Yours ever

A.A. Lovelace

To Augustus De Morgan

Sunday, 15 August [1841]   Ockham Park

Dear Mr De Morgan. You must be beginning to think me lost. I have been however hard at work, with the exception of 10 days complete interruption from company. I have now many things to enquire; First of all; can I spend an evening with Mrs De Morgan & yourself on Tuesday the 24th? On that day we go to Town to remain till Friday, when we move down to Ashley for 2 months at least. . .

I have been especially studying this subject of Circulating Force, & believe that I now understand it very completely. I found that I could not _rest_ upon it at all until I made the _whole_ of the subject out entirely to my satisfaction. . . Yours most truly   A.A. Lovelace

I N THE NEXT SERIES OF LETTERS Ada hypothesized a geometry of the "fourth dimension." Several popular books today deal with this subject: Rudy Rucker's _The Fourth Dimension_, Stephen Hawking's _A Brief History of Time,_ and Philip Davis's _Descartes' Dream_. Also note Ada's mention of Bernoulli numbers, which are explained later when Ada suggested to Babbage that they be used in her description of the Analytical Engine.

The remains of Ada's correspondence to Augustus De Morgan are generally scattered, skewed, and undated; when they are dated, the dates are often incorrect. For example, Ada sent two letters to De Morgan Sunday 6 July, and the other Monday 6 July; both appear from their contents to have been written in 1841.

A constant theme in Ada's letters to De Morgan was the concern that she was taking up his time needlessly. She asked him whether he received the pheasants and whether he would like to come to visit. All her intense mathematical activity and correspondence with De Morgan prompted her to speculate. Many of her speculations, from extending geometry to other dimensions to her description of the nature of a function, have turned out to be correct.

Her correspondence with De Morgan in November 1841 was almost daily; she was working feverishly, "drowning in Calculus." Ada may also have been writing other feverish letters to Dr. Kay that do not remain because after Ada died he wrote Lady Byron: "No passage of my life is so full of marvel as the friendship with which I was honoured by your daughter. I felt that such a friendship as that with which she had distinguished me, must cease to be demonstrative after my marriage."

Whatever the exact nature of their relationship was, it can only be hinted at. There are hints. On 21 October Dr Kay wrote to Ada: "I have bethought me a new name for you which is prompted by your waywardness, beauty, & intangibility – You always elude my grasp, and seem to delight in leading me into some bog, while I am gazing on you half in admiration, half in wonder, somewhat in apprehension, and altogether in kindness. Henceforth you are christened 'Will-o'-the Whisp' A delusive & beautiful light flickering with wayward course over every dangerous pitfall."

On 27 October Ada decided to go to town, meaning London. She wrote her mother a letter about Byron and returned to Ashley Combe, Porlock. Ada found it difficult to understand graphing a functional equation, a wave, and generating that wave by graphing it point by point.

Lord Byron, as mentioned in the Introduction, described emotional relationships in terms of mathematical shapes, "princess of the parallelograms," "squaring her notions." Ada went in the opposite direction. In a letter written on 27 November [1841] she used the personal characterization Kay attributed to her, a "Will-o'-the Whisp" (Kay misspelled Wisp) to describe the whole functional equation. By doing that she revealed not only her frustration, but her understanding.

Using modern mathematical, scientific, and economic terminology, she laid a personal characterization on a mathematical term, much as a seamstress lays a pattern on material. Then Ada used the word "tangibility" to emphasize the "Will-o'-the-Wisp" metaphor.

The collapse Ada felt in her verbal metaphor of tangibility is suggestive of a problem with the mathematical metaphors of modern physics, the dilemma that relates to the difficulty in measuring a wave function that changes continuously and causally (measuring at two specific points separated by time) and discontinuously and erratically, as a result of observation. The difficulty in observation is termed "the collapse of the wave-function."

To Augustus De Morgan

19 September [1841]

Dear Mr De Morgan. I have more to say to you than ever; (beginning with many thanks for your beautiful replies to my last packet)...

It cannot help striking me that this extension of Algebra ought to lead to a further extension similar in nature, to the Geometry of Three Dimensions; & that again perhaps to a further extension in some unknown region & so ad-infinitum possibly...

I enclose you also a paper I have written explaining a difficulty of mine in the Definitions of the Geometrical Algebra...

I hope you receive game regularly. Yours most truly

A.A. Lovelace

P.S. Did you ever hear of a Science called Descriptive Geometry? I think Monge is the originator of it.

To Augustus De Morgan

Wednesday, 27 October [1841] Ashley Combe, Porlock, Somerset

Dear Mr De Morgan. I have for the last fortnight been daily intending to write to you on mathematical matters; & now I do not think it worth while because I have an idea of being in Town on Tuesdy next for a day or two. And if I could see you on Weddy either by your kindly coming to me at 12 o' clock that day, or by my going to spend Weddy Evg in Gower St, it would answer the purpose much better. Besides having a list of par-

<u>ticular</u> little things to ask you about; I am now anxious to consult you again as to my <u>general</u> progress & way of going on. I have one or two little difficulties just now.

I believe we shall remain on here for some weeks longer. My intended journey to Town is only one particular business. And by the bye it is <u>not</u> <u>to</u> <u>be</u> <u>known</u> <u>that</u> <u>I</u> <u>am</u> <u>going</u>. My mother even has no idea of it; & I do not wish that she should. So I will thank you & Mrs De Morgan to mention nothing about it to anyone.

How is she? And <u>when</u> to be confined? – Yours most truly

A.A. Lovelace

To Augustus De Morgan

Monday, 8 November [1841]   Ashley-Combe

Dear Mr De Morgan. . . I am much obliged by your letter. I send a corrected version (now I believe <u>quite</u> <u>right</u>). . .

I should perhaps mention that lately I have had my mind a good deal distracted by some circumstances of considerable annoyance & anxiety to us; & I have certainly studied much <u>less</u> <u>well</u> & <u>more</u> <u>negligently</u> in consequence. Indeed the last few weeks I have not at all got on as I wished and intended; & I find that to <u>force</u> <u>myself</u>, (when disinclined & distracted [?]), <u>beyond</u> <u>a</u> <u>certain</u> <u>point</u> is very disadvantageous. So on these occasions <u>I</u> <u>just</u> <u>keep</u> <u>gently</u> <u>going</u>, without however attempting very much. I am hoping now to get <u>a</u> <u>good</u> <u>lift</u> again before long; as I think I am returning to a more settled & concentrated state of mind. I mention all this as an excuse for some errors & over-sights which I conceive are more likely just at present to creep into my performances than would usually be the case. . .

Pray congratulate Mrs De Morgan on the arrival & prosperity of <u>Pudge</u>. Your most truly   A.A.L.

To Augustus De Morgan

Sunday, 21 November [1841]   Ashley Combe

My Dear Mr De Morgan. I said <u>Weddy.</u> At least I meant to do so. On <u>Tuesday</u> I have already an engagement in the morning. Perhaps you have written <u>Tuesday</u> by mistake. But if you cannot come on Weddy, then I must put off my <u>Tuesday's</u> engagement, that I may see you <u>then</u>. If it is the same to you however, I should much prefer <u>Weddy</u>...

I have referred to <u>Numbers of Bernoulli</u> & to <u>Differences of Nothing</u>; in consequence of reading the Article <u>Operation</u>. And find that I must read that on <u>Series</u> also...

I will not trouble you further in this letter. But I have a <u>formidable</u> <u>list</u> of <u>small</u> <u>matters</u> down, against I see you. – Yours most sincerely

A.A. Lovelace

To Augustus De Morgan

27 November [1841]   Ashley Combe

Dear Mr. De Morgan. I have I believe made some little progress towards the comprehension of the Chapter on Notation of Functions, & I enclose you my Demonstration of one of the Exercises at the end of it...

I do not know when I have been so tantalized by anything, & should be ashamed to say <u>how</u> much time I have spent upon it, in vain. These Functional Equations are complete Will-o'-the-Wisps to me. The moment I fancy I have really at last got hold of something tangible & substantial, it all recedes further and further & vanishes again into thin air...

Really I do not give you a Sinecure. Your letters are however well bestowed, in as far as the use they are of to me, can make them so, and the great encouragement that such assistance is to me to continue my Studies with zeal & spirit.

We are to return to Surrey very soon. I expect to have occasion to trouble you again before we go, & after that I shall hope to see you & Mrs De Morgan in Town, where I intend to be for two or three days in about a fortnight.

Yours very truly

A.A. L.

9.

Scorn and Fury, Poetical Genius, Not Dropping the Thread of Mathematics, A Nice Colony of Friends
[1842]

I T APPEARS THAT ADA took a giant step back from her mathematical studies, for no more letters to De Morgan were found in the files for the rest of 1841. In February 1842, Dr. Kay married, and henceforth became known as Dr Kay-Shuttleworth.

Once again Ada was ill. She turned to poetry, the theater and music as more appropriate channels for her energies and intellect. These interests provoked strong reactions from her family. Neither her husband nor her mother approved of that direction. William wrote Ada many letters asking her not to drop her mathematical and scientific interests. The more William criticized Ada's musical and dramatic interests, the more she defended her position.

Many of these letters are not dated and from the inconsistency in tone, it may appear that some are out of sequence, but then Ada was not consistent. She often vacillated between being very practical like her mother and very wild like her father, especially during 1842, when she was trying to create a future that would meet both her intellectual and emotional needs.

To William, Lord Lovelace

Saturday, 4 o'clock, [February 1842]

I have posted your letter to the Hen. You have blundered about her stay in Town. . .

I did <u>not</u> forget the Medallion. <u>Wyon</u> is the man to take my likeness; but he has of late declined all private commissions. Wheatstone thinks however that when he has been introduced to me, & knows that <u>I</u> am the lady in question, he will not object. Wheatstone only mentioned a lady. There is no one, Wheatstone says, at all to compare with him for medallion likeness... But really I don't think I am pretty enough to be medallioned at all...

Wedding-cake has arrived from Mr & Mrs Kay Shuttleworth...

To William, Lord Lovelace

Thursday Night, [Undated, Spring, 1842]   St James' Square

Dearest William. I have had much satisfaction in my consultation with Dr L [Locock] as to my case altho' he takes a somewhat different view...

I am terribly tormented by smoke here; – in fact it is quite filthy & odious here. I have no peace with it: having only the choice of <u>suffocation</u> or <u>starvation</u>.

I have just returned from seeing the Merchant of Venice at Drury Lane. And I cannot say how gratified I have been – Macready's Shylock is so excellent, that really <u>you</u> must see it. I am highly pleased with all I see & hear of his undertaking in that Theatre. He seems likely to raise the tone & style of our stage most laudably; – & <u>Shakespeare's</u> <u>plays</u> have a chance of being <u>worthily</u> performed...

I have just had my first lesson from a Signor Faia, a highly reputable & suitable person in all respects. – He seems not a little pleased with me; & to anticipate that I may even attain <u>any</u> <u>degree</u> of perfection; having a wonderful <u>facility</u>...

I am just starting for Esher. So Goodbye.

To William, Lord Lovelace

Tuesday [April 1842]

My dearest Mate. I quite agree in the wisdom of your remarks;

but I think that I have perhaps led you slightly into an error as to the nature & intensity of my <u>dramatic</u> wishes & plans.

I consider the dramatic <u>representation</u> as only <u>one</u> ingredient (tho' an important & to me essential one), of far more enlarged views; & I would on <u>no</u> <u>account</u> make it my <u>main-stay</u>. . .

Now do you begin to comprehend my views? – . . . but I have genius enough to perceive that a great poet . . . (that is what <u>I</u> call a great Poet), must go thro' a vast and arduous training . . . Now, dear William, I had not intended to impart to you at present these recent occurrences; but I feel from your late letters, that no one is so worthy of it. I had feared your disapproval. . . But, Oh Heaven! may <u>you</u>, dear William, understand it all in its' <u>true</u> <u>light</u>! For I tremble, lest I might receive <u>any</u> check from <u>you</u>! It might utterly blast me, slow tho' sure in its' effects.

ADA DID HER SHARE of criticizing William by admonishing him for the way he dealt with the children and suggested to him that instead of teaching Byron in a classroom, he should "take him outdoors . . . conversing with him on the objects around him." After he had received many pages of emotional letters, William stopped humoring her. He was skeptical about her hopes for a musical and literary career. He related a story of a bird pecking at the picture on a Greek vase, thinking it was real. Ada, like the bird, was deluded.

William discussed the state of affairs with Lady Byron, which certainly did not please Ada, but she slowly resumed "doing her duty." However, Ada's attitude towards both her husband and her mother began to change. It was difficult for her to step back from either one, especially when they acted as a concerted force. And to add to Ada's torment at this time, Lady Byron kept the Medora issue alive for her. Elizabeth Medora was set up in a home not far from Ockham.

I have deleted many letters that referred to William's sister Hester, who was a major support for Ada. Later, in the 1880s,

Lady Anne Blunt (Annabella) recalled how her Aunt Hester brought joy to her childhood. Hester helped Ada with the children, and when she became engaged to Sir George Craufurd, Ada had mixed emotions.

She tried to keep in touch with her old friend Charles Babbage. She never felt that Babbage considered such subjects as mathematics, science, and technology as duty; they were joys to him. Her interest in mathematics could not be a self-sacrificing endeavor. Though there are no letters that explain why she returned to her mathematical studies, she did, most likely in the summer of 1842 after a year's absence.

To William, Lord Lovelace

Thursday, 1/2 past 4 o'clock [Undated, 1842]

Dearest Mate. I am as careful as you can wish, to burn your letters; but they would be quite safe at any rate, for there is trouble enough to make them out even for <u>me</u>; I am sure <u>no servant</u> <u>could</u> by any possibility do so. Now don't, dear Old Crow, fancy that a saucy Thrush is insulting <u>ou</u>, & revenge yourself by not writing. You know how I like to have your letters, & how I admire your handwriting. But tho' very <u>pretty</u> it never is very <u>legible</u>.

In consequence of the enclosed from the Hen, I went myself in the Chariot to meet her; which pleased her, & was more than she expected. I left her at Lord Byron's & went on to the Royal Institution to a Lecture, sending the carriage back to her for her use this afternoon. So you see the Bird does not neglect that <u>nice</u> <u>old</u> <u>Gentleman</u> the Hen!

Today I had my Singing Lesson at 10 o' clock, for an hour & a half. Then Wheatstone for 2 hours; then to the Railway: then the Lecture. And now I must set to work to practise my harp for 4 or 5 hours at least. . .

But you see I attend to my <u>business</u> in real <u>good</u> <u>earnest</u> despite there being very special Theatrical attraction just now too. . .

I am well & happy; & I hope doing my duty, & getting on in everything. . .

To Charles Babbage

Monday, 2 May [1842]   St James' Square

My Dear Babbage. Will you do me the favor of showing your Calculating Machine to an old friend of mine, who is on leave of absence from India, & is to return there immediately. It is Mr Henry Siddons, Grandson of the Mrs Siddons, & first cousin to Mrs Butler, & Adelaide Kemble

He is very desirous of just seeing the small portion that was completed, of your old machine. His wishes arise from the perusal of your 9th Bridgewater Treatise; & he would ask leave to call on you for that purpose any morning this week that you can fix.

I believe that the favour would be well bestowed by you. He is not one of the idle or merely inquisitive; altho', he himself is fully aware of, he cannot pretend or expect to comprehend much of the principles on which the machine is planned & executed. Yours ever,   A.A. Lovelace

To William, Lord Lovelace

Thursday, 6 o'clock [July 1842]   67 Regent St Cambridge

Dearest W. I have got a tiny Setting & Bed-room in a lodging house close by here. . . Sir G Craufurd was I believe in India some years; I suppose also there in the clerical capacity. He came to the title & property unexpectedly, in consequence of the death of his elder brother.

He is a bachelor, between 40 & 50. Hopes for H [Hester] I think . .

Gamlen is gone over to Brampton today, for a night. I am delighted at this; tho' I lose him here; for he does not return to Cambridge.

He holds me out hopes of a visit of a week to Ockham, this

summer or autumn. This would be to me charming; & hardly
less so to you.

Your sisters were quite amused & pleased with his delight
at so unexpectedly meeting me here yesterday. He took the
bird in his arms, & kissed her; & then turning to them, said,
"You know she is quite my own little girl; & as such I must
always treat her. But believe me too, I respect her as much as I
love her." . . .

Dear Me! If I could, what a nice colony of friends I would
have to live with me! I would have F. Knight, Dr Locock,
Gamlen, & I think Kay Shuttleworth. And _perhaps_ admit _you_
as 5th; tho' really of what use an old Crow could be to me I
know not.

You see the Bird is saucy today! – But yet she's a good bird
too, is she not, to write you such long letters . . .

DURING THE SUMMER OF 1842, Ada was still disturbed by
the "Paris Affair," or, more specifically, Elizabeth Medora
Leigh. Medora was a constant reminder of Ada's father's alleged
depravity. Ada had tried to help when she was in Paris by hiring
a French maid, Nathalie Beaurepaire, who was paid by Lady
Byron. Nathalie told Lady Byron about Medora's behavior and
activities. It became obvious to Nathalie that Medora was not a
"proper lady." Before Medora left for a short trip to France, Ada
suggested solutions to Medora's problems. She became her
mother's voice to Medora, as she would soon become Babbage's
voice to the scientific community. Elizabeth Medora would have
none of Ada's suggestions.

To William, Lord Lovelace

Tuesday Afternoon [Undated]

Dearest W. . . The Paris affair has turned out most miserably &
vexatiously. I cannot bear to think of it, & the _folly_ of so many
people.

I am endeavouring to do all you would most wish, dearest I am endeavouring to do all you would most wish, dearest W. My scientific & literary pursuits must ever be the main thing, evidently, for myself; & quite make everything yield now (excepting consideration of <u>health</u> & <u>exercise</u>) to these engagements.

Don't say, & don't think, that my resolutions cannot be trusted to. However, even if you <u>do</u>, there is the comfort of remembering that you are not <u>God</u>, <u>Providence</u>, or <u>Fate</u>, & that your fears & doubts cannot <u>make</u> me fail, if I do not fail of <u>my own accord</u>.

Still I would like you to be my <u>good</u> Fate, & to anticipate perseverance & success. Adieu.

Mr De Morgan has been with me all this morning.

To Lady Byron

Monday Afternoon, [18 July 1842]   Ockham

. . . I am setting about my various avocations. I don't think tho' that I have anything very lively or interesting to write to you today. I am very unwell, very pale, & have a crack against Annabella; with whose great pudding face, & eyes sunk & small with vile fat, I have been quite amazed & horrified.

Never mind the tirade. I am more than ever usually <u>knocked</u> <u>down</u> with a certain occurrence; but W – says that I am very agreeable, very gentle, &c, &c. I only wish that nasty child of mine had not grown so fat. –

I am anxious to hear about you, & where you are. I hope you do not miss me much. I fear I have written a dull letter, which is why I added the above observation. One cannot be always <u>gay</u>, tho' one may be always fairly happy.

To Lady Byron

Monday Night, [25 July 1842]   Ockham

Dearest Hen . . . I think we shall get a decent stud at last . . .

You are a nice stingy Old Hen; (especially about <u>horses,</u> & to <u>myself</u> more particularly . . .)

I wonder why I waste pen, ink & paper on such a Skin-Flint as you. You are not worth expending any one of the three upon.

I am afraid you are lonely this evening. I wish I were with you. And yet I am satisfied where I am. So Good Night. . .

THE DATING OF the next letter is difficult. It appears that Ada returned to the study of mathematics in the fall of 1842; however, there are no other letters in August 1842 from Ashley Combe. Ada did write about going to Ashley, so perhaps the only letters that remain from this period are to De Morgan.

Ada's letters reveal that her approach to mathematics was out of the ordinary, most likely because she questioned basic assumptions. De Morgan, who knew her capacity better than anyone else, stated unequivocally that Ada's "power of thinking from the beginning of my correspondence with her, has been so utterly out of common way for any beginner, man, or woman. Mrs Somerville's mind never led her into other than the details of mathematical work: Lady L [Lovelace] will take quite a different route."

The last letter in this series is on exhibit at Newstead Abbey, Lord Byron's ancestral home.

To Augustus De Morgan

Monday, 4 September [1842?]   Ockham

Dear Mr De Morgan. Will you send the enclosed to Mrs De Morgan. It explains the arrangements I have made in case she comes here, & also that Lord L – & myself have delayed our departure until Satdy next.

Now to the mathematical business: I think you have hit the nail on the head, altho' my confused notion of the differential was not the only piece of puzzle & mistiness which constituted the impediments towards my comprehension. . .

I cannot help here remarking a circumstance which I think is almost invariably true respecting all my difficulties & confusions in studying. . .

I therefore have lately begun to ask myself whenever I am stopped, whether I clearly understood what the <u>subjects</u> of the reasoning are; & to go over carefully the verbal & symbolic representative of a thing or an idea, with the question respecting each "now what does it mean, & how was it got? Am I sure of this, is each instance involved in the subject?" This may save me much future trouble. . .

To Woronzow Greig

Friday, 16 December [1842]   Ashley

Dear Greig. . . We are to return directly to Surrey. . . As to <u>myself</u>, I think further explanation is necessary to you. At this moment I can only say that I never dreamt of <u>excelling</u> in more than <u>two</u> things, viz: one <u>mental</u> & <u>one</u> purely <u>executive</u> & <u>active</u> pursuit.

Say for instance my <u>Harp</u> & <u>Singing</u>; & whatever <u>mental</u> pursuit I might choose ultimately. I say <u>Harp</u> & <u>Singing</u> because I reckon them as <u>one</u>. The same principles apply to both. In the <u>one</u> I am already advanced three-fourths of the way, & the other is not likely to be a matter of much difficulty owing to my having the most flexible voice <u>possible</u>.

I am not dropping the <u>thread</u> of Science & Mathematics; & this may probably still be my ultimate vocation. Altho' it is likely perhaps to have a formidable rival to its being other than just my pastime; should I take seriously with "<u>undivided</u> <u>mind</u>" to musical Composition.

Time must show. To say the truth, I have less ambition than I had. And what I <u>really</u> care most about is now perhaps to establish in my mind those <u>principles</u> <u>&</u> <u>habits</u> that will best fit me for the next state. There is in my nervous system such utter want of <u>all</u> ballast & steadiness, that I cannot regard my life or powers as other than precarious.

And I am just the person to drop off some fine day when nobody knows anything about the matter or expects it. I have, I hope, a perfect confidence, in every contingency that may arise. –

Yours ever   A.L. . . .

To Woronzow Greig

Friday Night, 31 December [1842]   St James' Square

Dear Mr. Greig. Do come at 5 o'clock tomorrow; stay & dine
with me & go to the Play. And now don't be <u>unhappy</u> about <u>me</u>.
I am doing very well indeed; – as well as possible. And I have
no notion or idea whatever of either taking myself <u>out</u> <u>of</u> <u>the</u>
<u>world</u>, or being a useless invalid <u>in</u> <u>it</u>. So be easy. – You know I
am a d — d <u>odd</u> animal! And as my mother often says, she never
has quite yet made up her mind if it <u>Devil</u> or <u>Angel</u> that
watches <u>peculiarly</u> over me; only that it <u>is</u> one or the other,
<u>without</u> <u>doubt</u>! – (And for <u>my</u> part, I am quite indifferent
<u>which</u>) –

But if you knew one half the <u>harum-scarum</u> extraordinary
things I do, you would certainly incline to the idea that I have a
Spell of <u>some</u> sort about me. I am positive that no other <u>She</u>
Creature of <u>my</u> <u>years</u> <u>could</u> possibly <u>attempt</u> many of my everyday performances, with any impunity.

I think I must amuse you when we meet, by telling you
some of them. – Yours ever   A.L.

To William, Lord Lovelace

Thursday 4 o'clock [1842]   St James' Square

Dearest W. I have nothing <u>very</u> particular to tell you. . .

Wheatstone has been with me a long while today, & has
taken my translation away with him, after reading it over with
me. I hope to receive the <u>proofs</u> of it for correction, by & bye as
I trust Taylor will not reject it. I am now translating a beautiful
Italian scientific paper.

Tonight I take Hester to see Miss Kemble in Norma. –

I seem likely to lead a very quiet life I think altogether. –
And I certainly care little about anything but the scientific &
the musical. –

To Charles Babbage

Sunday, [Undated] [Maybe 1843]   Ockham

The lamentably small quantity of <u>margin</u> has placed my ingenuity in full play how to make all my corrections distinct & legible.

Why do they not give one more room? –

I am much better today. My <u>intellect</u> will keep me alive; & <u>active</u> & <u>merry</u> into the bargain.

I verily believe I should be in a bad way but for my <u>great objects</u>. If I were in circumstances that permitted of my dwelling much or long on <u>myself</u> & my <u>sensations,</u> it would be a very unpromising business. But I have happily got fairly <u>entrâinée</u> [involved] now, into a course which leaves me little opportunity for mere <u>self</u> study & speculation; & which moreover gives me pressing motives to desire not only a mere continuance, but a highly active & efficient continuance, of life in this world for many more years to come. Science has thrown its' net over me, & has fairly ensnared the fairy, in whatever she is.

Depend upon it that I here express a very remarkable & a very <u>true</u> <u>truth</u>. –

And I am quite certain that none is perhaps so capable of feeling the justice & reality of my own idea on the subject, as yourself.

A.L.

At <u>three</u> tomorrow.

10.

Working Like the Devil, A Fairy in Your Service, What a General I Would Make, An Analyst and a Metaphysician
[1843]

ADA GAVE WHEATSTONE, who was working with Richard Taylor, the publisher of a scientific journal, her translation of L. F. Menabrea's description of Babbage's Analytical Engine, which was published in French in a Swiss journal in October 1842. According to Babbage's recollection in his autobiography, *Passages,* many years after Ada's death, he wrote: "Some time after the appearance of his memoir [article] on the subject in the 'Bibliothéque Universelle de Génève,' the Countess of Lovelace informed me that she had translated the memoir of Menabrea. I asked why she had not herself written an original paper on the subject with which she was so intimately acquainted? To this Lady Lovelace replied that the thought had not occurred to her. I then suggested that she should add notes to Menabrea's memoir: an idea which was immediately adopted."

Babbage scribbled a note on 7 February 1843 stating that he had a meeting with Ada which was "under new circumstances." On 15 February Babbage, along with Dr Kay-Shuttleworth, attended the marriage of Hester King to Sir George Craufurd. Ada then started to "work like the Devil" for Babbage.

Chapters 10 and 11 contain Ada's correspondence during the period that she was writing the Notes. Her letters to Babbage reveal the process and the nature of their creative collaboration. Chapter 12 contains excerpts from Ada's Notes which, with the help of Colonel Rick Gross, have been annotated and related to the modern-day computer language named in her honor.

Ada's task was not easy because by the time Babbage died, he had filled over thirty volumes with plans for the Analytical Engine. Ada's job was to synthesize his ideas in such a way that the British government and scientists would recognize the value of Babbage's revolutionary invention. The publication, when completed, including Ada's translation of Menabrea's article and her Notes, was referred to as the Memoir. When Ada was finished with the Memoir, Babbage wanted to send it to Prince Albert, who had an interest in science. Babbage wanted to include a preface detailing the history of the British government's non-support of his calculating engines.

The letters that Ada wrote to Charles Babbage are located (with a few exceptions) in the British Library. The sequence of her letters to him can only be guessed at since so many are not dated. I have arranged a few letters in a different order from that in which they appear in the collection at the British Library.

Some biographers of Ada and Babbage call into question Ada's contribution to the Notes, almost as if Babbage wrote them and Ada was merely his secretary. It is hard to understand why that question even arose. Babbage in his autobiography clearly stated that Ada wrote the Notes based on the material he gave her. It was a collaborative effort because it was a description of Babbage's plans for an Analytical Engine. However, according to Babbage, Ada corrected a mathematical error that he had made. When Babbage tried to alter any of her Notes, Ada had something to say about his editing ability. The only help Babbage gave Ada, according to him, was in completing the table for the Bernoulli numbers as she was very ill at the time.

Ada began her task of writing the Notes by asking pertinent questions and selecting a mathematical model that would highlight the difference between Babbage's first calculating engine, the Difference Engine, and the Analytical Engine.

Ada's selection of the Bernoulli numbers was a perfect example to highlight the difference. To calculate Bernoulli numbers, one must perform many operations, then take the results of those operations and use them in other operations. For example, add, then divide, then raise to a power, and on and on. No mere calculator or calculating engine like the Difference Engine could perform this feat. Only the Analytical Engine could calculate Bernoulli numbers without the intervention of a "human hand or head" because numerical information and operational instructions would be received by means of a punch card (or punched card), which Babbage had adapted from Jacquard. Jacquard's punch card instructed the loom how to weave designs into a fabric.

Just as Ada was grounded in selecting a specific mathematical model that would show the power of the Analytical Engine, she was also developing a metaphysical understanding of the Analytical Engine. She began to see not only the technical details, but also the whole picture, the concept, of what the Analytical Engine could do. This was no easy task since Babbage had volumes of designs and many sample iterations of what today might be referred to as computer programs. Yet Ada, questioning and arguing with Babbage and distilling the information he gave her, was able to put his remarkable idea for the Analytical Engine in its proper perspective.

In the midst of this very serious undertaking, Ada wrote delightful and outlandish letters to Babbage. The letters are not only filled with discussions about Bernoulli numbers and the Medora melodrama, but visions of herself as a fairy, puzzle-pate and general. She even made references to flirtations with her Somerset neighbour, Frederick Knight. Babbage became her confidant, and she became his "interpretess."

To Charles Babbage

Thursday Morning [1843]   Ockham

My Dear Babbage. I have read your papers over with great attention; but I want you to answer me the following question by return of post. The day I called on you, you wrote off on a scrap of paper (which I have unluckily lost), that the <u>Difference</u> Engine would do. . . (something or other) but that the <u>Analytical</u> Engine would do. . . (something else which is absolutely general).

Be kind enough to write this out properly for me; & then I think I can make some <u>very</u> good Notes.

I have been considering about Prince Albert; but I much doubt the expediency of it. However there is time enough to consider of this.

I am anxious to hear how you are. Yours ever   A.A.L.

A DA BEGAN TO MAKE headway with the Notes and sent some off for Babbage's inspection. As for her Note A, Babbage replied the next day: "If you are as fastidious about the acts of your friendship as you are about those of your pen, I much fear I shall equally lose your friendship and your Notes. I am very reluctant to return your admirable & philosophic Note A. Pray do not alter it . . . All this was impossible for you to know by intuition and the more I read your notes the more surprised I am at them and regret not having earlier explored so rich a vein of the noblest metal."

Babbage continued his compliments and wrote her that Note D was in her usual "clear style."

In 1840 Ada had started thinking about putting games into mathematical language when she wrote Babbage about the game Solitaire. Using indices as a means of tracing each step of an algorithm was a similar conceptual skill.

The Analytical Engine would receive information about number, operations, and variables by means of the punched card. Ada wanted Babbage to be very specific about how the Analytical Engine would handle variables. In J. M. Dubbey's *The Mathematical Work of Charles Babbage,* he describes how Ada had a slightly more elaborate and improved way than Menabrea of writing out the sequence of operations taking into account the variables. From Ada's questions, and the table included and annotated in Chapter 12, I believe Ada had the skills that today are important to programmers and programming languages. The most important thing for Ada in writing this description was not fame or fortune but following the Lovelace family motto "Labor ipse voluptas" (Labor is its own reward).

To Charles Babbage

Monday [10 July 1843]   Ockham

My Dear Babbage. I am working very hard for you; like the Devil in fact; (which perhaps I am).

I think you will be pleased. I have made what appear to me some very important extensions & improvements. Why I now write is to beg you will send down to the Square before tomorrow evening. Brookes's Formulae, & also the Report of the Royal Society on your machine. I suppose you can get it easily, & I particularly want to see it, before I see you on Weddy Morg. –

It appears to me that I am working up the Notes with much success; & that even if the book be delayed in it's [sic] publication, a week or two, in consequence, it would be worth Mr Taylor's while to wait. I will have it well & fully done; or not at all.

I want to put in something about Bernoulli's Numbers, in one of my Notes, as an example of how an implicit function, may be worked out by the engine, without having been worked out by human head & hands first. Give me the necessary data & formulae. Yours ever   A.A.L.

To Charles Babbage

Saturday, 6 o'clock [Undated]

My dear Babbage. I have been hard at work all day, intending to send you the Diagram & all, quite complete.

Think of my horror then at just discovering that the Table & Diagram, (over which I have been spending infinite patience & pains) are seriously wrong, in one or two points. I have done them however in a beautiful manner, much improved upon our

<u>first</u> edition of a Table & Diagram. But unluckily I have made some errors.

I send you all of this <u>final</u> note H, excepting the said Table & Diagram. I also return you Note C, in which (for a wonder), I can discover nothing to alter or mend. . . I also beg for Note A, in which I remember a wrong passage about <u>Variable</u>-cards. Now <u>pray</u> attend strictly to my requests; or you will cause me very serious annoyance.

I shall be up betimes tomorrow morning, & finish off the Table & Diagram; so as to send it [to] you by post; together with the amendments in what my servant shall bring me down tomorrow morning from you.

You will have therefore a budget on Monday Morg; and I intend to go to Town myself on Monday, for a few hours, in order to run over a few things with you finally. Be so kind as to be in the Square at two o'clock.

I fear you will think me <u>detestably</u> <u>persevering</u>. Yours ever A.L.

Let me know how you like my finishing up of H. Mind you scrutinise all of the <u>n's</u> very carefully; I mean those of sheet 4 and 5.

To Charles Babbage

Sunday, 6 o'clock [2 July 1843]   Ockham.

I have worked incessantly, & most successfully, all day. You will admire the <u>Table</u> & <u>Diagram</u> extremely. They have been made out with extreme care, & all the <u>indices</u> most minutely & scrupulously attended to. Lord L – is at this moment kindly <u>inking</u> <u>it</u> <u>all</u> <u>over</u> for me. I had to do it in pencil. . .

I cannot not imagine what you mean about the Variable-Cards; since I never either supposed in my own mind, that one Variable-card <u>could</u> <u>give</u> <u>off</u> more than one Variable at a time; nor have (as far as I can make out) expressed such an idea in any passage whatever.

I cannot find what I fancied I had put in Note A; so I return it whole & sound, for your speedy relief. . .

Lord L – has put up, I find, in a separate cover, all that

belongs to Note H. (He is quite enchanted with the <u>beauty</u> & <u>symmetry</u> of the Table & Diagram). No – I find I can put in Note D <u>with</u> H.

To Charles Babbage

Sunday Morning, 2 July 1843   Ockham

My Dear Babbage. Unless you really have <u>necessary</u> business to transact with me tomorrow, pray do <u>not</u> come to see me; for I am full of pressing & unavoidable engagements; & moreover, I shall obliged to be in Town on Friday next, & could then see you at 12 o'clock – . . .

I am reflecting much on the work & duties for you & the engine, which are to occupy me during the next two or three years I suppose; & I have some excellent ideas on the subject.

I intend to incorporate with one department of my labours, – a complete reduction to a system, of the principles & methods of <u>discovery</u>, – elucidating the same with examples. I am already noting down a list of discoveries hitherto made, in order myself to examine into their <u>history, origin, & progress</u>. One first & main point, <u>whenever</u> & <u>wherever</u> I introduce the subject, will be first to <u>define</u> & to <u>classify</u> all that is to be legitimately included under the term <u>discovery</u>. Here will be a fine field for my <u>clear, logical,</u> & <u>accurate,</u> mind, to work its' powers upon; & to develop its' <u>metaphysical</u> genius, which is not least amongst its' qualifications & – characteristics. –

Let me find a note tomorrow when I arrive, which I expect to do between twelve & one. I should like to <u>know</u> whether to expect you or not. Yours   A.L.

To Charles Babbage

Tuesday Morning [4 July 1843]   Ockham

My Dear Babbage. I now write to you expressly on <u>three</u> points; which I have very fully & leisurely considered during the last 18 hours; & think of sufficient importance to induce me to send a servant up so that you may have this letter by half after six this evening. . .

Firstly: the few lines I enclosed you last night about the connexion of (8) with the famous Integral, I by no means intend you to insert, unless you <u>fully</u> approve the doing so.

It is perhaps very dubious whether there is any sufficient <u>pertinence</u> in noticing <u>at</u> <u>all</u> that (8) is an <u>Integral</u>. . .

Secondly: Lord L – suggests my <u>signing</u> the translation & the Notes; by which he means, simply putting at the end of the former: "<u>translated</u> <u>by</u> <u>A. A.L</u>;" & adding to each note the initials A.A.L.

It is not my wish to <u>proclaim</u> who has written it; at the same time that I rather wish to append anything that may tend hereafter to <u>individualise,</u> & <u>identify</u> it, with other productions of the said A. A. L.

My third topic, tho' my last, is our most anxious & important: –

I have yesterday evening & this morning very amply analysed the question of the <u>number</u> of Variable-Cards, as mentioned in the final Note H (or G?). And I find that you & I between us have made a <u>mess</u> of it; (for which I can perfectly account, in a very natural manner). I enclose what I wish to insert <u>instead</u> of that which is now there. I think the present <u>wrong</u> passage is only about eight or ten lines, & is I believe on the <u>second</u> of the three great sheets which are to <u>follow</u> the Diagram. . .

It does not signify whether the operations be in <u>cycles</u> or not. . . . In Note H, the erroneous lines are founded on the hasty supposition that the cycle, or recurring group, of <u>Operation</u>- Cards (13 . . . .23), will be <u>fed</u> by a cycle, or recurring group, of <u>Variable</u>-Cards.

I enclose what I believe it <u>ought</u> to be.

If already gone to the printer, we must alter that passage in the proofs, unless you could call at the printers & there paste over the amendment. –

I can scarcely describe to you how <u>very</u> ill & harassed I felt yesterday. Pray excuse any abruptness or other unpleasantness of manner, if there were any.

I am breathing <u>well</u> again today, & am much better in all respects; owing to Dr. L's remedies. He certainly does seem to understand the case, I mean the _treatment_ of it, which is the main thing.

As for the _theory_ of it, he says truly that _time_ & _Providence_ alone can develop that. It is so _anomalous_ an affair altogether. A _Singular Function,_ in very deed!

Think of my having to _walk,_ (or rather _run_), to the Station, in _half_ _an_ _hour_ last evening; while I suppose _you_ were feasting & flirting in luxury & ease at your dinner. It must be a very pleasant merry sort of thing to have a _Fairy_ in one's service, mind & limbs! – I envy you! – _I,_ poor little Fairy, can only get dull heavy _mortals,_ to wait on _me_! – Ever Yours

A.L.

To Charles Babbage

Tuesday [Undated]   Ockham

My Dear Babbage. I hope you will approve of what I send. I have taken _much_ pains with it. I have explained that there would be, in this instance & in many others, a recurring group or cycle of _Variable_ as well as of _Operation_ Cards; . . . I think I have done it admirably & diplomatically. (_Here_ comes in the _intrigante_ & the _politician_!)

Ever yours   A.L.

To Charles Babbage

Wednesday, 5 July [1843]   Ockham Park

My Dear Babbage. I am much obliged by the contents of your letter, in all respects. Should you find it expedient to substitute the amended passage about the Variable-Cards, there is also _one_ other _short_ sentence which must be altered similarly. This sentence precedes the passage I sent yesterday by perhaps half a page or more. . .

"Why does my friend prefer _imaginary_ roots for our friendship?" – Just because she happens to have some of that very imagination which _you_ would deny her to possess; & therefore she enjoys a little _play_ & _scope_ for it now & then. Besides this,

I deny the <u>Fairyism</u> to be entirely <u>imaginary</u>; (& it is to the <u>fairy</u> similes that I suppose you allude).

That <u>brain</u> of mine is something more than merely <u>mortal</u>; as time will show; (if only my <u>breathing</u> & some other et-ceteras do not make too rapid a progress <u>towards</u> instead of <u>from</u> mortality). –

Before ten years are over, the Devil's in it if I have not sucked out some of the life-blood from the mysteries of this universe, in a way that no purely mortal lips or brains could do.

No one knows what almost <u>awful</u> energy & power lie yet undevelopped in that <u>wiry</u> little system of mine. I say <u>awful</u>, because you may imagine what it <u>might</u> be under certain circumstances.

Lord L, – sometimes says "what a <u>General</u> you would make!" Fancy me in times of social & political trouble, (had <u>worldly</u> power, rule, & ambition been my line, which now it never could be).

A <u>desperate</u> spirit truly; & with a degree of deep & fathomless <u>prudence</u>, which is strangely at variance with the <u>daring</u> & the <u>enterprise</u> of the character, a union that would give me unlimited sway & success, in all probability.

<u>My</u> kingdom however is not to be a <u>temporal</u> one, thank Heaven! – . . .

I am doggedly attacking & sifting to the very bottom, all the ways of deducing the Bernoulli Numbers. In the manner I am grappling with this subject, & connecting it with others, I shall be some days upon it.

I shall then take in succession the <u>other</u> subjects that have been suggested to me during my late labours, & treat them similarly. –

<u>Labor</u> <u>ipse</u> <u>voluptas</u> is in <u>very</u> deed my motto! – And, (as I hinted just now), it is perhaps well for the world that my line & ambition is over the <u>spiritual</u>; & that I have not taken it into my head, or lived in times & circumstances calculated to put it into my head, to deal with the sword, poison, & intrigue, in the place of x, y, & z. . .

Your <u>Fairy</u> for ever

A.A.L. . .

To Charles Babbage

Thursday [6 July 1843]   Ockham

My Dear Babbage. I send you the first sheet all corrected. I have taken much pains with it, & I think it very much improved.

The printer has made one or two <u>paragraphs</u> where none ought to exist; & has also <u>not</u> put some words in <u>Italics</u> that ought to be so expressed. I have endeavoured to indicate all this, as I best might.

I send you four Foot-Notes, which are referred to in the proper places. I think you will like them; especially the first one about Pascal's Machine. – I hope to send you the remainder of the translation tomorrow. – My plans are again all altered. I go on Monday for the <u>day</u> only. Will you come at <u>three</u> o'clock.

I do not suppose that the Notes will take half the corrections which the translation does. I took so much more pains with them. I hope not, for it is damnably troublesome work, & plagues me. Pray let me know if my corrections are intelligible. . .

F Knight reappeared from Holland on Tuesday, so he spent Wednesday Morg with me, & was very delightful. He is anxious about my publication, & only fears my writing anything <u>inexperienced</u>.

I see I am more his ladye-love than ever. He is an excellent creature, & deserves to have a nice ladye-love. – Yours   A.L.

P.S. I mean to put A.A.L. to all the Notes, but to leave the translation without.

To Charles Babbage

Tuesday, 5 o'clock [11 July 1843]   St James' Square

I find that I do <u>not</u> come up on Friday next. But if you will give me Monday Evening (I shall stay the night), it will be desirable. –

Meanwhile I shall get on with the corrections, & send the papers back to you as early as possible; only hoping that nothing in them will oblige me to have your assistance. I do not think this likely. –

I hope you will attend carefully to my criticisms about the Preface. I think them of consequence. If Lord L – suggests any further ones, you shall hear. Perhaps he may. Ever yours

A.L.

To Charles Babbage

Thursday, 6 o'clock [13 July 1843]

My Dear Babbage. Will you come at nine on Satdy morning, & stay as long as we find requisite. I name so early an hour, because we shall have much to do I think. – And it certainly <u>must</u> not be later than <u>ten</u> o'clock.

I have been very unwell indeed; partly with distressing indigestion & partly with this most miserable & changed weather. – This is why you have heard nothing more from me...

I send you a note from F. K. [Frederick Knight]. It will show you the tone of writing between us; & the sort of footing we are on. Are you not amused at "your Ladyship" which just means, by the way that I am <u>anything</u> but <u>My</u> <u>Ladyship</u> to him!...

Am I very naughty to send you such a caller-up of many & dubious speculations and associations? – No. Ever yours   A.L.

To Charles Babbage

Friday, 4 o'clock [July 21]   Ockham

My Dear Babbage. I am in much dismay at having got into so amazing a quagmire & botheration with these <u>Numbers,</u> that I cannot possibly get the thing done today. I have no doubt it will all come out clear enough tomorrow; & I shall send you a <u>parcel</u> up, as early in the day as I can. – So do not be uneasy. (Tho' at this moment I am in a charming state of confusion; but it is that sort of confusion which is of a very <u>bubble</u> nature). I am now going out on horseback. Tant mieux

Yours puzzle-pate

To Charles Babbage

Saturday, 3 o'clock [22 July 1843]   Ockham

My Dear Babbage. I send you all excepting four pages which I cannot get done today, as they necessitate one or two troublesome alterations. You will perceive therefore that the two parts of what I send do not <u>follow</u>. I shall send the rest by post tomorrow.

You ought to get this tonight & an additional shilling is promised upon <u>immediate</u> delivery. I must now explain one or two things. I am much annoyed at your having altered my Note. You know I am always willing to make <u>any</u> required alterations myself, but that I cannot endure another person to meddle with my sentences. If I disapprove therefore, I hope I may be able to alter in the <u>revise</u>, supposing you have sent away the proofs & notes.

Then I cannot agree to your not having effaced the <u>paragraphs</u>. In <u>one</u> instance, at any rate, if not in all, it is very necessary that the paragraph <u>should</u> be effaced; as it makes a division in the sense where there should be a perfect continuity.

In short I am somewhat disturbed about the matter altogether.

And I must then beg you to deliver to me tout suit plus vête, all the documents I am at present to have in order to commence work upon.

I think much about them & all other scientific matters, and I find that my plans & ideas keep gaining in clearness; & assuming more of the <u>crystalline</u> & less & less of the <u>nebulous</u> form. Yours   A.A.L.

P.S. I have been very suffering, & more ill than ever yet. But today I have rallied considerably. Hang the whole affair.

ADA HAD TRIED TO HELP her mother by hiring the French maid, Nathalie Beaurepaire, for Medora. When the maid and her husband discovered that Medora's daughter Marie was

illegitimate, and that Medora was not a "proper lady," they were concerned that it might reflect on them. They sought another appointment expecting a character reference from Lady Byron, who paid their salary. Not only did Lady Byron refuse to do that, but she accused the Beaurepaires of embezzlement. At that point, in defense of her mother, Ada became further involved in the situation by going to the French Embassy to protect her mother's position. This occurred during the very hectic time that she was completing the Notes. I have deleted Ada's description of the visit to the Embassy and excerpts that show how Lady Byron tried to divert Ada's attention from the work she was doing with Babbage. Doris Langley Moore in her biography of Ada (see Bibliography) described the situation vividly and accurately.

To Lady Byron

Tuesday Morning, 25 July [1843]   Ockham

Dear Mama. . . I am endeavouring to give you a succinct & clear impression of the order & succession in which the various parties have been concerned in this affair . . . I shall say no more today about this horrible affair; excepting that you may be sure I fully enter into all your views about it, & into the harassing demand it is on your strength at present; and that my logical & analysing mind is endeavouring to extract all possible good out of this shocking thirty years' tale, by putting every circumstance concerning it (& all my own share in any portion of it) into the great laboratory of my brain, & deriving deep & profitable lessons therefrom; lessons which may continue to develop for the rest of my existence perhaps. Let this be a comfortable reflection for you at least. –

As for me & my affairs, I have much to say; but really cannot today. – Be assured however that it is all on the whole of a satisfactory nature.

As to my health, it has been during the last week in a stranger state than ever. Dr L [Locock] says that as to an opinion, one may as well attempt to give one on the nature of an inhabitant of the moon, or of any wholly unknown order of beings; he said to me so simply & candidly yesterday, when I was relating to him some (certainly very remarkable phenomena), & asked him, "Now, how can one account for that?" "To say the truth, it is perfectly incomprehensible on any known principles; and in fact I can't pretend to <u>explain</u> <u>any</u> part of your case. The utmost I can do is to study the sequences as to the facts; viz: that one event or measure seems to be followed by <u>good</u>, another by <u>mischief</u>, & so forth."

There is at least some <u>amusement</u> in being so curious a riddle; & as I often <u>suffer</u> a great deal, I endeavour to think of every compensation I can extract.

I do not believe I shall ever henceforth be very free from suffering, for any long period: & I have made up my mind at once to this probability. Then I am perfectly content, <u>if</u> this is the necessary condition of all that wonderful & available mental power which I see ground to believe I am acquiring. I conceive that my state of health is the inevitable <u>condition</u> attached to the nature of my mind, & will never be an <u>impediment</u> to the development of this. I will willingly bear <u>anything</u>, if this be so. What would be to me terrible, would be mind & activity <u>impeded</u> by health.

Give <u>me</u> <u>power</u> with <u>pain</u> a million times over, rather than <u>ease</u> with even <u>talent</u> (if not of the highest order).

To Charles Babbage

Tuesday Morning [25 July 1843]   Ockham

My Dear Babbage. The bearer will I hope deliver this by nine this evening. He is to return here as early tomorrow as you can let him have an answer. – What I want to know is this: can you be with me in Town at four on Thursday, in order that I may <u>read</u> <u>over</u> aloud, with you, all the Notes. For I cannot feel satisfied, (on re-perusing them), I find; without going over them <u>with</u> <u>you</u>; before they are finally printed off. . .

Can you afterwards give me Thursday <u>evening</u>, to go to the Opera. If my servant can have a reply from you <u>tonight</u>, he will be off by daylight tomorrow morning. If not, he must come as early as he can tomorrow.

I keep back <u>your</u> Note; wishing to consider it a little more. I think it unobjectionable, as far as I have <u>yet</u> considered it. Pray take care that the printing is so managed as to separate distinctly the <u>translator's</u> notes, from either <u>your</u> note, or one there is of Menabrea's own . . .

I shall not put my initials to my Notes. But I wish them to be <u>Translator's</u> <u>Notes</u> . . .
Yours ever

A.L.

To Charles Babbage

Wednesday Evening, 10 o'clock [26 July 1843]

I send you what I have done of Note E, which is not <u>nearly</u> all. So you must not judge of it, as it is. I am becoming sadly <u>over-worked</u>, & have scarcely brains left for anything. –

I wonder how you will like my further <u>addition</u> to the upper indices. I half fear <u>not</u>. But I can cancel it, if you disapprove. No more tonight, for I can neither talk, write, nor think, common sense. And yet I feel more like a <u>fairy</u> than ever. (But I suppose <u>that</u> idea is <u>uncommon,</u> & not <u>common,</u> sense). Yours

Addle pate

To Charles Babbage

Thursday Morning, 27 July [1843]   Ockham

My Dear Babbage. I cannot get on satisfactorily with either the proofs or the revise, unless I have my own manuscripts for the former, & the corrected proofs for the latter. . .

I am happy to find that the <u>Notes</u> will require very little correction indeed. – To say the truth, I am rather <u>amazed</u> at them, & cannot help being struck quite <u>malgrè</u> <u>moi</u>, with the really masterly nature of the style, & its superiority to that of the Memoir itself.

I have made Lord L – laugh much, by the dryness with which I remarked, "Well, I am very much satisfied with this first child of mine. He is an uncommonly fine baby, & will grow to be a <u>man</u> of the first magnitude & power."

I approve your alteration in the preface, excepting that I think the word "<u>so</u>" comes in both awkwardly & superfluously. Pray efface it, & let it stand, "<u>of the money to be expended</u>." That little word spoils it. – . . .

Lord L – seems pleased beyond measure, with the very <u>learned</u> & <u>knowing aspect</u> of my baby's physiognomy, which he has glanced at. Yours   A.L.

To Charles Babbage

Friday, 5 o'clock [28 July 1843]   St James' Square

The beginning of Note G (by which I mean the Table & all that <u>precedes</u> it) never has been returned into my hands; a small part of the remainder <u>was</u>, but <u>that</u> I speedily gave you back, & there it is, now printed. –

The missing part <u>must</u> be either at your house or at the printer's; & it seems to me <u>very</u> unlikely that <u>you</u> should have retained it. So altogether I would wager almost anything that it is at the <u>office</u>; or that if lost, it has been lost <u>there</u>. –

At the same time, I have always fancied you were a little harum- scarum & inaccurate now & then about the exact <u>order</u> & <u>arrangement</u> of sheets, pages, & paragraphs &c; (witness that paragraph which you so carelessly <u>pasted over</u>!)

I suppose that I must set to work to write something <u>better</u>, if I can, as a substitute. The <u>same precisely</u> I could not recall. I think I should be able in a couple of days to do something. However I should be deucedly inclined to <u>swear at you</u>, I will allow.

I desire my messenger to wait; as it is possible you may have something to communicate more agreeable.

I go soon after seven. I believe I shall <u>not</u> be in Town myself on Monday as I expected. Yours   A.L

To Lady Byron

Thursday Morning [August 1843]   Ockham

. . . I certainly feel some relief & satisfaction in turning to the packet of <u>clear, forcible</u> & <u>logical</u> documents now before me for my final revision; after the <u>tortuous</u> & <u>nefarious</u> documents & affairs which have recently so painfully engaged much of our energy & attention. My <u>first</u> <u>born</u> is characterized chiefly by a <u>strong</u> <u>sense</u> & union of the most minute & laborious accuracy, in particulars, with a colouring & undercurrent (rather <u>hinted</u> <u>at</u> & <u>suggested</u> than definitely expressed) of <u>large</u>, <u>general</u>, & <u>metaphysical</u> views. He is not <u>eloquent</u> or <u>brilliant</u>, but he shows indication of much <u>latent</u> power, & of a most <u>indomitable</u> <u>industry</u> which despises no even apparently trivial minutia.

He will make an excellent <u>head</u> of (I hope) a <u>large</u> family of brothers & sisters; to whom he will impart a certain <u>staid</u> & <u>solid</u> character, for which they will be much indebted to him, (tho' probably no one may ever perceive or acknowledge his quiet & insensible influence). . .

To Charles Babbage

Monday Afternoon [Undated]

There is not much correction for Note A; (I send you the whole of it); And of these the chief part I think are merely <u>paragraphs</u> <u>to</u> <u>be</u> <u>effaced,</u> & <u>stops</u> <u>to</u> <u>be</u> <u>inserted</u> <u>or</u> <u>altered</u>. I cannot refrain from expressing my amazement at my own child. The <u>pithy</u> & <u>vigorous</u> nature of the style seem to me to be most striking; and there is at times a <u>half</u>-<u>satirical</u> & <u>humorous</u> <u>dry-</u> <u>ness</u>, which would I suspect make me a most formidable <u>reviewer</u>. I am quite thunder-struck at the <u>power</u> of the writing. It is especially unlike a <u>woman's</u> style surely; but neither can I compare it with any <u>man's</u> exactly. . .

Likewise the Notes should have <u>A. A. L.</u> appended to them. I do not mean the Foot-notes; only Notes A, B, C, D, E, F, G; the illustrious <u>seven</u>! –

You have now the whole of the <u>Revise</u>. I trust that <u>all</u> of Note G was found. There is but a <u>very</u> little bit of it indeed, yet sent to me. I can correct the <u>proof</u> of it in an hour or two, when I get it.

Expect a parcel from me tomorrow, with the remaining proofs of the Notes.   A.A.L.

To Charles Babbage

Sunday, 30 July [1843]   Ockham

I am beyond measure vexed to find that instead of inserting my <u>corrected</u> Table in the Revise . . . they have left it exactly as it was before. Pray see about it immediately. It is exceedingly careless & annoying.

Out of <u>several</u> <u>corrections</u> made, not one is inserted; neither are the Upper Indices added; nor the little Foot-Note. I send you back all the latter part of the Revise, & the corresponding <u>proofs</u>, that you may look to the matter forthwith. I cannot account for such negligence. . .

I do not think you possess half <u>my</u> forethought, & power of foreseeing all <u>possible</u> contingencies (<u>probable</u> & <u>improbable</u>, just alike). –

I am glad to see the sheets I return you so <u>clean</u> on the whole.

Tomorrow I expect to send you up the rest of the Revise, & Note A by my governess, in the middle of the day; & more by post.

I will work most diligently; but I wish to revise the Notes myself. You might send some one down here the moment you get them; & I would attend <u>immediately</u>, & send them back by the same or some other special messenger – . . .

How <u>very</u> careless of you to forget that Note; & how much <u>waiting on</u> & <u>service</u> you owe me, to compensate.

I am in good spirits; for I hope another year will make me <u>really</u> something of an <u>Analyst</u>. The more I study, the more irresistible do I feel my genius for it to be.

I do <u>not</u> believe that my father was (or ever could have been) such a <u>Poet</u> as <u>I</u> <u>shall</u> be an <u>Analyst</u>; (& Metaphysician); for with me the two go together indissolubly. – Yours   A.L.

To Charles Babbage

Tuesday Afternoon [1 August 1843]   Ockham

. . . Note B has plagued me to death; altho' I have made but little alteration in it. Such alterations as there are however, happen to have been very tiresome & to have demanded minute consideration & very nice adjustments.

It is a very excellent Note.

I wish you were as accurate, & as much to be relied on, as I am myself.

You might often <u>save</u> me much trouble, if you were; whereas you in reality <u>add</u> to my trouble not infrequently; and there is at any rate always the anxiety of <u>doubting</u> if you will not get me into a scrape; even when you don't.

By the way, I hope you do not take upon yourself to alter any of my corrections.

I <u>must</u> beg you not. They all have some very sufficient reason. And you have made a pretty mess & confusion in one or two places (which I will show you sometime), where you have ventured in my <u>M.S.'s</u>, to <u>insert</u> or <u>alter</u> a phrase or word; & have utterly muddled the sense.

I could not conceive at first in one or two places what had happened to my sentences; tho' I soon saw they were <u>patch-work</u> & not my own; and found it so, on referring to the M.S. I fear you will think this a very <u>cross</u> letter. Never mind. I am a good little thing, after all. Yours ever

          A. A. L.

Later. P. S. It is impossible to send you anything but Notes B and C; (& this partly owing to some wrong references & blunderations of your own). –

Do not be afraid, for I will work like the Devil early tomorrow morning. –

To Charles Babbage

Wednesday, 4 o'clock [2 August 1843]   Ockham

After working almost incessantly, since 7 o'clock this morning, until I am <u>forced</u> to give in from sheer inability to apply longer, I find only the sheet I enclose is quite completed. I shall however send a servant up tomorrow morning by a ten o' clock train, to take you all the rest; so that you will have it almost as soon as this letter.

You cannot conceive the trouble I have had with the trigonometrical Note E. –

In fact no one but me, I really believe, would have doggedly stuck to it, as I have been doing, in all <u>wearing</u> minutiae.

I am very uneasy at not hearing from you, as I have expected to do both yesterday & today; & fear some disaster or other. I hope <u>all</u> of Note G is forthcoming; & I also hope you have received all my communications safely.

I think <u>you</u> had better do the <u>second</u> <u>revise</u> of the translation for me. If you will compare it carefully with my <u>first</u> <u>revise</u>, it can hardly be necessary I think for <u>me</u> to go over it again.

I suppose I ought to take it for granted that <u>no</u> <u>news</u> <u>is</u> <u>good</u> <u>news;</u> but I am in a sad fidget. – Yours ever

                                                        A.L.

11.
Multitudinous Charlatans and the Enchantress of Numbers
[1843]

ADA WAS PLAGUED by many problems – writing the Notes, her illness, problems with the children, and the melodramatic issue of Medora, which was becoming more complicated each day. Ada turned to her cousin, Robert Noel, who was living in Germany, and described the need for a tutor for the children, her hopes for a profession, and speculations on where her future scientific endeavors might lead. In addition to the Notes, Ada wrote many pages about these issues, all carefully thought out and expressed.

Then difficulties arose with Babbage. Ada had asked him to do the second revision, yet it is apparent that she was involved in the final draft with the printers (whether this is the second or third is not clear). The major issue was the preface that Babbage wrote describing the non-support of the British government toward the completion of the Difference Engine and his innovative plans for the Analytical Engine. Babbage wanted the preface printed as part of the Memoir. When Ada read the final draft of the preface, she refused to have it included. She was furious.

Richard Taylor (the publisher) wrote a letter to Babbage at this time confirming that he agreed with Ada's wish not to have the preface printed. Babbage apparently then asked Ada to withdraw the article and write an entirely new one. Ada did not mince words. According to her, Babbage was acting on principles that were "suicidal."

Both Ada and Lord Lovelace wanted to take a direct part in helping Babbage transform his innovative ideas for the Analytical Engine into a working model. Because Babbage was considered a poor player at the political game, Ada wanted to take over this function to ensure that the Analytical Engine would become a reality. She wrote Babbage a sixteen-page letter highlighting the very different perceptions that men and women often have. This is the first time that the entire letter has been published.

The following letter, perhaps one of the most important, turned up in, of all places, California. After reading an article I wrote, a Silicon Valley executive contacted me and has kindly allowed me to include this letter. It is a gem.

To Charles Babbage

Sunday, 6 August [1843]   Ockham

My Dear Babbage. I did not make you any communication on Friday, because I did not feel I could do so satisfactorily to myself or to you, without another day of leisure to reflect. On the <u>one</u> <u>point</u> of <u>not</u> <u>withdrawing</u> the translation & Notes from the Memoir, or consenting to its' <u>separate</u> publication, I was entirely & finally decided; as I think neither for <u>your</u> <u>advantage</u> nor my own, to do so; added to my opinion that it would under the circumstances be dishonorable & unjustifiable.

But in <u>other</u> respects, I have felt very anxious to obtain your co-operation & cordial assent & concurrence.

It was my intention therefore to write to you very strongly on some points in which I consider you mistake your own interests. I will not however, now do so; at any rate until I hear what the <u>present</u> plan is; for my representations may be unnecessary & irrelevant. –

Having decided <u>as</u> <u>an</u> <u>axiom</u> that the <u>Memoirs</u> are to contain the paper, I intended to leave it to <u>you</u> (only subject to Lord <u>L's</u> approbation) whether it should come out in <u>this</u> number, or be delayed until the next to give you more time for thinking over matters. – This I still do.

Be assured that I am your best friend; but that I never <u>can</u> or <u>will</u> support you in acting on principles which I conceive to be not only wrong in themselves, but <u>suicidal</u>.

This sentence will excite your <u>deprecation</u>, I am well aware; & you will inwardly exclaim: "<u>how</u> <u>she</u> <u>misunderstands</u> <u>me</u>!" –

No more of this just at this moment, for I have perhaps already said too much. –

But, before I undertake any further labors in conjunction with you, I must have an explicit understanding on one or two points; & do not anticipate that you will hesitate much to agree to my conditions. Yours   A.L.

To Lady Byron

Tuesday, 8 August [1843]   St James' Square

Dear Mama. . . Lady Mahon being now out of Town, & I believe taking no present part in this affair, I considered that further communication from me to her, would come better in a week or two weeks from the time I received her reply just at the moment. . .

I must tell you that another reason why I have not been writing to you (as I did not perceive an immediate call for it), is that I have been harassed & pressed in a most perplexing manner by the conduct of Mr Babbage. We are at fact <u>at</u> issue: I am sorry to have to come to the conclusion that he is one of the most <u>impracticable</u>, <u>selfish</u>, & <u>intemperate</u> persons one can have to do with. I do not anticipate an absolute <u>alienation</u> between us; but there must ever be a degree of coolness & reserve I fancy in the future. I have had in W [William]'s absence, to act quite unadvised in the matter; but I am happy to find that W – & Wheatstone entirely approve my conduct & views. I declared at once to Babbage, that no power should induce me to lend myself to any of his quarrels, or to become in any way his <u>organ</u>; & that I should myself communicate in a direct manner with the editors on the subject, as I did not choose to commit a dishonorable breach of engagement, even to promote <u>his</u> advantage (if it <u>were</u> to his advantage which I doubted).

<u>He</u> was <u>furious;</u> <u>I</u> imperturbable & unmoved. He will never forgive me. I had tried to conciliate & quietly to <u>advise</u> and

<u>suggest</u>, until I found that it was necessary to be very deter-
mined & explicit. Pray forgive my forcing on you at <u>this</u>
moment, these painful circumstances in another matter.

I only want you to understand that all my <u>time</u> & my <u>energy</u>
have been miserably absorbed the last few days; for what
between Babbage & the editors, both pressing hard in different
directions, I have been torn to pieces; & as I heard nothing
more from <u>any</u> one, of the E. L. affair I really endeavoured to
<u>forget</u> for a few days all its tortuous & villainous
implications. . .

I must hope that I may <u>develop God's truth more fully for
the use of mortals</u>. With this <u>single</u> object, if I have but the
determination to adhere to it in <u>purity</u> & <u>steadfastness,</u> I shall
be able to weather all the storms; & to leave a <u>name</u> for the
race & the family which may <u>screen</u> & <u>cloak over</u> even <u>its'</u> mani-
fold iniquities & tortuousities, when all these (if they ever do)
come fully to light. – . . .

To Robert Noel

Wednesday Afternoon, 9 August 1843   Ockham Park

My Dear Robert. . . Since Lord Lovelace wrote his note (here-
with enclosed) this morning, he & I have conversed earnestly
on the subject of Herr Kraemer, & have in fact come to stronger
conclusions respecting him, than we contained in Lord L's note.
These Lord L – wishes me therefore to state. We think. . .we
had better decline entering on an engagement with him, at
such a distance, & under such circumstances. My own impression of his <u>letter,</u> is by no means agreeable; and I should expect
he would prove to be somewhat <u>impracticable,</u> & <u>proud</u>.

Should you decide against him, we must still beg of you the
great favor to be on the look-out for us. Our case is becoming
rather pressing . . .The <u>real</u> ground of the very independent way
of conducting our family arrangements, ought to be
understood. It is neither the result of <u>pride;</u> nor of <u>indifference</u>
to our own children & their habits. But I am now myself a completely <u>professional</u> person, to speak plainly; & am engaged in

studies & in literary & scientific avocations, which render me
quite unable (were I even fitted by <u>nature</u>, which I am <u>not</u>), to
associate much personally with my children, or to exercise a
favorable influence over them by attempting to do so. . .

I shall have the pleasure of sending you, (if you will tell me
<u>how</u>), a copy of my translation of Monr Menabrea's description
of Babbage's Calculating Engines, to which I have appended
very copious Notes of my own, that are in fact longer & more
abstruse than the original Memoir itself. This engagement has
been in some respects arduous & troublesome; and it will probably bring me in but little return of reputation or fame, (which
were indeed no part of my motive when I undertook it): for
there is more of a <u>quiet</u> <u>patient</u> <u>labour</u> & <u>industry</u> in it, than of
brilliancy or attractiveness. I intentionally keep myself <u>way</u>
<u>back</u>. I had better feel my way gradually. I have plenty of
<u>imagination</u> and <u>eloquence</u>, when the right time shall come.
Meanwhile I wish to <u>build</u> upon strong foundations of <u>logic</u>,
<u>industry</u>, & <u>real</u> <u>study</u> & <u>training</u>. But I am glad to have got
<u>launched</u>, in however <u>humble</u>, & <u>dry</u> a form.

I wish now to know how far you may think yourself <u>able</u> &
<u>willing</u>, to organize a plan I have for you; which I fancy you
exactly fitted for fulfilling, & is a great desideratum in this
country. I believe that many researches are going on in Germany, as to the <u>microscopical</u> structure & changes in the <u>brain</u>,
<u>nervous</u> <u>matter</u>, & also in the <u>blood</u>. Now, we in this country,
need <u>data</u>, on this subject more than almost any. . .

My kindest remembrances to Mrs R. N.; & believe me ever,
with many thanks. Most sincerely yours   A.A. Lovelace

To Charles Babbage

Monday, 14 August 1843   Ockham Park

My Dear Babbage. You would have heard from me several days
ago, but for the <u>hot</u> work that has been going on between me &
the printers. This is now all happily concluded. I have endeav-
oured to work up everything to the utmost perfection, <u>as</u> <u>far</u> <u>as</u>
<u>it</u> <u>goes</u>; & I am now well satisfied on the whole, since I think

that <u>within</u> <u>the</u> <u>sphere</u> <u>of</u> <u>views</u> I set out with, & in accordance with which the whole contents & arrangement of the Notes are shaped, they are very complete, & even admirable. I could <u>now</u> do the thing <u>far</u> <u>better</u>; but this would be from setting out upon a wholly different <u>basis</u>. –

I say you would have heard from me before. Your note (enclosed on Monday with my papers &c), is such as demands a very full reply from me, the writer being so old & so esteemed a friend, <u>&</u> <u>one</u> <u>whose</u> <u>genius</u> I <u>not</u> <u>only</u> <u>so</u> <u>highly</u> <u>appreciate</u> <u>myself,</u> <u>but</u> <u>wish</u> <u>to</u> <u>see</u> <u>fairly</u> <u>appreciated</u> <u>by</u> <u>others</u>.

Were it not for this desire (which both Lord L – & myself have more warmly at heart than you are as yet at all aware of), coupled with our long-established regard & intercourse, I should say that <u>the</u> <u>less</u> <u>notice</u> <u>taken</u> <u>by</u> <u>me</u> <u>of</u> <u>that</u> <u>note</u> – <u>the</u> <u>better</u>; & it was only worthy to be thrown aside with a smile of contempt. The <u>tone</u> of it, it is impossible to misunderstand; & as I am myself always a very "<u>explicit</u> <u>function</u> <u>of</u> <u>x,</u>" I shall not pretend to do so; & shall leave to <u>you</u> (if you please it) to continue the "<u>implicit</u>" style which is exceedingly marked in the said note.

As I know you will not be <u>explicit</u> enough to state the <u>real</u> state of your feelings respecting me at this time, I shall do so for you. You feel, my dear Babbage, that <u>I</u> have (tho' in a negative manner) <u>added</u> to the list of injuries & of disappointments & mis-comprehensions that you have already experienced in a life by no means smooth or fortunate. You <u>know</u> this is your feeling; & that you are deeply hurt about it; & you endeavour to derive a poor & sorry consolation from such sentiments as "Well, she don't <u>know</u> or <u>intend</u> the injury & mischief if she has done" &c.

You say you did not wish me to "break my engagement, but merely to ask to be released from it." My dear friend, if the engagement was such that I had no right to break it <u>without</u> <u>leave,</u> I had still <u>less</u> <u>right</u> to appeal to the <u>courtesy</u> of parties, in order to obtain an apparent sanction & excuse for doing that which their <u>justice</u> & <u>sense</u> <u>of</u> <u>their</u> <u>own</u> <u>rights</u> could not have conceded. There is no greater sin, or deeper <u>double-dealing</u> in this world, than that of endeavouring thro' the influence of secondary motives to get the apparent support & consent of others towards that which on a <u>higher</u> & more <u>general</u> motive would be inadmissable. Your reply to this will be, that my principle is <u>just, good,</u> & <u>great</u>; but that it did not apply to the particular case; in as much as the editors would themselves have been glad of an excuse to be released, under the circumstances. You must allow me to state that I took measures for ascertaining that point beyond all possibility of doubt, & that I found it to be very much otherwise.

You will deny & dispute this; or more probably you will immediately perceive grounds <u>why</u>, (from various unworthy arrière-pensées) the persons concerned might still wish to retain the article. Remember however, that when you do this, you have <u>shifted your original ground</u>; & that your question then becomes not whether Lady L – ought to oblige two parties, <u>you</u> & <u>the editors</u>, who both tho' on different grounds wish to dispose of my publication thro' another channel than that originally proposed, but whether Lady L – ought tacitly to lend herself to certain possible or probable unworthy motives entertained by the editors. Now to this the reply is perfectly plain in the opinion of all parties accustomed to fair & honorable dealings, uninfluenced by secondary motives. My engagement was <u>unconditional,</u> & had no reference to the <u>motives</u> of the parties with whom I contracted it. I have therefore no right to withdraw it on grounds <u>subsequently</u> thought of. If I had undertaken to do the thing specially <u>for</u> you, in addition to its being <u>for</u> them, the case would have been wholly different. But with the circumstance of your happening to be a private friend of my own, & of my therefore being too happy & delighted to make prior engagement <u>especially</u> pleasing & useful to you, <u>they</u> had nothing to do. Consequently, because my private friend wished it, (however justly), this could form no <u>real</u> & equitable ground for withdrawing the article.

I have now touched on all the grounds which can be taken on the supposition of it's <u>really being pernicious to your interests</u> that I have thus allowed the article to appear. This however I cannot agree to or believe; & were you not influenced by a set of feelings which are very different from those that I myself, & the minds whom I most esteem, can consider wise, justifiable, or in harmonious accordance with man's moral nature, <u>you</u> would not think so. Mind, I do not say that <u>your</u> views may not be in reality higher, juster, & wiser, than my own. But my moral standard, such as it is, I must stick to; as long as it <u>is</u> my moral standard. It would not be of any use for me to endeavour making you see thro' <u>my</u> glasses; for, (besides the fact that they may be as far or farther than yours, from refracting & reflecting quite truly), no one <u>can</u> instanter alter the views & modes of feeling of a <u>life</u>. But I <u>do</u> wish you to understand the fact, that <u>I</u> <u>believe</u> myself (however erroneous that belief may be), to have forwarded <u>your</u> interests far more by allowing the article to appear than I should have done by any of the courses you suggested. I <u>have</u> a right to expect from you the belief that I do sincerely & honestly take this view. For if <u>your</u> knowledge of <u>me</u> does not furnish sufficient grounds for doing so, then I can only say that <u>no</u> mutual knowledge of any two human beings in this life, can give stable & fixed grounds for faith & confidence. Then Adieu to <u>all</u> trust, & to everything most generous, in this world! –

I must now come to a practical question respecting the future. <u>Your</u> affairs have been, & are, deeply occupying both myself & Lord Lovelace. Our thoughts as well as our conversation have been earnest upon them. And the result is that I have plans for you, which I do not think fit at present to communicate to you; but which I shall either develop, or else throw my energies, my time & pen into the service of some other department of truth & science, according to the reply I receive from you to what I am now going to state. I do beseech you therefore deeply & seriously to ponder over the question how far you can subscribe to my conditions or not. I give to <u>you</u> the <u>first</u> choice & offer of my services & my intellect. Do not lightly reject them. I say this entirely for <u>your</u> <u>own</u> sake, believe me.

My channels for developping & training my scientific & literary powers, are various, & some of them very attractive. But I wish my old friend to have the <u>refusal</u>.

Firstly: I want to know whether if I continue to work <u>on</u> & <u>about</u> your own great subject, you will undertake to abide wholly by the judgement of myself (or of any persons whom you may <u>now</u> please to name as referees, whenever we may differ), on <u>all</u> <u>practical</u> matters relating to <u>whatever</u> <u>can</u> <u>involve</u> <u>relations</u> <u>with</u> <u>any</u> <u>fellow-creature</u> <u>or</u> <u>fellow-creatures.</u>

Secondly: can you undertake to give your mind <u>wholly</u> & <u>undividedly,</u> as a primary object that no engagement is to interfere with, to the consideration of all those matters in which I shall at times require your intellectual <u>assistance</u> & <u>supervision</u>; & can you promise not to <u>slur</u> & <u>hurry</u> things over; or to mislay, & allow confusion & mistakes to enter into documents, &c?

Thirdly: If I am able to lay before you in the course of a year or two, explicit & honorable propositions for <u>executing</u> <u>your</u> <u>engine,</u> (such as are approved by persons whom you may <u>now</u> name to be referred to for their approbation), would there be any chance of your allowing myself & such parties to conduct the business for you; your own <u>undivided</u> energies being devoted to the execution of the work; & all other matters being arranged for you on terms which your <u>own</u> friends should approve?

You will <u>wonder</u> over this last query. But, I strongly advise you not to reject it as chimerical. You do <u>not</u> know the grounds I have for believing that such a contingency may come within my power, & I wish to know before I allow my mind to employ its energies any further on the subject, that I shall not be wasting thought & power for no purpose or result.

At the same time, I must place the whole of your relations with me, in a fair & just light. Our motives, & ways of viewing things, are very widely apart; & it may be an anxious question for you to decide how for the advantages & expediency of enlisting a mind of my particular class, in your service, <u>can</u> over-balance the annoyance to you of that divergency on perhaps many occasions. My own uncompromising principle is to endeavour to love <u>truth</u> & <u>God</u> <u>before</u> <u>fame</u> & <u>glory</u> or <u>even</u> <u>just</u> <u>appreciation</u>; & to believe generously & unwaveringly in the <u>good</u> of human nature, (however dormant & latent it may often seem).

<u>Yours</u> is to love truth & God (yes, deeply & constantly); but

to love <u>fame, glory, honours, yet</u> <u>more</u>. You will deny this; but in all your intercourse with <u>every</u> human being (as far as I know & see of it), it is a <u>practically</u> <u>paramount</u> sentiment. Mind, I am not <u>blaming</u> it. I simply state my belief in the <u>fact</u>. The fact may be a very <u>noble</u> & <u>beautiful</u> fact. <u>That</u> is another question.

Far be it from <u>me</u>, to disclaim the influence of <u>ambition</u> & <u>fame</u>. No living soul ever was more imbued with it than myself. And my own view of duty is, that it behooves me to place this <u>great</u> & <u>useful</u> quality in its <u>proper</u> <u>relations</u> & <u>subordination;</u> but I certainly would not deceive myself or others by pretending that it is other than a very important motive & ingredient in my character & nature.

I wish to add my mite towards <u>expounding</u> & <u>interpreting</u> the Almighty, & his laws & works, for the most effective use of mankind; and certainly, I should feel it no small <u>glory</u> if I were enabled to be one of his most noted prophets (using this word in my own peculiar sense) in this world. And I should undoubtedly prefer being <u>known</u> as a benefactor of this description, to <u>being</u> equally great in fact, but promulgating truths from obscurity & oblivion.

At the same time, I am not sure that 30 years hence, I may put even so much value as <u>this,</u> upon human fame. Every year adds to the unlimited nature of my trust & hope in the Creator, & decreases my value for my relations with mankind <u>excepting</u> <u>as</u> <u>His</u> <u>minister;</u> & in <u>this</u> point of view those relations become yearly more interesting to me. Thro' my present relations with <u>man,</u> I am doubtless to become fit for relations of another order hereafter; perhaps <u>directly</u> with the great Power Himself. Of course my view respecting every even <u>casual</u> social contact & intercourse, takes a corresponding colour; & will do so increasingly, if <u>that</u> view should become more confirmed.

My dear friend, if you knew what <u>sad</u> & <u>direful</u> experience I have had, in ways of which you cannot be aware, you would feel that <u>some</u> weight <u>is</u> due to my feelings about God & man. As it is, you will only smile & say, "poor little thing; she knows nothing of life or wickedness!" –

Such as my principles are, & the conditions (founded on

them), on which alone you may command my services, I have now stated them; to just such extent as I think is absolutely necessary for any comfortable understanding & cooperation between us, in a course of a systematized & continued intellectual labour. It is now for <u>you</u> to decide. Do not attempt to make out to yourself or me that our principles entirely accord. They do <u>not</u>, nor <u>cannot</u> at present, (for people's views as I said are not to be altered in a moment).

Will you come <u>here</u> for some days on Monday. I hope so. Lord L – is very anxious to see & converse with you; & was vexed that the Rail called him away on Tuesdy before he had heard from yourself your own views about the recent affair.

I sadly want your <u>Calculus</u> <u>of</u> <u>Functions</u>. So <u>Pray</u> get it for me. I cannot understand the <u>Examples</u>.

I have ventured inserting to one passage of Note G a small Foot-Note, which I am not sure is <u>quite</u> <u>tenable</u>. I say in it that the engine is remarkably well adapted to include the <u>whole</u> <u>Calculus</u> <u>of</u> <u>Finite</u> <u>Differences,</u> & I allude to the computation of the <u>Bernoullian</u> <u>Numbers</u> <u>by</u> <u>means</u> <u>of</u> <u>the</u> <u>Difference</u> <u>of</u> <u>Nothing</u>, as a beautiful example for its' processes. I hope it <u>is</u> correctly the case.

This letter is sadly blotted & corrected. Never mind that however.

I wonder if you will choose to retain the lady-fairy in your service or not. Yours ever most sincerely.

A.A.L.

ADA'S DIFFICULTIES WITH BABBAGE began to be resolved. The preface was not included in the Memoir; Babbage's views were printed anonymously the following month. Babbage did not agree to Ada's proposal for their future working relationship; however, her honesty did not destroy their friendship, but changed it. She hardly had time to dwell on all these issues for she went off with her family to Ashley Combe and invited Babbage to join her there.

To Lady Byron

Tuesday 5 o'clock, 15 August [1843]   St James' Square

... No one can estimate the trouble & <u>interminable</u> labour
of having to revise the printing of <u>mathematical</u> formulae. This
is a pleasant prospect for the future, as I suppose many hundreds & thousands of such formula will come forth from my
pen, in one way or another.

You will receive a few copies (amongst a hundred that are
printed separately for me). But <u>where</u> and <u>how</u> should I send
them? ...

I am uncertain as yet how the Babbage business will end.
He has written <u>unkindly</u> to me. For many reasons however, I
still desire to <u>work</u> upon his subjects & affairs if I can do so
with any reasonable prospect of <u>peace</u>. I have written to him
therefore, very explicitly; stating my own <u>conditions</u>, without
which I positively refuse to take any further part in <u>conjunction</u>
with <u>him</u>, upon any subject whatever. He has so strong an idea
of the <u>advantage</u> of having <u>my</u> pen as his servant, that he will
probably yield; though I demand very strong concessions.

If he <u>does</u> consent to what I propose, I shall probably be
enabled to keep him out of much hot water; & to bring his
engine to <u>consummation</u>, (which all I have seen of him & his
habits the last 3 months, makes me scarcely anticipate it ever
<u>will</u> be, unless someone really exercises a strong coercive influ-
ence over him). He is beyond measure <u>careless</u> & <u>desultory</u> at
times. – I shall be willing to be his Whipper-in during the next
3 years, if I see fair prospect of success. Much of this is W's
suggestion; (altho' W – thinks B's conduct to me has recently
been <u>very</u> <u>blamable</u>).

To Lady Byron

Wednesday, 22 August [1843]   Ockham

Dearest Mama ... The "publication" named by Mrs Jameson is
of course the translation & the Notes... W – & I have treated it
quite as a matter of course, not worth either making a mystery

of or particularly proclaiming. I think it very natural that many persons must be acquainted with the fact that I have been writing something or other. And we are by no means desirous of making it a secret, altho' I do not wish the <u>importance</u> of the thing to be exaggerated & overrated.

As the publication will be <u>followed</u> <u>up</u> by others . . . & as I am now completely tied down & committed to the scientific & literary line, we are rather desirous than otherwise that there <u>should</u> be an impression of such being the case. William especially conceives that it places me in a much <u>juster</u> & <u>truer</u> position & light, than anything else can.

And he tells me that it has already placed <u>him</u> in a far more agreeable position in this county. Besides the many other motives which concur to urge me on to perseverance & success in a studious & literary career, I must name how very important an addition it is to their weight that I see W – looks to it as what is to place <u>him</u> (even more than perhaps myself) in the most advantageous & natural position, from its' various indirect effects.

Oh dear! how mercilessly he carried off my proofs & revises to some of his friends who came here; despite my remonstrances as to their blotted & unintelligible state!

Babbage & I are I think more friends than ever I have never seen him so agreeable, so reasonable, or in such good spirits!

Babbage's reply to Ada's invitation to come to Ashley:

9 September 1843

My Dear Lady Lovelace. I find it quite in vain to wait until I have leisure so I have resolved that I will leave all other things undone and set out for Ashley taking with me papers enough to enable me to forget this world and all its' troubles and if possible its' multitudinous Charlatans – every thing in short but the Enchantress of Numbers.

My only impediment would be my Mother's health which is not at this moment quite so good as I could wish.

Are you at Ashley? and is it still convenient with all your other arrangements that I should join you there? – and will next Wednesday or next Thursday or any other day suit you: and shall I leave the [?] road at Taunton or at Bridgewater and have you got Arbogast Du Calcul Des Derivations with you there at Ashley. I shall bring some books about that horrible problem – the three bodies which is almost as obscure as the existence of the celebrated book "De Tribes Impostoribus." So if you have Arbogast I will bring something else.

Farewell my dear and much admired Interpretess.

Evermost Truly Yours
C Babbage

12.

The Analyst and the Metaphysician, and the Analytical Engine: A Selection from Ada's Notes

[1843]

> Mechanics is the paradise of the mechanical
> sciences because by means of it one comes to
> the fruits of mathematics.
> Leonardo da Vinci (1452-1519)

> I am a philosopher. Confound them all –
> Birds, beasts and men: but no, not womankind. –
> Lord Byron
> quoted by Babbage on the title page
> of his autobiography, *Passages*

BABBAGE'S IDEA FOR THE Analytical Engine was the conceptual birth of the computer revolution. There were four components to the Analytical Engine – input, storage, processing, and output. The input medium was the punched card. There were two sets of cards – variable and operational cards. Though there was no programming in the modern sense, by arranging the cards one could program the engine to perform a repeating cycle or process, taking numbers from the store. Babbage planned to store over 1000 fifty-digit numbers. The numbers were then processed in what Babbage called the "mill." In Babbage's *Passages* he stated that there were three mechanisms for the output of numerical information: an apparatus for printing on paper, a means for producing a stereotype mould of the tables or results it computes, and a mechanism for punching on blank pasteboard cards or metal plates the results of any of its computations.

Babbage covered thousands of pages with designs and diagrams. In that form, it would be difficult to absorb the information or support the building of a prototype. To describe how a system that had not been built would work is very difficult (that essentially was done in Menabrea's description). To relate that description to its value and its use and abuse is a difficult and critical task as well, e.g., having had in 1940 a clear statement describing the power of atomic energy, its potential use and abuse, and having that statement be meaningful today. Ada's Notes are still thought-provoking over 150 years later, especially in light of the interaction between the computer and nuclear power and our desperate need to know not only technology, but the ramifications of technology.

Babbage supplied the concept and design, and Ada, being both an analyst and metaphysician, put that concept and design in an appropriate context on both micro and mega levels. She asked critical questions that many of us who are not professional mathematicians, scientists, or software engineers would ask. By asking those questions she has given us a methodology and a language to understand the content and concept of a technological innovation. She integrated what we now refer to as digital or scientific skills of reason and analysis, from verbal to numerical, with the poetical skills of imagination and metaphor.

Ada's Notes foreshadowed the capability of the modern computer and the impact such a development would have on the language of science. The Notes were written for an educated Victorian audience and are probably not of interest to many people today. Those who are interested can read the original, which now has been reprinted in several books (see Appendix I). The selection presented here highlights some of the issues discussed at the time and how they relate to the modern computer and to the software language *Ada*. (To differentiate Ada Lovelace from the software language *Ada*, the latter is italicized in this chapter.) It is important to mention once again that this chapter, the annotation of the excerpts from Ada's Notes, is a collaboration between Colonel Rick Gross, United States Air Force, and me, and represents our views.

All quotations and page numbers refer to the original Memoir, which was printed in Scientific Memoirs, Selections from The Transactions of Foreign Academies and Learned Societies and from Foreign Journals, edited by Richard Taylor, F.S.A., Vol III London: 1843, Article XXIX. *Sketch of the Analytical Engine invented by* Charles Babbage *Esq. By* L. F. Menabrea, *of Turin, Officer of the Military Engineers* [From the Bibliothèque Universelle de Génève, No. 82 October 1842].

To start with, Ada added a footnote to her translation. She emphasized the difference between Pascal's machine, which can be compared to a calculator, and Babbage's Analytical Engine, which can be compared to a modern day computer. Ada translated what Menabrea wrote: "For instance, the much-admired machine of Pascal is now simply an object of curiosity, which, whilst it displays the powerful intellect of its inventor, is yet of little utility in itself. Its power extended no further than the execution of the first four operations . . ." Ada augments Menabrea's statement and clearly defines the boundaries of Babbage's Analytical Engine.

From Ada's footnote to her translation of Menabrea's work on p. 670:

This remark seems to require further comment, since it is in some degree calculated to strike the mind as being at variance with the subsequent passage (page 675), where it is explained that *an engine which can effect these four operations* [+, −, x, ÷] can in fact effect *every species of calculation* . . . The explanation lies in this: that in the one case the execution of these four operations is the *fundamental starting-point*, and the object proposed for attainment by the machine is the *subsequent combination of these* in every possible variety. . . The one *begins* where the other *ends*. . .

On p. 687 Ada made a mistake in the translation that was not caught by either Babbage or Wheatstone, who, as can be seen from Ada's correspondence, were supposed to be proofing the translation and Notes. Ada translated "cosine" incorrectly. However, Herschel Babbage, years later, corrected the mistake with another mistake, 1/0. While others have focused and made an issue of a minor typo, we would rather focus on what Ada did do.

In her first "Philosophical Note A," which Babbage liked so much, Ada defined the boundaries of the Analytical Engine, and the details of how the Analytical Engine would perform its tasks. She emphasized that the Difference Engine, Babbage's first calculating engine, was designed primarily for calculating and printing tables, but the Analytical Engine was a mechanical and conceptual leap.

From Ada's Note A, p. 691

The Analytical Engine, on the contrary, is not merely adapted for *tabulating* the results of one particular function and no other, but for *developping and tabulating* any function whatever. In fact the engine may be described as being the material expression of any indefinite function of any degree of generality and complexity. . .

Ada had now emphasized the fundamentally different capability of the Analytical Engine, that is, to be able to store a program (a sequence of operations or instructions) as well as data (informational values themselves). At this point, she began to recognize and to amplify the increased responsibility this new capability placed upon the machine's user, to specify the stored program both precisely and in complete accordance with the user's interest. Her recognition of this increased responsibility is a remarkable insight, in that the magnitude of this specification task (a task we refer to today as *software development*) is only now being appreciated.

It is accordingly most fitting that the programming language *Ada*, developed in the early 1980s by the U.S. Department of Defense, provides the most precise facilities for this software development (specification) task of any general-purpose software language for large-scale problems existing today.

In the following passage, Ada explained the difficulty of the software development task, that is, the difficulty of communicating to the machine what it is we expect it to do. But note that in so doing, she also extolled the power of mathematical language when it is precise. Thus, a software language capable of great precision in specification (like the *Ada* language) also provides great power.

Indeed, throughout this translation one is struck by the appreciation Ada exhibited for the principle that power comes from disciplined creativity. Neither her analyst nor metaphysician persona is allowed to overcome the other, resulting in a synergy of amazing potential. The powerful, innovative *Ada* software language is a fitting namesake. Its advanced features have been implemented in a framework that encourages their use in a structured, repeatable *software engineering* process. Indeed, Dr Frederick Brooks, a renowned modern software authority, forecasted that the *Ada* language's "greatest contribution will be that switching to it occasioned training programmers in modern software-design techniques."[1]

From Note A, p. 693

The confusion, the difficulties, the contradictions which, in consequence of want of accurate distinctions in this particular, have up to even a recent period encumbered mathematics . . . It may be desirable to explain, that by the word *operation*, we mean *any process which alters the mutual relation of two or more things*, be this relation of what kind it may. This is the most general definition, and would include all subjects in the universe . . .

They will also be aware that one main reason why the separate nature of the science of operations has been little felt, and in general little dwelt on, is the *shifting* meaning of many of the symbols used in mathematical notation. First, the symbols of *operation* are frequently *also* the symbols of the *results* of operations . . .

Secondly, figures, the symbols of *numerical magnitude*, are frequently *also* the symbols of *operations*, as when they are the indices of powers [e.g., 2 and 3^2] . . . [In] the Analytical Engine . . . whenever numbers meaning *operations* and not *quantities* (such as indices of powers), are inscribed on any column or set of columns, those columns immediately act in a wholly separate and independent manner . . .

One of Ada's first letters to De Morgan, which does not remain, dealt with acoustics. De Morgan directed Ada to the *Penny Encyclopedia* to find out more about the relationship between mathematics and music. Ada's great love was music and she speculated how the Analytical Engine might deal with it. We have highlighted in bold type sections which have been quoted often. For example, guest editor Denis Baggi's introduction to the July 1991 issue of *Computer* (devoted entirely to computer-generated music) began with an acknowledgment that Ada was the first to have suggested such an application.[2]

It is perhaps coincidental in this regard, but still appropriate, that one of the advanced features of the software language *Ada* is its strong typing capability. Strong typing allows an *Ada* software developer to define within the *Ada* language named mathematical objects (such as musical constructs, e.g., "tones") and a set of operations appropriate to those objects (e.g., "play," "store," etc.). Having done so, the developer can then refer to these objects and operations directly and abstractly, avoiding the requirement levied by less advanced languages to encode manually such objects and operations into alphanumeric values (a process both error-prone and cumbersome). The software language *Ada* thus supports Ada's suggestion that a machine like the Analytical Engine could operate directly on music.

From Note A, p. 694

Again, it [the Analytical Engine] might act upon other

things besides *number*, were objects found whose mutual fundamental relations could be expressed by those of the abstract science of operations, and which should be also susceptible of adaptations to the action of the operating notation and mechanism of the engine . . . **Supposing, for instance, that the fundamental relations of pitched sounds in the science of harmony and of musical composition were susceptible of such expression and adaptations, the engine might compose elaborate and scientific pieces of music of any degree of complexity or extent.**

Once Ada had made the distinction between numbers and the operations to be performed, it was not difficult for her to project further how the Analytical Engine would then be capable of giving two types of results – numerical and symbolic (e.g., algebraic). Because the Analytical Engine could generate new programs as well as numbers, it opened up a vast new territory for the analysis of information.

Here again, the *Ada* software language contains somewhat unique facilities corresponding in a sense to Ada's insight. One such *Ada* facility is the generic subprogram, a template for future software generation. Having defined a generic subprogram for data of one type, the *Ada* software developer can create new copies automatically tailored to data of other types.

A second unusual *Ada* facility, exception handling, reflects in a different but related way Ada's vision of the Analytical Engine's superiority over the Difference Engine. *Ada* exception handlers can be defined by the developer to deal in a controlled way with what Parnas and Wuerges called "undesired events,"[3] those combinations of input data that might otherwise cause aberrant program behavior. In this sense the *Ada* language exception handler operates at a level of control above the program itself, confirming Ada's foresight.

From Note A, p. 696

The former engine [the Difference Engine] is in its nature strictly *arithmetical*, and the results it can arrive at lie within a very clearly defined and restricted range, while there is no finite line of demarcation which limits the powers of the Analytical Engine. These powers are co-extensive with our knowledge of the laws of analysis itself, and need be bounded only with our acquaintance with the latter. Indeed we may consider the engine as the *material and mechanical representative* of analysis, and that our actual working powers in this department of human study will be enabled more effectually than heretofore to keep pace with our theoretical knowledge of its principles and laws, through the complete control which the engine gives us over the *executive manipulation* of algebraical and numerical symbols.

In the seventeenth century, imagination was used interchangeably with fancy. However, by the nineteenth century, Wordsworth and Coleridge came to identify imagination with the creative processes in poetry and discovery. Imagination was considered the highest faculty. Ada continued along the Coleridgean path and used her imagination to speculate on how the Analytical Engine might be a path as well to "higher truth." In the following passage Ada looked at the Analytical Engine from a metaphysical point of view and explained its potential to aid science.

From Note A, p. 696

Those who view mathematical science not merely as a vast body of abstract and immutable truths, whose intrinsic beauty, symmetry and logical completeness, when regarded in their connexion together as a whole, entitle them to a prominent place in the interest of all profound and logical minds, but as possessing a yet deeper interest for the human race, when it is remembered that this science constitutes the language through which alone we can adequately express the great facts of the natural world, and those unceasing changes of mutual relationship which, visibly or invisibly, consciously or unconsciously to our immediate physical perceptions, are interminably going on in the agencies of the creation we live amidst: those who thus think on mathematical truth as the instrument through which the weak mind of man can most effectually read his Creator's works, will regard with especial interest all that can tend to facilitate the translation of its principles into explicit practical forms.

Ada repeated the distinction between the two engines again and again because many people criticized Babbage for not continuing to work on his first calculating engine, the Difference Engine, and instead putting all his efforts into the Analytical Engine. It is a distinction that even some people today have difficulty understanding.

In simple terms, the Analytical Engine used punch or punched cards, like the first modern mainframe computers, as an input device. It had a "store" to store numbers. It was not until the mid-1960s that the modern computer could store as many digit numbers as did the Analytical Engine. The Analytical Engine had a "mill" where the information was processed and is similar to the Central Processing Unit (CPU) in the modern computer.

Finally, the Analytical Engine used several methods to print out information, even in graph form. It was not programmable in the modern sense of that word. It was to be programmable in the software by arranging the punch cards by repetition of cycles. Ada emphasized this distinction by using a metaphor (highlighted in bold type) as accurate as one her father might have written.

From Note A, p. 696

The distinctive characteristic of the Analytical Engine, and that which has rendered it possible to endow mechanism with such extensive faculties as bid fair to make this engine the executive right-hand of abstract algebra, is the introduction into it of the principle which Jacquard devised for regulating, by means of punched cards, the most complicated patterns in the fabrication of brocaded stuffs. It is in this that the distinction between the two engines lies. Nothing of the sort exists in the Difference Engine. **We may say most aptly that the Analytical Engine *weaves algebraical patterns* just as the Jacquard-loom weaves flowers and leaves.**

Another critical distinction was the ability to deal with conditional operations or "if" statements. The ability of the engine to act on an "if" statement without the intervention of a human hand separated it from all mere calculating machines. It was a quantum leap that Ada recognized. The Analytical Engine could calculate a problem and put it in the "store," retrieve the answer, and use it in another problem; as a result it was capable of both analysis and synthesis.

From Note A, pp. 696-697

The bounds of *arithmetic* were however outstepped the moment the idea of applying the cards had occurred; and the Analytical Engine does not occupy common ground with mere "calculating machines." It holds a position wholly its own; and the considerations it suggests are most interesting in their nature. In enabling mechanism to combine together *general* symbols, in successions of unlimited variety and extent, a uniting link is established between the operations of matter and the abstract mental processes of the *most abstract* branch of mathematical science. A new, a vast, and a powerful language is developed for the

future use of analysis, in which to wield its truths so that
these may become of more speedy and accurate practical
application for the purposes of mankind than the means
hitherto in our possession have rendered possible.

From Note A, p. 697

We will touch on another point which constitutes an
important distinction in the modes of operating of the Difference and Analytical Engines. In order to enable the former to do its business, it is necessary to put into its
columns, the series of numbers constituting the first terms
of the several orders of differences for whatever is the particular table under consideration. The machine then works
upon these as its data. But these data must themselves
have been already computed through a series of calculations by a human head . . . In other words, an *analysing*
process must have been gone through by a human mind in
order to obtain the data upon which the engine then *syn-
thetically* builds its results . . . [The] Analytical Engine is
equally capable of analysis or of synthesis.

Ada attempted to answer a persistent question about the Analytical Engine: Of what possible use could such an engine be?
She then emphasized the practical value of such a machine.

Who should develop it? Babbage was frustrated that no one
in England was supportive of his ideas for the Analytical Engine. Ada tried to protect Babbage from engendering anger in
the British community by insisting that the preface detailing
the lack of support of the British government not be included in
the Memoir. She wrote Babbage that inclusion was suicidal. Instead, Ada attempted to gain support for his idea for the Analytical Engine by evoking patriotic sentiment.

In her letters to Annabella and Livy in 1834, she tried to
evoke a passion for a joint mission, an esprit de corps. In the following passage Ada used patriotic feeling to enlist supporters

for the Analytical Engine. She predicted accurately that if the government were not supportive, it would lead to the "completion of the undertaking by some *other* nation or government."

From Note A, pp. 699-670

Those who incline to very strictly utilitarian views, may perhaps feel that the peculiar powers of the Analytical Engine bear upon questions of abstract and speculative science, rather than upon those involving every-day and ordinary human interests. These persons being likely to possess but little sympathy, or possibly acquaintance, with any branches of science which they do not find to be *useful* (according to *their* definition of that word), may conceive that the undertaking of that engine, now that the other one is already in progress, would be a barren and unproductive laying out of yet more money and labour; in fact, a work of supererogation. Even in the utilitarian aspect, however, we do not doubt that very valuable practical results would be developped by the extended faculties of the Analytical Engine; some of which results we think we could now hint at, had we the space; and others, which it may not yet be possible to foresee, but which would be brought forth by the daily increasing requirements of science, and by a more intimate practical acquaintance with the powers of the engine, were it in actual existence.

From Note A, p. 700

With whomsoever or wheresoever may rest the present causes of difficulty that apparently exist towards either the completion of the old engine, or the commencement of the new one, we trust they will not ultimately result in this generation's being acquainted with these inventions through the medium of pen, ink and paper merely; and still more do we hope, that for the honour of our country's reputation in the future pages of history, these causes will not lead to the completion of the undertaking by some *other* nation or government.

One can read into the following quotations the germ of perhaps the most important advance in software development in the past twenty years, an idea variously referred to (in its many forms) as *abstraction, modularity, separation of concerns, information hiding,* or *object-oriented design.* The essential component of this idea is the separation of a software action specification from its implementation, and the *Ada* software language contains novel facilities to encourage precise execution of this separation. Every *Ada* subprogram is divided into a *specification* (that carefully describes the subprogram's behavioral interface with other system components, that is, "what" the subprogram does) and a *body* (that instructs the machine what to do to effect the subprogram, or "how" the subprogram is to work). The power conferred by this separation allows the *Ada* language very important powers, among them (1) to permit early integration of subprograms based only on the specification parts, a boon in large system design; and (2) to allow system updating by changing only subprogram bodies, avoiding the costly effects of having this change "ripple" through the system.[4]

Other *Ada* language constructs, such as *packages*, also facilitate the separation of concerns. Indeed, it may be said that the separation of concerns is a principle underlying the *Ada* language's entire design. Today's software problems are problems of complexity (i.e., of scale), and that complexity management is the critical need in modern software development. Of all the *Ada* language's contributions, none is more important than the ability it conveys to separate "those things which are in reality distinct and independent, and [unite] those which are mutually dependent."

From Note A, p. 700

M. Menabrea, on the contrary, exclusively developes the analytical view; taking it for granted that mechanism is able to perform certain processes, but without attempting to explain *how*; and devoting his whole attention to explanations and illustrations of the manner in which analytical laws can be so arranged and combined as to bring every branch of that vast subject within the grasp of the assumed powers of mechanism. It is obvious that, in the invention of a calculating engine, these two branches of the subject are equally essential fields of investigation, and that on their mutual adjustment, one to the other, must depend all success. They must be made to meet each other, so that the weak points in the powers of either department may be compensated by the strong points in those of the other.

From Note B, p. 706

The further we analyse the manner in which such an engine performs its processes and attains its results, the more we perceive how distinctly it places in a true and just light the mutual relations and connexion of the various steps of mathematical analysis, how clearly it separates those things which are in reality distinct and independent, and unites those which are mutually dependent.

Charles Babbage had adapted the idea of the punched card from the Jacquard Loom. Rather than relying on verbal explanations, Ada invited the reader who wished to see how the punched card and the Jacquard Loom worked to visit the exhibit of the machine at two different locations in London. Babbage, by adapting the punched card to the Analytical Engine, had made an improvement in the way punched cards could be used in giving the loom instructions. Ada related that improvement to art, using a metaphor once again to reinforce her meaning.

It should be noted that carefully specified software (such as the loom-cards) is eminently capable of being reused in ways (such as "backing") other than those originally intended. Such software reuse is an exceptionally economical means of software development; not only does it save the cost of redeveloping similar software, but it also allows use of already tested software, saving the cost of error repair. Some predict that the 1990s will be the decade in which software reuse becomes the principal software development mechanism, and that the *Ada* software language, which simplifies software reuse because of its precise interface specification and generic subprogram facilities, will lead the way.

From Note C, p. 706

The mode of application of the cards, as hitherto used in the art of weaving, was not found, however, to be sufficiently powerful for all the simplifications which it was desirable to attain in such varied and complicated processes as those required in order to fulfil the purposes of an Analytical Engine. A method was devised of what was technically designated *backing* the cards in certain groups according to certain laws. The object of this extension is to secure the possibility of bringing any particular card or set of cards into use *any number of times successively* in the solution of one problem...

It has been proposed to use it for the reciprocal benefit of that art, which, while it has itself no apparent connexion with the domains of abstract science, has yet proved so valuable to the latter, in suggesting the principles which, in their new and singular field of application, seem likely to place *algebraical* combinations not less completely within the province of mechanism, than are all those varied intricacies of which *intersecting threads* are susceptible. By the introduction of the system of *backing* into the Jacquard-loom itself, patterns which should possess symmetry, and follow regular laws of any extent, might be woven by means of comparatively few cards.

In the first excerpt from Note D, Ada commended the use of indices, a now-basic technique for reducing complexity in the processing of regular data structures. All software language and computer hardware provide facilities for indexed iteration. To further illustrate the concept, Ada included at the end of Note D a table tracing execution of a set of indexed instructions.

Number of Operations.	Nature of Operations.	Variables for Data.						Working Variables.									Variables for Results.	
		$^1V_0$	$^1V_1$	$^1V_2$	$^1V_3$	$^1V_4$	$^1V_5$	$^0V_6$	$^0V_7$	$^0V_8$	$^0V_9$	$^0V_1$	$^0V_{11}$	$^0V_{12}$	$^0V_{13}$	$^0V_{14}$	$^0V_{15}$	$^0V_{16}$
		+	+	+	+	+	+	+	+	+	+	+	+	+	+	+	+	+
		0	0	0	0	0	0	0	0	0	0	0	0	0	0	0	0	0
		0	0	0	0	0	0	0	0	0	0	0	0	0	0	0	0	0
		0	0	0	0	0	0	0	0	0	0	0	0	0	0	0	0	0
		0	0	0	0	0	0	0	0	0	0	0	0	0	0	0	0	0
		m	n	d	m'	n'	d'										$\dfrac{dn'-d'n}{mn'-m'n}=x$	$\dfrac{d'm-dm'}{mn'-m'n}=y$
1	×	m	......	......	......	n'	......	mn'										
2	×	......	n	......	m'	......	......		$m'n$									
3	×	......	......	d	......	......	......			dn'								
4	×	......	0	......	......	......	d'				$d'n$							
5	×	0	......	......	......	......	0					$d'm$						
6	×	......	......	0	0	......	......						dm'					
7	−	......	......	......	......	......	......	0	0					$(mn'-m'n)$				
8	−	......	......	......	......	......	......			0	0				$(dn'-d'n)$			
9	−	......	......	......	......	......	......					0	0			$(d'm-dm')$		
10	÷	......	......	......	......	......	......							$(mn'-m'n)$	0		$\dfrac{dn'-d'n}{mn'n}=x$	
11	÷	......	......	......	.... .	......	......								0			$\dfrac{d'm-dm'}{mn'-m'n}=y$

DIAGRAM TO NOTE D

Her table further refined "Menabrea's notation of V_0, V_1, V_2 ... as far as lower suffices are concerned, to denote location, but also introduced higher suffices ^0V, ^1V, ^2V to denote the state of the variable column. Any column which is given a number is labelled ^1V, and if this number is altered during the operation it becomes successively ^2V, ^3V... Lady Lovelace [Ada] justifies her upper suffix notation by remarking ... it is better to record the events as $^{m+1}V_n = {}^mV_p + {}^mV_n$, rather than the confusing $V_n = V_p + V_n$."[5]

The second excerpt goes further. While her discussion of indexing assumed control of the Analytical Engine by a single sequential instruction stream, Ada displayed in this second excerpt remarkable insight into the vastly more complex milieu of multiple parallel instruction streams. Because of the explosion of the numbers of possible conditions that must be taken into account, software development for such parallel and simultaneous instruction streams strains the current state of the art.

From Note D, p. 709

There are several advantages in having a set of indices of this nature; but these advantages are perhaps hardly of a kind to be immediately perceived, unless by a mind somewhat accustomed to trace the successive steps by means of which the engine accomplishes its purposes. We have only space to mention in a general way, that the whole notation of the tables is made more consistent by these indices, for they are able to mark a *difference* in certain cases, where there would otherwise be an apparent *identity* confusing in its tendency . . . It is also obvious that the indices furnish a powerful means of tracing back the derivation of any result; and of registering various circumstances concerning that *series of successive substitutions*. . .

In the excerpt from Note D, Ada referred to the parallel but independent activities of parts of the Analytical Engine, but it is then only a short step to imagine multiple parallel whole Analytical Engines interacting simultaneously. The *Ada* software language is one of only a few such languages that explicitly includes *tasking* constructs to allow software developers to specify and control the interaction of parallel independent *tasks*. As Ada correctly noted, the complexity of such specification is especially great, to the extent that the design of the *Ada* software language has been criticized for including its necessarily complex (and thus costly) tasking features. In light of the exceptional metaphysician's insight Ada displayed in this excerpt, however, it seems that it would have been ironic to deny the *Ada* language this facility of vastly greater (and all the while controlled) expression.

From Note D, p. 710

It must be evident how multifarious and how mutually complicated are the considerations which the workings of such involve. There are frequently several distinct *sets of effects* going on simultaneously; all in a manner independent of each other, and yet to a greater or less degree exercising a mutual influence. To adjust each to every other, and indeed even to perceive and trace them out with perfect correctness and success, entails difficulties whose nature partakes to a certain extent of those involved in every question where *conditions* are very numerous and inter-complicated; such as for instance the estimation of the mutual relations amongst *statistical* phenomena, and of those involved in many other classes of facts.

In the excerpt from Note E, Ada related how the Analytical Engine would compute a trigonometric function. Then she expanded the visual image she had used of weaving and symmetry to highlight the *cycle*, a conceptual building block of programs for both the Analytical Engine and later the computer.

From Note E, p. 716

. . . Wherever a *general term* exists, there will be a *recurring group* of operations, as in the above example. Both for brevity and for distinctness, a *recurring group* is called a *cycle*. A *cycle* of operations, then, must be understood to signify any *set of operations* which is repeated *more than once*. It is equally a *cycle*, whether it be repeated *twice* only, or an indefinite number of times; for it is the fact of a *repetition occurring at all* that constitutes it such. In many cases of analysis there is a *recurring group* of one or more *cycles*; that is, a *cycle of a cycle*, or a *cycle of cycles*. . .

From Note F, p. 720

There is in existence a beautiful woven portrait of Jacquard, in the fabrication of which 24,000 cards were required.

The power of *repeating* cards, alluded to by M. Menabrea in page 680, and more fully explained in Note C, reduces to an immense extent the number of cards required. It is obvious that this mechanical improvement is especially applicable wherever *cycles* occur...

Of all the material in the translation, the following Note has probably engendered the most controversy in light of its denial of the possibility of creating original knowledge through "artificial intelligence." While we have highlighted in bold type the passage most often quoted, the whole passage summarized precisely and with remarkable insight the limits and the potential of both the Analytical Engine and the computer.

The first paragraph has proven to be prophetic in the introduction of the *Ada* software language by the U.S. Department of Defense. In the early 1980s the exceptional features of this advanced language caused too many to yield to the temptation to overrate and oversell it as a panacea for software ills. As a result, there was widespread impatience with fledgling *Ada*-to-machine language translators (*compilers*) and other supporting software *tools*, denying the *Ada* language a normal maturation period. This period was followed by a protracted period of undervaluing *Ada* that continues to this day, manifesting itself in a tendency for many to ignore an accumulating body of evidence that the *Ada* software language is a remarkable, useful, and superior technology.

From Note G, p. 722

It is desirable to guard against the possibility of exaggerated ideas that might arise as to the powers of the Analytical Engine. In considering any new subject, there is frequently a tendency, first, to *overrate* what we find to be already interesting or remarkable; and, secondly, by a sort of natural reaction, to *undervalue* the true state of the case, when we do discover that our notions have surpassed those that were really tenable.

The Analytical Engine has no pretensions whatever to

originate any thing. It can do whatever we *know how to order it* to perform. It can *follow* analysis; but it has no power of *anticipating* any analytical relations or truths. Its province is to assist us in making *available* what we are already acquainted with. This it is calculated to effect primarily and chiefly of course, through its executive faculties; but it is likely to exert an indirect and reciprocal influence on science itself in another manner. For, in so distributing and combining the truths and the formula of analysis, that they may become most easily and rapidly amenable to the mechanical combinations of the engine, the relations and the nature of many subjects in that science are necessarily thrown into new lights, and more profoundly investigated. This is a decidedly indirect, and a somewhat *speculative,* consequence of such an invention. It is however pretty evident, on general principles, that in devising for mathematical truths a new form in which to record and throw themselves out for actual use, views are likely to be induced, which should again react on the more theoretical phase of the subject. There are in all extensions of human power, or additions to human knowledge, various *collateral* influences, beside the main and primary object attained.

There have been rumors for several years that Ada did not write the first program or these Notes – that her contribution has been exaggerated. I have specifically asked for evidence from those making such allegations. As yet I have not received any evidence that would lead me to change my conclusion that Ada wrote these Notes and the first table of instructions of appropriate complexity for the Analytical Engine.

Babbage had no question about Ada's contribution. He recognized her importance. After Ada's death, he wrote to her son Byron: "In the memoir of Mr. Menabrea and still more in the excellent Notes appended by your mother you will find the only comprehensive view of the powers of the Anal. Engine which the mathematicians of the world have yet expressed."[6]

He summarized his high regard for what Ada had done in *Passages*:

> We discussed together the various illustrations that might be introduced: I suggested several, but the selection was entirely her own. So also was the algebraic working out of the different problem, except indeed, that relating to the numbers of Bernoulli, which I had offered to do to save Lady Lovelace the trouble. This she sent back to me for an amendment, having detected a grave mistake which I had made in the process. . . These two memoirs taken together furnish, to those who are capable of understanding the reasoning a complete demonstration – That the whole of the developments and operations of analysis are now capable of being executed by machinery.[7]

As to the fate of the Analytical Engine, when Babbage wrote *Passages* in 1864, he expressed some optimism:

> If I survive some few years longer, the Analytical Engine will exist, and its work will afterward be spread over the world. . . Half a century may probably elapse before anyone without those aids which I leave behind me, will attempt so unpromising a task.[8]

It was over seventy years before a working computer was built. In 1991, the computer industry, both hardware and software, represented the third largest industry in the world. In I. Bernard Cohen's excellent introduction to the 1990 revised *A Computer Perspective, Background to the Computer Age,* he states: "Even more astonishing may be the transition from minis to micros and the emergence of the computer as an all-purpose machine to serve such different purposes as industry, commerce and banking, as well as science and engineering. Hardly anyone in the early 1950's and even later would have predicted that one and the same all-purpose machine would be designed and manufactured to serve efficiently both the needs of business and engineering."[9]

Yet, Ada had the foresight in 1843 to envision the Analytical Engine fulfilling both a metaphysical scientific purpose and an analytical practical engineering purpose. Because of her contribution, she deserves her proper place in history as a "pioneer of computing." In *Pebbles to Computers, The Thread*, Stafford Beer states his view of Ada's contribution: "Augusta Ada, The Countess of Lovelace, was the poet Byron's daughter – who understood perhaps better than Babbage himself, where all this . . . would finally lead."[10]

13.
Fairy Guidance,
My Metaphysical Child,
Caged Bird
[1843-1844]

AS SOON AS ADA RECEIVED the Memoir, at the beginning of September 1843, she sent copies to various friends, including Mrs Somerville, who praised Ada for her accomplishment. Ada received a letter at this time from John Kemble, a respected philologist and the editor of a philosophical review. According to his letter, there must have been a skirmish in the battle of the sexes. Ada was quite upset at how he had categorized women's capabilities, and Kemble, being a gentleman, apologized for leaving the impression of undervaluing the intellectual capabilities of women. It is an attitude that many women are concerned about today, and Ada had tried to set him straight.

She was not quite sure what her intellectual destiny would be, or where her interests would take her. After Babbage and Wheatstone left Ashley Combe, Ada was in a "fairy" mood. She joined her mother on a trip to the environs of Bristol. Ada found that she could not leave her problems behind, especially since Lady Byron was prodding her to tend to the tutor problem.

William stayed at Ashley Combe tending to his many duties: fashioning the landscape, planting trees, and constantly building. He started digging tunnels under the house for the servants to walk in during bad weather, and he erected towers made of pink-colored bricks. Ada was concerned that he would be lonely and was delighted to hear he had a visit from Andrew Crosse, a Somerset neighbor, with his son. Crosse was an experimenter in electricity and had a reputation for being strange. William was so perturbed at how long it took both Crosse and his son to answer a question that he preferred not to have their company.

Ada wanted to spend more time with William, to explore the countryside with him; however, William preferred spending time on his architectural pursuits. He was pleased that Ada was cheering up her mother. Both William and Lady Byron considered Ada "<u>Our</u> <u>Bird</u>" and believed they now had her firmly in their control. Ada searched for her own way but was constantly thwarted by her ill health. She took comfort in the development of her children, especially her "metaphysical child."

To Lady Byron

Wednesday [Mid August, 1843]

Dearest Hen... That <u>good</u> little <u>trustworthy</u> creature Annabella, exhibits most interesting traits of character; far beyond her years I think. –

If you go to Clifton for any <u>time</u>; might I not join you there do you think? I have however made engagements for Babbage & Wheatstone to pass some time at Ashley; & could not of course break <u>these</u>. Babbage comes <u>immediately</u> to us, on our arrival. Wheatstone I believe <u>later</u>.

We send you a parcel containing <u>three</u> copies of your literary <u>grandchild</u>, The rest you can have when you are settled again.

To Charles Babbage

Sunday, 10 September 1843

My Dear Babbage. Your letter is <u>charming</u>, and Lord L – & I have smiled over it most <u>approbatively</u>. You must forgive me for showing it to him . It contains such <u>simple</u>, <u>honest</u>, <u>unfeigned</u> admiration for myself, that I could not resist giving <u>him</u> the pleasure of seeing it. I send you De Morgan's <u>kind</u> & <u>approving</u> letter about my article. I never expected that <u>he</u> would view my crude young composition so favourably.

You understand that I send you his letter in strictest <u>confidence.</u> He might perhaps not like you to see his remarks about the relative <u>times</u> of the invention of the two engines. I am going to inform him of my grounds of feeling satisfied of the literal correctness of my statement on that point. I cannot say how much his letter has pleased me.

You are a brave man to give yourself wholly up to Fairy-Guidance! – I advise you to allow yourself to be unresistingly bewitched, neck, & crop, out & out, whole seas over, &c, &c, &c, by that curious little being!

To Lady Byron

Friday, 15 September [1843]   Ashley [Combe]

I was so <u>amazed</u> when I read the beginning of your letter this morning, at the absolute identity of the <u>principle</u> expressed in it, to that which <u>I</u> had expressed (tho' in a different form) to <u>you</u> in my last, that I could not help exclaiming to <u>Babbage</u> "<u>this</u> <u>is</u> <u>most</u> <u>extraordinary</u>!" & relating to him the circumstance.

There are however so many very remarkable circumstances that have occurred during the latter weeks and months, & which I cannot pretend to unravel, at present, but which something tells me I shall find the real clue to all in good time, that this merely <u>adds</u> one to their number. I am very much <u>afraid</u> as yet of exerting the powers I <u>know</u> I <u>have</u> <u>over</u> <u>others</u>, & the <u>evidence</u> of which I have certainly been <u>most</u> <u>unwilling</u> <u>to</u> <u>admit</u>, & in fact for a long time considered to be quite fanciful & absurd. I am an utter novice at present, on the threshold of a new world; & I feel my best plan is to wait modestly & humbly for God to teach me, & not to anticipate that teaching, but rather to keep <u>behind</u> . . . Those powers are not <u>ripe</u>, & my <u>habits</u> & <u>principles</u> are still far too young, now, & green . . .

I had better continue to be simply the High-Priestess of Babbage's Engine, & serve my apprenticeship faithfully therein, before I fancy myself worthy to approach a step higher towards being the <u>High</u> <u>Priestess</u> of God Almighty Himself. And one has a fearful universe of <u>habits</u> to acquire. Many get <u>habits</u> first, & great principles <u>afterwards</u>. But here am I (who always did everything topsy-turvy, & certainly ought to have come into the world <u>feet</u> <u>downwards</u>) with <u>principles</u> highly & largely developped, but <u>habits</u> alas that are either non-existent or <u>positively</u> <u>bad</u>, & (hardly a single good one).

So one must <u>drag</u> one's habits (however unwillingly), <u>after</u> & <u>up</u> <u>to</u> one's principles, before one thinks oneself worth anything whatever. –

By the way I am particularly <u>ill</u> at present. . . But the time will come, when all this will be very different . . .

WHEN MR KRAEMER, Robert Noel's suggestion, did not work out as a tutor, Lady Byron helped to select a proper tutor so that Ada would have time to devote to her profession. Dr William Carpenter was chosen to supervise the education of the children with the aid of a Miss Cooper and masters for singing, riding, etc. Carpenter was a Unitarian, a physician, and a professor who is credited with various written works on physiology and the unconscious mind. Lady Byron was supposed to be his guide. When Ada met Carpenter, she was flirtatious, but when Carpenter took the flirtation seriously and had difficulty in deciding whether or not to take the position, Ada specified the terms.

By the beginning of 1844, once Carpenter was in place, Ada's views towards the children relaxed. Her attitude towards her husband and mother depended on the extent of pressure or support she received from them. Ada was still experimenting, trying to find the appropriate path for her intellectual endeavors; meanwhile, she had to attend to William's complaints.

To Lady Byron

Friday [Undated, late 1843]   Ashley

My Dear Grand-Hen. Only a line just to tell you that I am enjoying the <u>peace</u> & <u>rest</u>, like a Paradise. We are taking rides, & I am studying <u>health</u> in everything; temperance in all departments, regularity, freedom from hurry & fuss, &c, &c. You will see me <u>very</u> <u>slim</u> & <u>fairyish</u>, when I return. . .

I have a <u>volume</u> of Dr C [Carpenter]'s by me, which I must answer tomorrow. We shall agree to all he wishes. William does not quite like the condition about the children being only <u>one</u> <u>month</u> at Ashley; that is to say it goes <u>against</u> <u>the</u> <u>grain</u>; & rather <u>hurts</u> him. I feel for his little favorite crotchets; & tender points; & I think I manage to console him about this one pretty well. – He is a good crow, (tho' he <u>does</u> try to murder his thrush now & then). The attempts on my life & limbs are very droll, (in retrospect). –

By the bye, you cannot think what a delight it is to me that Dr Carpenter & my own dear <u>Old</u> <u>Arab</u> <u>Horse</u> [Dr Locock] have met, & seem to have agreed about me & all things. Congratulate me upon this. It is worth it. . .

To Lady Byron

Tuesday, 11 o'clock [undated, 1844?]   Ockham

. . .You cannot think how charmed I am with my <u>metaphysical</u> child, & how I have thought of her. If she will only be kind enough to be a metaphysician & a mathematician instead of a silly minikin dangling <u>Miss</u> in leading strings, I shall love her <u>mind</u> too much to care whether her <u>body</u> is male female or neuter.

But really, all joking apart, I feel that there is that in her which I shall <u>delight</u> to commute with as she comes to maturity, (& which has nothing to do with the sex either way). William begins too to feel her superiority. He say that he hopes that she will marry a man whose position & circumstances may be such as to place his wife above the necessity of giving her intellect & energies to mere daily affairs of life; that if A's mind is capacious & superior, it would be a shame that it were not free to follow out its own bent & studies. He says that he thinks she <u>might</u> be tolerably happy at home until 20, provided she liked study & <u>had</u> <u>pursuits</u>.

In short what <u>he</u> dreads in a girl, is evidently a <u>purposeless</u> <u>desultory</u> Miss, whose interests merely consist in flirting, embroidering, or perhaps (as a great God-send) the piano & miniature painting. What he would like is a <u>business-like</u>

young lady; and yet she must be a <u>busy-lady</u>, & she must be <u>feminine</u> & <u>elegant</u> in manner & appearance. But a <u>business-like</u> young lady is the right expression.

You will be vastly amused at this letter; & at our drawing anticipations that the <u>female</u> <u>misfortune</u> <u>may</u> turn out quite overwhelming. . .

I had rather not leave the sick old crow today. The poor old fellow would be lonely & moping on his perch; (altho' Byron would be <u>some</u> resource to him).

Wednesday, 2 o'clock [Undated]   St James' Square

. . . Dr Locock came this morning, & was satisfied; altho' I feel very over-full again today, & am not a bit reduced in any way. He has desired me to take a very good walk, which I am forthwith going to set about. He wishes to reduce me by exercise, & laudanum (judiciously administered), in preference to another bleeding. – He is probably right. . .

It is disagreeable enough, but I don't think my health will remain so uncertain much longer; & then (as Dr L [Locock] said himself), people will soon forget the past Lady L – is the present one.

To William, Lord Lovelace

10 o'clock, 10 April [1844]   St James' Square

I have thought of you with no small distress, dearest W – , & I feel I have not one word to say for myself. I hope you will not fail to see me on Friday, before you go to Ashley.

I have had <u>no</u> <u>intention</u>, I can truly & honestly say, of teasing & hurting you. The consequence was that when I found I <u>had</u> (most <u>undesignedly</u>) had those effects, I felt beyond measure exasperated with you <u>for</u> <u>having</u> <u>felt</u> <u>hurt</u>. – I am not pleading for the justice or fairness of this. Far from it. I merely mention it as a fact. . .

It is my <u>first</u> wish, dearest mate, to make your happiness & comfort; but I assure you it is not easy; simply because <u>you</u> give me no helping hand. I know that this is from <u>diffidence</u> on your part, to a certain extent. But it is a diffidence very pernicious to our mutual happiness & which makes <u>my</u> game a difficult one.

   <u>Pray</u> write to me, if only 6 words. I am quite miserable about you because I know you are unhappy, & fancy you have an unkind bird.

A DA'S HEALTH WAS SO POOR that after a stint at the dentist, Dr Landzelle, she headed for Brighton hoping to get her health in order. Brighton became a favorite retreat for Ada. Yet, even at a distance, she tried hard to take care of family needs. Her letters to William were newsy and coaxing and described Brighton seaside adventures in 1844, complete with bathing costumes. She suggested to William that he build a swimming pool because "You know all <u>caged</u> Birds require a large saucer to dip into."

To William, Lord Lovelace

Friday Morning 9 o'clock [August 1844]

                        38 Bedford Square, Brighton

Dearest W. I little thought when I wrote you my note on Weddy by Dr Carpenter, what I should have to go thro' with my teeth. I was seized with paroxysms of pain in the jaw that had been operated upon, that afternoon, & had to pass <u>some</u> <u>hours</u> at the Dentist's . . . I never shall forget the agonies I endured for some hours. I hope to write you a better account tomorrow morning. My head & stomach are all wrong still . . . But I may recover from this rapidly enough, when once I take a good turn again.

   So, my Dear, don't be vexed! I think much about <u>ou</u>. I hope you take out your young to ride with you sometimes; (not interfering with Dr C [Carpenter]'s hours however). I hope that you don't wholly neglect <u>Jack</u> either, & also that you give <u>Tag</u> <u>Rag</u> plenty of work. <u>Your</u> careful riding does both his health & temper a world of good. And I am sure you won't jerk up his mouth in the way I dislike.

I pick up all the household & domestic knowledge I can, in every way. I feel more & more sure that I can not only reduce greatly our expenses, but actually <u>increase</u> our pleasures & comforts notwithstanding.

To Lady Byron

Saturday 1 o'clock [1844]   Ockham

. . . Dr L [Locock] can tell you all about the improvement <u>here</u>. You write in good spirits, so I feel satisfied. I have got sadly quakey & frightened of late about the poor old Hen. I don't know <u>what</u> I should do without her chuckling & meddling. I think she may get on however a good many years yet. . .

I had a conversation with Miss Cooper last evening, which was <u>more</u> satisfactory than I expected. She has in her the material for firmness; & she seems quite inclined to <u>put</u> <u>it</u> <u>out</u>, now that she has <u>seen</u> William's manners with the children, & <u>heard</u> my decisive tone on the subject. . .

They find <u>William</u> a very different sort of master; & I think that their being under him for a time is an excellent thing. . . Altho' I dare say they do not <u>learn</u> nearly as much; for I do not think W – has a particularly enlightened or skillful method of instruction; & besides that, he has not above 20 minutes to give to each of the two. But he drills them famously. I don't think he is over-<u>patient</u>, but tant mieux. I know he has been very sharp with <u>Annabella</u>, & spoken to her in a tone she is not used to at all. But she has been very impertinent to him. She is much awed by some measures <u>I</u> have taken in consequence also. I sent her word that I should not speak to her until I heard that she had satisfied her father by proper respect, obedience & attention for 2 or 3 days; that she owed respect to <u>all</u> her masters & would be <u>made</u> to pay it willingly or unwillingly, but that I considered her being wanting towards her <u>father</u> when <u>he</u> was so very kind as to give her his time & trouble as being unpardonable, & I could not easily forget it.

14.

Planetary Systems,
Not a Snail-Shell But
a Molecular Laboratory,
A Newton for the
Molecular Universe
[1844]

SINCE ADA WAS CONSTANTLY ILL, she wondered about the influence of the mind over the body. Ada was being fed a constant dose of laudanum by the physicians, which did not please her mother. In the autumn of 1844 Lady Byron suggested that Ada read Harriet Martineau's *Letters on Mesmerism* explaining how mesmerism relieved her of the necessity for opiates and cured her cancerous tumors.

Ada was open to explore new ideas and was interested in mesmerism. She questioned Dr Locock about his views on the subject. He explained his views and continued to give her "silver drops of opiates." She wrote the following letters, no doubt, under the influence of laudanum, where she headed into the cosmos, returned to earth to take care of her practical needs, and then orbited back into outer space. She created her own universe of slavery and freedom, of comets and planets, and even asked her mother to become a planet. Ada wondered why she had been created, was it just for her mother's entertainment?

To Lady Byron

[Undated Fragment, most likely 1844]

. . . Dr Locock is a decided believer in certain <u>physical</u> effects of mesmeric influence, but wholly disbelieves in all those assigned phenomena which are classed under the terms <u>lucid-</u><u>ity</u> or <u>clairvoyance</u>. He thinks that certain remarkable effects already known to occur in some <u>diseases</u>, & also some other effects already known to occur in <u>natural</u> <u>somnambulism</u>, are often produced by mesmeric influence. –

He believes <u>no</u> <u>further</u> than this, because he says he has never had <u>any</u> <u>evidence</u> <u>whatever</u> for doing so, but <u>quite</u> <u>the</u> <u>reverse</u>; besides thinking it a priori very <u>improbable</u> that there should be <u>during</u> <u>human</u> <u>life</u> the possibility of producing states which are independent of the barriers of <u>Space</u> & <u>Time</u>. – As for <u>Satanic</u> <u>agency</u>, it is so laughable to <u>conceive</u> of <u>his</u> imput- ing such a cause to any such phenomena whatever, that one can say at once it is <u>absolutely</u> <u>impossible</u>. I think it <u>exceedingly</u> probable that he has <u>joked</u> on the subject, & that some pious believer in Satan has taken it all for gospel & earnest. He is just the man to be <u>tickled</u> by such an idea.

His present theory (I <u>think</u>) about those effects of Mesmerism in which he <u>does</u> firmly believe, is that they are the result of <u>mental</u> <u>impression</u> & <u>cause</u>, but not the less <u>real</u> for <u>that</u>. He told me that after all he <u>knows</u> to have occurred thro' purely <u>mental</u> agency, by means of both Irving & Prince Hol- henhole, he feels inclined to impute mesmerical phenomena to the <u>same</u> agency, <u>until</u> <u>he</u> <u>finds</u> <u>positive</u> <u>proof</u> <u>of</u> <u>some</u> <u>one</u> <u>being</u> <u>mesmerized</u> <u>without</u> <u>their</u> <u>own</u> <u>knowledge</u>. That he con- siders the test. –

Dr L [Locock] is not a man too <u>violent</u> or <u>abusive</u> about any one or anything. He might be <u>coldly</u> <u>contemptuous</u> & set things & authorities at nought, very likely. Mesmerism has <u>not</u> suc- ceeded upon <u>him</u>, altho' he has often tried. – In this he & I are just in the same case. –

I know that he feels much contempt for the <u>credulity</u> of many of the <u>public</u>, & of some of <u>his</u> <u>own</u> <u>profession</u>, & that if he met with patients inclined to <u>gulp</u> down <u>marvels</u> without philosophical evidence of their probability, this feeling would be very <u>apparent</u>. –

I should say that he, Dr Forbes, & Dr Carpenter, are <u>all</u> <u>three</u> as nearly as possible in the same state of mind about

Mesmerism. All of them doubt if mesmeric effects will ever be produced when the mesmerer is ignorant of what is going on.

And from the facts I have recently read of, I must say I doubt this myself; or am at least inclined to doubt it. –

I remember Dr Locock's saying about Miss M's [Martineau] first letter that there was nothing in it at all absurd, respecting mesmerism, altho' she betrayed in it an ignorance of medicine & physiology. He said more, & specified further, but I do not recollect what with sufficient exactness to write it down. The general impression left on my mind was that he wholly disbelieved that any organic disease ever had been or ever could be cured by Mesmerism, but that he did think states of health both had been, & could be benefitted by its' measures.

Dr Locock considers that the effect has been on her general health only, & that the tumours either still exist, or have been absorbed owing to the Iodine. He says that uterine tumours often shift about so as to cease causing inconvenience. Dr Forbes said ditto.

To Lady Byron

Thursday 10 October [1844]   Ashley Combe

I have been thinking much about the Mesmerism in Miss Martineau's case. I have long had a strong suspicion that I am myself a victim to those mesmerical experiments in 1841; & as more facts come to my knowledge about others, & also as my advancing studies on the Nervous System show me that the simply organic or reflex (including the great ganglions of the stomach) portion of the Nervous System acts wholly independently of sensations & of the mental, I become more persuaded that I was mesmerized, & that all my ill health had its' foundations in that. This is a hopeful view, because if so, time will certainly restore all.

My belief is that in certain cases effects on the simply organic system take place instead of on the sensational, or mental systems; and that mine was such a case. –

I have been rather annoyed about Annabella, who has been

in what I can graphically designate as a <u>rampant</u> state. . .the
moment Annabella turns insolent, she excites in me the irresistible determination to <u>annihilate</u> her. I think this effect on
me will be less the case perhaps, when she becomes of an age
to be capable of feeling more the <u>general</u> <u>weight</u> of my character & influence. It is now an awkward period <u>between</u> baby
<u>stick</u> law & the full force of <u>grown-up</u> motives. One is still
obliged to appeal a good deal to the merely immediate.

Well, from all this you see that <u>Byron</u> is now <u>up</u>, & <u>Anna-
bella</u> is <u>down</u>. Ralph is in the <u>neuter</u> degree of my favor. –

The weight of all my past inequities begin to press on me. I
am not joking, & often I have to remember that a continued
<u>dwelling</u> on regrets is loss of power & of time. I am sure that
<u>Scripture</u> repentance is not <u>such</u>. What makes my difficulty is
the <u>too</u> <u>much</u> <u>freedom</u>, that I wrote about yesterday.

Would that I were a <u>slave</u>, (providing I had but a kind &
just master)! – But I seem to myself as if <u>condemned</u> <u>to</u> <u>liberty</u>;
as if I were ordered by Providence to be a wandering & erratic
<u>star</u> amongst the boundless Heavens, in vain seeking for
entrance into some one of the <u>planetary</u> <u>systems</u>, in vain <u>pray-
ing</u> <u>to</u> <u>obey</u> <u>some</u> <u>Sun</u>. –

No, I was a daring & a presumptuous young spirit; so God
has said to me:

"Thy Sun thou must now make for thyself, or else wander
for ever thro' the wide firmament!" – Solemn decree. –

That idea might be developped into a fine poem: The Dis-
obedient & Wandering Star. (Not the Wandering <u>Jew</u>). I would
rather say the <u>presumptuous</u> than the <u>disobedient</u>, I think. I
<u>never</u> <u>was</u> <u>disobedient</u>. Always I shall contend <u>that</u>. –

What an awful re-action tho', from the <u>lawless</u> & <u>liberty-
seeking</u> state! – Let no one envy this awful condemnation to
create my own Sun & my own Orbit & Planetary System; tho'
[an] <u>inglorious</u> destiny, if <u>ever</u> accomplished. But that <u>is</u> <u>such</u>
an <u>If</u>. –

I grow so fond of my old Hen, who understands all I can say
& think so much better than <u>any</u> <u>one</u>. I once was pleased to
think she was the <u>last</u> person who could comprehend me, or <u>to</u>

whom it was safe to commit myself. –

If ever I succeed in creating my Sun, will the Hen be one of my Planets revolving round it in company with me? – I invite her. Nor let her think lightly of this.

I know but one other person whom I feel as fully fitted for me to communicate with as yourself, had he had sufficient of my society & sufficient leisure for knowing me. You will guess at once that I mean Dr Locock. – He does not I think as well understand some points, because he really has not had the opportunities & the data. But I feel he would, if he had. So I hope you would accept him for a Brother Planet.

I question if I am quite as much attached, in a certain way, to any one else; and I hope that will be developped, in the next world, if not in this. Our paths at present here below are somewhat diverse. Not that that is a circumstance which lessens the feeling of attachment, where character is the foundation on both sides. How I wish to live to earn his well founded esteem. His fullest measure of esteem I do not consider that I have, or deserve to have as yet. –

Well, I have ordained a Hen & a Horse for two of my Planets, & I think at present I will go no further in the list. Gamlen would be my next I think. Mrs Somerville also perhaps. But no Babbage or even Dr King. No, I can think of none others, as yet.

Oh! I must arrange some Comets too, by & bye. No complete planetary system without. Heavens! how shall I get any comets? I think I must myself be the chief Comet & not merely one of the Planets. Yes – that will do.

At least I am an amusing Bird, if not a very wise one, with my repentances, my Suns, Planets, Comets, &c, &c, &c.

I really believe that you hatched me simply for the entertainment of your old age; that you might not be ennuyée...

S INCE ADA'S USE OF DRUGS has been the subject of both the fiction and nonfiction accounts of her life, a good dose of modern medical opinion is in order. Dr Locock's prescriptions of opiates might have caused Ada's dependence on opiates; however, recent research reported in *Scientific American* (February 1990) has called into question the addictive nature of opiates when prescribed for pain and terminal illness. When the patient does not need opiates, he can withdraw from them without serious withdrawal symptoms, as will be seen with Ada. On the other hand, opiates needed for pain, as in Ada's case, act like a sponge; very ill patients can absorb enormous amounts that would be deadly for an addict.

Ada had a difficult time, under these conditions, finding an appropriate path for her intellectual interests. There were major problems with the tutor, Dr Carpenter. Ada attempted to deal with them, but neither William nor Lady Byron was cooperative. In late 1844 or early 1845 the Lovelaces were making plans to move to a new estate, East Horsley Towers. During 1844 Carpenter had laid out quite a bit of money fixing up a house at Ockham that Lady Byron had promised to cover. There was no accommodation for Carpenter or his family at Horsley, but Ada was confident that some solution would be found.

Ada considered various scientific subjects that would be appropriate for her to explore. She no longer considered the Analytical Engine as a possibility since Babbage did not want her help in that area. After Ada wrote the Notes and had the argument with Babbage, the nature of their relationship changed. It became much closer emotionally and less involved technologically, though Ada was still supportive of Babbage's continuing efforts for the Analytical Engine. Where else could she turn but to her own body, racked with pain.

She could have moaned and groaned and evoked sympathy for her plight but instead used it as an opportunity to understand physiology. She would not tune out with mesmerism, but tune in to her own body. Her "susceptible frame" would be her inspiration, but she needed to do practical experiments under the guidance of a professional scientist. Ada was impressed by the work of Michael Faraday, and she approached him to help and guide her.

To Lady Byron

Monday 10 o'clock [Autumn 1844]   St James' Square

I received your letter too late this morning to send down by the 10 o'clock coach; (the post being always late on <u>Monday's</u>). . . The facts are as follows: I got <u>worse</u> on Satdy; till by a fortunate <u>accident</u> (& not having seen him for 4 days), Dr Locock called about 4 o'clock. He had never actually <u>seen</u> me under such a crisis of suffering, & indeed he seemed really shocked. He made up his mind <u>at once</u>, & certainly results have proved as he predicted. He insisted, & would hear no objections, for once, on giving me Laudanum directly, 25 drops – (or 20 <u>minims,</u> if you know the distinction), desiring me to go to bed & to keep <u>very</u> <u>warm</u> & <u>very</u> <u>quiet</u>; 10 drops more of Laudanum to be taken if there were not a decided effect in the head & on the general state in 3 or 4 hours time. There was no occasion thus to <u>repeat</u> the dose, nor have I had to do so since, as yet. After an hour & a half, the head sensations began to abate, & by morning the change was great & decided, & there has been little variation or relapse since Laudanum seems to take down the <u>swelling</u> really in a magical manner. This is the second time it has done so within these 10 days. I thought it an accidental coincidence the first time; but I do not think so now. . .

I think he has got at the thing <u>at last</u>. – I must tell you that latterly – the last 2 or 3 years – Opium had seemed strangely to <u>disagree</u> with me. But I now understand why this has been, & why it deceived me. I was all the time taking <u>wine</u> or other <u>stimulant</u>; & the two things made a terrible jumble.

To be very quiet, & to encounter no excitements, is necessary on a Laudanum day, & indeed on the following one. But as I am <u>at any rate</u> incapacitated, I may as well be so by the <u>preventive</u> or <u>remedial</u> measure, as by the natural illness itself. –

The opium has a remarkable effect on my eyes, seeming to <u>free</u> them, & to make them <u>open</u> & <u>cool</u>. Then it makes me so philosophical, & so takes off all <u>fretting</u> eagerness & anxieties. It appears to <u>harmonize</u> the whole constitution, to make each function act in a <u>just</u> <u>proportion</u>; (with <u>judgement</u>, <u>discretion</u>, <u>moderation</u>). . .

Dr L – by the bye dropped out on Satdy that he considers those swellings to be decidedly a <u>watery</u> <u>deposit</u>. I conclude the opium can only act on them <u>indirectly</u>. Surely good <u>Gin</u>, (if ever I take any Alcohol again in my life), would be good for me. . .

To Lady Byron

Monday, 11 November [1844]   Ashley Combe

I return you Miss M [Martineau]'s letter, which I forgot to put in yesterday. –

I hope she & I shall enter on <u>mesmerical</u> <u>correspondence</u>. I hope you will have approved of my letter to her. I endeavour, in writing to her, to say nothing I should care to have <u>published</u> even.

I go on <u>well</u>. The equilibrium gradually returning, the pendulum daily oscillates less outrageously. My grand difficulty is <u>warmth</u>. I told you that I have been for some weeks <u>tending</u> towards chaos; (the peculiar circumstances of the company, wine, &c having merely enhanced & hastened the coming disturbances). The fact is that when <u>warmth</u> leaves the face of the earth, <u>I</u> shall always <u>tend</u> towards illness & suffering. A warm <u>climate</u> would doubtless be the greatest possible <u>comfort</u> to me, it would be life itself to <u>me</u>. It oils all the hinges, does instead of food, makes all go <u>harmoniously</u> & easily.

Not that I believe my <u>life</u> would be lengthened by an <u>hour</u>, thro' a warm climate. I call it a <u>comfort</u> to me; not a <u>necessary</u>. . . Now, under these circumstances, I don't mean to sit down a <u>shivering</u> <u>fool</u>; but I shall act on the principle of <u>Mahomet</u> <u>going</u> <u>to</u> <u>the</u> <u>mountain</u> <u>since</u> <u>the</u> <u>mountain</u> <u>can't</u> <u>or</u> <u>won't</u> <u>come</u> <u>to</u> <u>Mahomet.</u> In other words: a <u>warm</u> <u>climate</u> I can't have. Therefore I must manage to find <u>substitutes</u>, & to do <u>in</u> <u>other</u> <u>ways</u> what the Sun would do in a direct manner for me.

My notion is Galvanization in <u>winter</u>, & sunbathing in <u>summer</u>, are the things for <u>me</u>. I think I have given you a <u>clear</u> & very logical sketch of my present views concerning <u>that</u> <u>portion</u> <u>of</u> <u>the</u> <u>material</u> <u>forces</u> <u>of</u> <u>the</u> <u>world</u> entitled <u>the</u> <u>body</u> of A.A.L.

Do you know it is to me quite delightful to have a frame so <u>susceptible</u> that it is an <u>experimental</u> <u>laboratory</u> always about me, & inseparable from me. I walk about, not in a Snail-Shell, but in a <u>Molecular</u> <u>Laboratory</u>. This is a new view to take of one's physical frame; & amply compensates me for <u>all</u> the sufferings, had they been even greater.

By the bye, Faraday expresses himself in absolute amazement at what he (I think most happily & beautifully) designates the "<u>elasticity</u> of my <u>intellect</u>."

Even from the little <u>correspondence</u> we have lately had, he seems quite <u>strangely</u> impressed with this characteristic; & says that he feels <u>himself</u> a "<u>mere</u> <u>tortoise</u>" in comparison. – . . .

It is evidently his impression that I am the <u>rising</u> <u>star</u> of Science. You know I am not a bit my own agent as to my scientific progress & objects. I am simply the <u>instrument</u> for the divine purposes to act <u>on</u> & <u>thro'</u>; happening to be appropriate for that object. Like the Prophets of old, I shall but <u>speak</u> <u>the</u> <u>voice</u> I am inspired with. . .

I am a <u>Prophetess</u> born into the world; & this conviction fills me with <u>humility</u>, with <u>fear</u> & <u>trembling</u>!

I tell you my views, because, <u>unless</u> I do so, it is scarcely giving you fair play, (in your <u>peculiar</u> relationship to me that is). If you know not the <u>colour</u> of my mind, you may speak <u>inappropriately</u> to me. Was not <u>that</u> my <u>early</u>, & for a time, <u>fatal</u> error towards you? I feared & <u>mistrusted</u> you, & endeavoured <u>therefore</u> to <u>mystify</u> you as to all my <u>real</u> feelings. And a pretty chaos I made of it. . .

I tried to serve <u>two</u> <u>masters</u>, <u>God</u> & <u>The</u> <u>World</u>; <u>until</u> the warning voice of pain & sufferings <u>recalled</u> me. – Happy those indeed, who are so <u>imperatively</u> commanded . . . I wished that before we meet, you should know to the <u>full</u> extent, my turn of mind. Tho' <u>more</u> <u>yours</u> than I ever was in my life, yet <u>am</u> I less <u>yours</u> too. . . I owe you a deep debt of gratitude, & much have I yet to listen to & learn from you as to mere human experience, & your experience & ideas. But I have taken leave of all mortal influence, even yours.

I no longer desire to shun the silken carpets of the rich & luxurious of the earth. Can I not carry a spirit there which shall penetrate even the deadening blunting vapors of aristocratic self-indulgence? – And are not these ones most in need of a Prophet of God? –

One must study them, for it is not by direct speaking & suggestions that one can do good to such. But, they may be mesmerized. And depend on it, I am a great mesmerizer, tho' may never sit down to a mesmerie séance. . .

William's mind & disposition appear to me to become more beautiful & singular every day. I think he will be one day my chosen pet amongst mortals, (which a husband by no means necessarily is). All the angles are rubbing down, more & more. –

[Undated Fragment, most likely early November, 1844]

There may possibly be simply a different law for the propagation of impressions thro' their substance. The molecules may move differently amongst each other. The Creator may have ordained that difference of sensation shall accompany each different law of molecular movement of this description.

And here lies a deep mystery as yet. A Newton for the Molecular Universe is a crying want; but the nature of the subject renders this desideratum of improbable fulfilment. Such a discovery, (if possible at all), could only be made thro' very indirect methods; – & would demand a mind that should unite habits of matter of fact reasoning & observation, with the highest imagination, a union unlikely in itself.

15.

A Calculus of the Nervous System, A Hospitable Chaos, The Traitor, Too Much Mathematics
[1844]

MICHAEL FARADAY COULD NOT HELP Ada perform experiments because he was ill and was unaware of how sick Ada was. He encouraged her with her "unbaulked health and youth in body & mind" to pursue science and her goals. Some of Ada's alarming symptoms were described in polite company using the catch word at the time, "gastritis." Hester, Andrew Crosse, and Faraday all complained about various forms of "gastritis."

Since Ada was at Ashley Combe in the autumn of 1844, she turned to her Somerset neighbor, Andrew Crosse. He was considered strange both by the scientific community, who accused him of promoting theories of spontaneous generation, and by his neighbors, who called him the "sound and lightning man." Crosse was performing experiments in growing crystals and producing sound by electromagnetism. Ada was fascinated by electricity and anxious to learn as much as she could.

Andrew Crosse went to Ashley Combe to accompany William and Ada on the twenty-mile journey back to his home, but William decided not to go at the last moment. Ada went off with Crosse, over the Quantock hills, sharing with him some of her ideas and her desire to perform scientific experiments. He suggested to her that she translate the works of her friend, Sir Gardner Wilkinson, an Egyptologist, into German. Most likely she carried with her the volume of *The Vestiges of the Natural History of Creation,* about the origin of the species, which Greig had given her, and discussed it later at the Crosse household with

John Crosse. Babbage was so impressed with Ada's talents that when he recommended the book to William, he asked William whether Ada had read it, that is, "if she had not written it."

To Woronzow Greig

Friday, 15 November 1844   Ashley Combe

My Dear Mr Greig. Altho' I cannot write today as I would wish, yet a line I must give you to say how acceptable is the Vol. It is the very thing I had been wanting & wishing for, I thinking how I could soonest get it.

I am so much occupied at this moment, in preparation & arrangements for <u>writing</u>, & also (I am sorry to say) in recovering with a <u>very</u> <u>unsteady</u> progress from an attack of my but too common <u>Gastritis,</u> that I cannot say to you all I could desire.

You do not know perhaps the service you are doing me, in thus keeping my objects in mind, & in <u>collecting</u> for me. Anything & everything you can kindly continue to collect & think of for me, which may bear directly or indirectly on my views, is so much very material assistance to my thoughts & labours. Your <u>letters</u> have been invaluable to me, just at the present juncture.

So pray scruple not to write as much & as freely as you can, on such topics. . .

I have my hopes, & very distinct ones too, of one day getting <u>cerebral</u> phenomena such that I can put them into mathematical equations; in short a <u>law</u> or <u>laws,</u> for the mutual actions of the molecules of <u>brain;</u> (equivalent to the <u>law</u> <u>of</u> <u>gravitation</u> for the <u>planetary</u> & <u>sideral</u> world). – . . .

L [Lovelace] knows <u>all</u> my plans & views & seems to think them not absurd, and that if not <u>feasible</u> <u>in</u> <u>themselves</u>, they may lead to what is, in the course of the investigations. The grand difficulty is in the <u>practical</u> <u>experiments</u>.

In order to get the exact phenomena I require, I must be a most skillful <u>practical</u> <u>manipulator</u> in experimental tests; & that, on materials difficult to deal with; viz: the brain, blood, & nerves, of animals.

In <u>time,</u> I will do all, I dare say. And if not, why it don't signify, & I shall have amused <u>myself</u> at least.

It appears to me that none of the physiologists have yet got on the right tack; I can't think <u>why</u>.

Have you heard about Miss Martineau & the Mesmerism? There can be <u>no</u> doubt of the facts, I am persuaded. I have seen her letters, some of them.

All this bears on <u>my</u> subjects.

It does not appear to me that <u>cerebral</u> matter need be more unmanageable to mathematicians than <u>sideral</u> & <u>planetary</u> matters & movements, if they would but inspect it from <u>the right</u> <u>point</u> <u>of</u> <u>view</u>.

I hope to bequeath to the generations a <u>Calculus</u> <u>of</u> <u>the</u> <u>Nervous</u> <u>System.</u>

With Many Many thanks, Ever yours   A.A.L.

To Andrew Crosse

[Undated, most likely 16 Nov 1844]

Dear Mr. Crosse, – Thank you for your kind and cordial letter. . . On Monday the 18th then, we expect you, and on Wednesday 20th we will all go to Broomfield. Perhaps you have felt already, from the tone of my letter, that I am more than ever now the bride of science. Religion to me is science, and science is religion. In that deeply-felt truth lies the secret of my intense devotion to the reading of God's natural works. . . And when I behold the scientific and so-called philosophers full of selfish feelings, and of a tendency to war against circumstances and Providence, I say to myself: *They* are not true priests, *they* are but half prophets – if not absolutely false ones. They have read the great page simply with the physical eye, and with none of the spirit *within*. The intellectual, the moral, the religious seem to me all naturally bound up and interlinked together in one great and harmonious whole . . . That God is one, and that all the works and the feelings He has called into existence are ONE; this is a truth (a biblical and scriptural truth too) not in my opinion developed to the apprehension of most people in its really deep and unfathomable meaning. There is too much tendency to making *separate* and *independent bundles* of both the physical and the moral facts of the universe. Whereas, all and everything is naturally related and interconnected. A volume could I write on this subject ... I think I may as well just give you a hint that I am subject at times to dreadful physical sufferings. If such should come over me at Broomfield, I may have to keep my room for a time. In that case all I require is to be *let alone.* With all my wiry power and strength, I am prone at times to bodily sufferings, connected chiefly with the digestive organs, of no common degree or kind...

Ever yours truly,

A.A. Lovelace

To William, Lord Lovelace

Saturday morning, about 1/2 past nine [22 November 1844]

Broomfield

Finding no <u>symptoms</u> of either breakfast (or cloth being laid), or of human beings, I have sat down to write to <u>you</u>, in my <u>shawl</u> & <u>boa</u> in their <u>very</u> cold Sitting Room.

I was down at nine, having been told there would then be a breakfast. We all sat up reading & talking philosophy till <u>one o'clock</u> last night. I suppose <u>that</u> is the secret of the dawdle this morning. My head is very <u>muzzy</u> this morning, from that cause I think; & I shall take the liberty <u>this</u> evening of calling my hosts to a recollection of <u>Time</u>. The droll thing was we were discussing the metaphysics of <u>Time</u> & <u>Space</u>; & in so doing we forgot <u>real</u> Time & Space...

Our journey was agreeable. I was so admirably clad that I did not feel the cold.

In the course of it, I was able to give Crosse a complete outline & vista of all my scientific plans & ideas. He seems to think there is much merit in them & remarked "I see no mere enthusiasm in all this. It is all so <u>quietly</u> <u>reasoned</u>, so soundly <u>based</u>."

I find my visit here is of <u>more</u> importance to me than I anticipated. The eldest son John is giving me information as to

the scientific doings in Germany which it is of the <u>utmost</u>
importance I should be in possession of, & he will undertake, if
I choose, to be my <u>organ</u> to any extent he can, in procuring me
every means of keeping <u>au</u> <u>courant</u> as to <u>German</u> mathematics
& Natural Philosophy. He is a most <u>extensively</u> read, & also a
very clever young man. I can get from & by means of him, what
I could from <u>no</u> one else. He is to be 6 months at Berlin next
year, & he will occupy himself in <u>catering</u> for me. He knows
much not only about German metaphysics & theology, but
about their <u>physiology</u> &c...

To William, Lord Lovelace

Sunday, 24 November [1844]   Broomfield

Dearest Crow. This is certainly a most extraordinary domicile
to visit at. It appears to me to be the most <u>unorganized</u> domestic system I ever saw.

All seems to happen by <u>chance</u> in a manner. <u>Two</u> members
of the family also are particularly <u>little</u> agreeable, & have what
I term a <u>bar</u> <u>sinister</u> about them; – a something or other of a
<u>deep</u> & <u>sinister</u> <u>reserve</u> which is withering, viz: <u>Miss</u> Crosse, &
Mr <u>Robert</u> Crosse – the 2nd son.

All this is just so much of a novel field for observation &
analysis of the <u>human</u> atom, and as the interests of my avocations will doubtless oblige me at times to be more or less a
guest in this dwelling, I am obliged to study how to fall into the
circumstances for the time being, in the most easy & agreeable
manner.

There is at least <u>one</u> very unusual & agreeable
circumstance. I am treated without <u>let</u> or <u>hindrance</u>, & left to
do exactly as I like.

Nobody thinks <u>anything</u> of me, or puts themselves out of
their way concerning me. This is just what I want. I am a
nobody here; altho' treated with all proper & necessary respect.

The eldest son is a <u>frank</u> & <u>cordial</u> person; & we take to
each other I think.

He has a mine of reading & references in him to me quite

invaluable. <u>Me</u> he evidently regards more as he would <u>a young man</u> than as a fine lady. I do not mean to say that he is wanting in any point of manners due to a <u>woman.</u> Far from it, but the <u>lady</u> & the <u>woman</u> are quite merged in his simple consciousness of the <u>intellect</u> & <u>pursuits</u>. He addresses <u>them</u>, not <u>Lady Lovelace</u>. . .

There is in Crosse the most <u>utter</u> lack of <u>system</u> even in his Science. At least so it strikes <u>me</u>. I may be mistaken. Perhaps I don't see <u>enough</u>, as yet, to discover his <u>system</u>. He says himself that he is in unusual confusion & transition-state.

I have quite a difficulty to get him to show me what I want. <u>Nothing</u> is ever <u>ready</u>. All chaos & chance. –

To William, Lord Lovelace

Monday, 25 November [1844]   Broomfield

Dearest Mate. All well, but not much <u>time</u>. I could stay here a <u>fortnight</u> with advantage.

I have made the <u>whole family</u> laugh heartily with my witty fun about the <u>chaotic</u> nature of the establishment & proceedings. Old Crosse delights in my <u>quizzing</u> him. The <u>playful</u> <u>Bird</u>, you know!! He is very harmless however, I assure you.

Young John Crosse is an excellent <u>mathematician</u> as well as <u>metaphysician</u> &c; & he <u>works</u> my brain famously for he opposes everything I advance, <u>intentionally</u>; but with perfect good humour. This is very useful & good for me. He will be an addition to my catalogue of <u>useful</u> & <u>intellectual</u> friends, in many respects.

I fully feel all you say my dear, about order, system, &c. Indeed, <u>here</u> I see an example of a <u>total want</u> of it, & <u>how much much</u> more might have been done <u>had</u> there been system & order. . .

Today is a gem. It is a sad drawback that we breakfast about 11 o'clock; it loses full half the day.

There is no <u>order</u>. Everyone straggles down whenever he pleases. You cannot conceive what an <u>odd</u> house it is altogether. The post &c <u>all</u> is <u>by</u> <u>chance</u>, & at <u>all</u> <u>sorts</u> of hours. I never saw the like. . .

To Andrew Crosse

[Undated, but most likely 28 November 1844]

My Dear Mr. Crosse, – I found my gold pencil this morning in
the pocket of the gown I wore on Tuesday evening. I believe I
had put it there to *prevent* losing it, as I went up to bed that
night. My journey was very wretched, – so cold, so late, so
dreary. I could not help lending my cloak to a lady who was my
companion, and who seemed to me more delicate and in need
of it than myself. This did not, however, add to my own physical
comfort. Many times after it became dusk did I think of your
hospitable 'chaos,' and wish myself back, and imagine to myself
if you were all sitting down to dinner, and if you missed me at
all or not. In short, I had in my own brain a very comical chaos
composed of what I had left behind, and a thousand heterogeneous ideas, all of them but half alive and stagnant through
physical cold. . . I have no time to say more, nor indeed, have I
anything particular to say as yet. My gold pin does not come
forth – but it is not a thing of much consequence. If a stray
gold pin, however, does develop itself, don't fancy it is an *electrical* production, but send it to me. My kind recollections to the
various heterogeneous atoms (organic and inorganic) of your
chaotic mass. – Yours ever   A.A.L.

To William, Lord Lovelace

Friday (2 o'clock), 29 November [1844]   St James' Sqre

My Dear Crow. I feel rather disappointed at not hearing from
you this morning. I wonder why you did not write me a line, &
yet I have no business to expect <u>daily</u> communications from
you.

I have had Wheatstone with me the last 5 hours . . . He has
given me much important information, & still more important
<u>advice</u>. He is anxious I should take such a position as may
enable me to influence <u>Prince</u> <u>Albert</u>, who is (he knows) a <u>very</u>
clever young man. John Crosse told me the same thing, which
he knew from the <u>first</u> <u>rate</u> men of science in Germany.

The Prince's whole & sole desire was to be at the head of a

scientific circle in England, & he has expressed his utter morti-
fication at the opposition & cold water which has been thrown
on all his desires in this respect.

Wheatstone says none but some woman can put him in the
right way, & open the door to him towards all he desires; that a
woman can say that which any man would get into a scrape by
doing. Wheatstone does not wish me to think of doing anything
immediate.

By no means. But he says it would occur in the natural
course of things that if I can take a certain standing in the
course of the next few years, the Prince would on some occasion speak to me about science, and that in that case; if I happily seize the moment, I may do for science an inestimable
benefit; for that all the Prince wants is a sensible advisor &
suggester, to indicate to him the channels for his exercising a
scientific influence.

He is very clever they say, but in a slow way; not a brilliant
man. All this is very curious; & it is odd enough that both John
Crosse & Wheatstone should have given me the same account
within a week, tho' derived from very different sources.

Oddly enough too, Wheatstone has spoken to me of the
great importance of studying the German philosophy & science.
Altogether my visit to Broomfield seems to have been very
opportune & to have laid the foundations for much that is
wanted for me just at this epoch of my progress...

As far as the German studies are concerned, they cannot be
carried on while upon a visit; & it is at home only that I should
make any real progress in such. If young Crosse stays with us,
some hours can be daily given for the time- being, to that purpose; but when one is visiting a family one must be diluted a
little amongst all the members of it, of course; besides which
the electrical experiments are a main engrosser of one's attention at Broomfield. Add to this that the irregularity of the family habits are a most serious drawback both to my health, & to
anything like study there. Wheatstone burst out laughing at
the very idea of my having stayed there any time, & yet Wheatstone is no man of luxuries certainly. He says that it is the

strangest & most <u>uncomfortable</u> house he ever stayed in.

There are certainly inconceivable <u>oddities</u> there. For instance; the <u>Water-closet</u> can only be got at <u>thro' the Drawing Room</u>; & of course it is perfectly evident the errand one is going on, since the exit leads nowhere else. <u>I</u> don't mind that sort of thing the least, when it is inevitable, & I take everything cooly & as a matter of course. That is the only way. Sometimes they <u>lock up</u> the Water-Closet, & then one has to make a hue & cry after the key. . .

Now it was almost impossible to set seriously to <u>anything.</u> Thus, I soon determined that I must try & get what I want with <u>young</u> Crosse, at my home.

Wheatstone has given me <u>some</u> very striking counsels. I did not think the little man had such <u>depth</u> in him. I can't <u>write</u> it all to you, or even a small part, but I know you will agree fully, with him when you do hear it.

The plan for my writing on Babbage's subject clearly <u>won't</u> do. Don't be vexed at this; a subject is fixed on instead, so it will make no difference, & I can as easily do the one as the other. . .

The electrical telegraph is laying down on <u>our</u> Southampton Rail, & by & bye Wheatstone says that we shall be able to send any message to Town for a shilling, & <u>get</u> an <u>answer</u>. There will be a secretary at the terminus to write down & dispatch notes to all parts of Town.

For instance, I might from Bridgewater the other day (had the telegraph reached to that station) have sent word in two seconds to London.

"I shall arrive by the two o'clock Train, instead of the 12 o'clock. Send my carriage for the latter hour. A.A.L.". . .

Think what a delight Wheatstone says that sometimes friends hold conversations from one terminus to the other; that one can <u>send</u> for anyone to speak to one. For instance, I might desire a tradesman to go directly to the Nine Elms' Station, & might discuss an <u>order</u> with him about goods &c. Wonderful agent and invention!

Wheatstone doubts <u>clairvoyance</u> greatly, tho' he believes in all the <u>physical</u> effects of Mesmerism. Certainly the <u>wonders</u> require to be <u>sifted</u> very rigidly.

Babbage roars with laughter about the state of the <u>Church.</u> He says he never could have conceived such a state of mutual tearing into (not 2 or 3) but <u>hundreds</u> of shreds & atoms. He is <u>uneasy</u> about it, fearing it will all <u>go</u> <u>too</u> <u>fast</u>, which he don't wish. He thinks that we must all turn Church people to stop the crash. That is a joke of his, you understand. . .

I have written you a long letter & yet not a quarter of what I might say. . .

ADA MUST HAVE ENJOYED reading the article in the *Illustrated London News*, January 1845, about Wheatstone's telegraph and how helpful it was in solving a murder. So many exciting developments were occurring at the time, and Ada wanted to know about all of them. To pursue research about the latest scientific developments, she needed to have access to the latest scientific information, which was not readily available to a woman. Despite Mrs Somerville's bust being on display at the Royal Society, Mrs Somerville had not been allowed into the library of that institution. Ada asked Greig to help her obtain permission.

She went to London to discuss the matter with him only to have the discussion turn to her alleged amorous liaisons. She discovered that she was the subject of rumors, most likely dealing with her relationship with Frederick Knight; however, the rumors might have been prompted by her recent visit to the Crosse household.

Ada had hardly begun her scientific endeavors when once again she became ill, this time with a very specific complaint. Mr Taylor, her physician, found a very serious ailment that would have prevented Ada from having any amorous affair, and this ailment eventually took her life.

To Woronzow Greig

Thursday, 5 December 1844   St James' Square

Dear Mr Greig. I should have liked extremely to go to the Play
tomorrow night with you, but I must leave Town tomorrow afternoon.

I think you could do me a service, unless you see in it anything <u>objectionable</u>. Pray consider well over it: –

When Lovelace became a member of the Royal Society
several years ago, it was entirely on <u>my</u> account. But the inconvenience of <u>my</u> not being able to go there to look at particular
<u>Papers</u> &c which I want, continually renders the advantages I
might derive quite nugatory. – Could you ask the Secretary if I
might go in now & then (of a <u>morning</u> of course) to hunt out the
things I require, being <u>censé</u> to do so in <u>L's</u> name & <u>for</u> <u>him</u>, tho'
it would be <u>really</u> for <u>myself</u>? As you <u>know</u> the Secretary, you
can judge if he is a discreet man, who would not <u>talk</u> about the
thing or make it <u>notorious</u>; one who in short could understand
<u>why</u> & <u>how</u> I want to get the entrée to their library in a quiet &
unobtrusive manner.

I assure you it would be to me an inestimable advantage. I
suppose there are <u>certain</u> hours when I should not be liable to
meet people there. Perhaps early in the mornings...

But I really have become as much tied to a <u>profession</u> as
<u>you</u> are. And so much the better for me, I always required this.

I am trying to discover <u>the</u> <u>Traitor</u>. It is not because I
think that particular instance of false report of much consequence to us, or that I am annoyed much at <u>that</u> <u>one</u> <u>special</u>
thing having been promulgated. It is so absurd that it <u>could</u>
not gain <u>much</u> currency.

But it is of consequence to know <u>who</u> is the untrustworthy
& malicious individual whom one ought on no account to harbour as a <u>spy</u> under our roof. –

And <u>if</u> ever I discover for <u>certain</u> who it is, I shall <u>tell</u> <u>him</u>
the above, the very first time we meet by accident (if it be 10
years hence); – doing so in <u>my</u> provokingly <u>cool</u> way, without
<u>feeling</u> or <u>temper</u>; just fixing my great eyes on him, & saying

my say in the most <u>gentle</u> way, taking care that <u>several</u> persons hear it. – No one could do this so well as <u>I</u> could, & it would be exceedingly amusing. My Mother quite chuckled over my notion.

There is the advantage of being rather of a <u>cold-blooded</u> temperament. No insult, no impertinence, ever can <u>excite</u> me. So I can <u>venture</u> on what others must not trust themselves to attempt. Yours ever   A.A. Lovelace

To William, Lord Lovelace

Thursday Morning, 5 December [1844]   St James' Square

Dearest Mate. How <u>sensible</u> are your letters always. –

I am sorry that owing to the Hen's blunder as to the <u>time</u> (of the Traitor's visit to Ockham), you have thus had the trouble of making out a useless list of visitors. . .

A friend of my mother's & of ours dined at Murray's & heard there <u>as public news</u> the report of this base-minded visitor; but could not discover the name of the person, nor even the sex. Only that every one had <u>believed</u> the report, because the informant stated that he (or she) had just come from Ockham & <u>knew it all for positive fact</u>. It must have been a <u>man</u> without doubt. . .

It is a most base & scandalous insinuation, of a <u>general</u> nature. The reporter gave <u>no facts</u>. Indeed he <u>could</u> not, unless he had absolutely <u>invented</u> them.

Now it is really of importance to detect who it <u>could</u> be; for one ought <u>not</u> to harbour a Serpent unconsciously in one's household; one who will fabricate; or at any rate maliciously <u>pervert</u> every real incident. . .

To Lady Byron

Friday Afternoon [Undated but between late 1844-1845]
                                              St James' Square

I am in a disagreeable plight rather. I have not been able to <u>stir</u> all day, waiting for Dr Locock, whom it was very necessary I

should see on account of a <u>local</u> complaint, of which I have
thought nothing hitherto; but finding it become worse, I wished
to consult him about it; & he finds, after making a complete
<u>examination</u> internally, that I am in a most <u>sad</u> state, requiring
great care.

My <u>general</u> state of health he is quite delighted with; but
this disorder might affect <u>that</u>, if it were not seen to. It is one
of decided <u>debility</u>, he says.

I believe at present I must not <u>ride</u> at all. . .

To William, Lord Lovelace
<u>Thursday</u> <u>Night</u>

Dearest Mate. What a <u>charming</u> letter from you today my Dear!
– With <u>such</u> a <u>diagram</u>!! – <u>delicious</u>!! –

You are indeed kind about me. Mr Taylor says it is unlikely
the Abscess will close for some time . . . It is a sad nuisance to
have a great sore under one, – & it is tender, & crippling; but it
seems like a <u>perfect</u> case, compared with the past. –

Mr Taylor seems to wonder that I take it all so quietly, & I
am so <u>little</u> rendered helpless by it. He says most people would
be in bed, & not move hand or foot; – instead of which he finds
me <u>usually</u> <u>dressed</u> & always ready to <u>hobble</u> <u>about</u> for my own
little wants when possible. – In fact he would scarcely have
thought it possible had he not seen it.

He said this evening, "Upon my word Ma'am, if <u>this</u> can't
keep you quiet, I don't know <u>what</u> <u>can</u>; for a more painful dis-
abling thing that you have had, I know not." . . .

To Sophia De Morgan
21 December [1844]   Ashley Combe

Dear Mrs De Morgan. You will I know be very interested in
hearing how I have gone on. I have been <u>very</u> <u>ill</u> <u>indeed</u>, since I
saw you. It has been a critical state; but it has all ended as it
should; & I am now going on charmingly. –

Dr Locock was admirably right in <u>all</u> his opinions &

advice. . . <u>Many</u> <u>causes</u> have contributed to produce the past derangement; & I shall in future avoid them. <u>One</u> ingredient, (but only one among many) has been <u>too</u> <u>much</u> <u>Mathematics</u>.

I need hardly say that since I returned here I have been <u>utterly</u> <u>unable</u> to think even of my Studies. I yesterday resumed them; but for some time I must only give from 1/2 an hour a day to an hour a day. Pray tell Mr De Morgan all this; (he must wonder at not having heard from me). . .

I am so thankful at the alarm about <u>adding</u> <u>to</u> <u>my</u> <u>family</u> being a <u>false</u> <u>one;</u> that I don't the least mind all I have suffered. I think <u>anything</u> better than <u>that.</u>

Yours most sincerely   A.A. Lovelace

16.
Vestiges,
Obedient with Safety,
<u>*Poetical Science*</u>
[1845-1846]

S INCE NEITHER HER MOTHER nor her husband was sympa-
thetic to her complaints of ill health, Ada turned to Woronzow Greig for sympathy, only to have it backfire. Just as Ada in
her Notes used both analytical and metaphysical approaches,
she used the same strategy in her attempt to explain to Greig
how he had come to a mistaken conclusion about her personal
life. She accused him of taking a momentary attitude, a biopsy,
and extrapolating it to her overall state of mind. He was taking
her attitude out of context. Her warning about the dangers of
erroneous conclusions can be applied to scientific as well as general information. Not only is analysis important, but it is necessary to make sure that conclusions are drawn on the whole
picture, and not a skewed sample. She tried to put her own life
into proper perspective.

Ada's feelings towards her husband vacillated. After ten
years of marriage, she was satisfied with her lot, but she had
some misgivings. When she was under the influence of laudanum, she thought William was an angel, but in reality she was
not at all sure she could "feel him to her mind," or understand
his persona.

Everything was up in the air, especially her intention to be a
"professional." Difficulties with the children's education loomed
again. Dr Carpenter left in bitterness when neither Lady Byron
nor William met his housing needs. Miss Cooper stayed on, but
the children began to take up more time, and other arrangements had to be made. Lady Byron took Ralph to Esher to live

with her and hired Mr Herford to tutor him. Annabella joined her brother at Esher, and Byron was sent off to Dr and Mrs King. Money problems arose as indicated by Ada's letters to her accountant, Mr Wharton.

Ada's intellectual endeavors were relegated to helping John Crosse with an article he was writing for Molesworth's journal, *The Westminster Review*. The article was about a book called *Vestiges*, which Ada had discussed with Crosse when she was at Broomfield, and many of Ada's ideas were incorporated into the article. Ada continued to follow the latest scientific developments, asking Babbage about Faraday's latest discovery. In September 1845, Faraday had demonstrated that when a light is passed through a special kind of heavy glass, between the poles of a powerful magnet, the plane of polarization of light is twisted.

To Woronzow Greig

Friday, 7 January [1845]   Ockham

My Dear Greig. . . I suppose you received my letter from Esher, of <u>Tuesday</u> last. –

Now you are going, I dare say, to think me a strange unaccountable mysterious being, in what I am going to say; which is that I must beg you to believe, that you have <u>no</u> <u>data</u> <u>whatever</u> for forming any complete or true judgement of either <u>me</u> or <u>my</u> <u>position</u>. – I must entreat you <u>not</u> to torment yourself, or to expend on me a sympathy which I assure you is <u>not</u> needed. My own ideas of matrimony, & of the <u>matrimonial</u> institution altogether, are <u>very</u> <u>peculiar</u>; & as I do not explain what these are, you <u>cannot</u> form any just idea how far I am to be <u>pitied</u> or not.

<u>No</u> man would suit me as a husband; & tho' some might be a shade or two <u>less</u> <u>personally</u> repugnant to me than others, yet in the <u>social</u> point of view I enjoy <u>as</u> <u>it</u> <u>is</u> more liberty (which is as necessary to <u>me</u>, as it is to some species of <u>birds</u>, who pine & die if <u>confined</u>) than <u>most</u> men might allow me; – (altho' <u>there</u> <u>are</u> some who would be as liberal, but in this country they are

the <u>minority</u>). I am therefore entirely satisfied; inconsistent as this declaration may seem with some things that I said before. –

You will do me the favor to <u>suspend</u> all opinions of my case & position for some years longer. – If you do otherwise, you <u>cannot</u> avoid falling into serious error. My character & feelings are but <u>partially</u> known to you. I have a peculiar dislike to making <u>myself</u> a topic of conversation & discussion, consequently I seldom <u>open</u> <u>out</u> at all, (& <u>completely</u> <u>never</u>). –

Some years hence it is not impossible that you may see many points you do not & <u>can</u> not at present penetrate... I daresay that you will fancy, even now, that you perfectly understand me, & all I say. – I simply warn you that you had better <u>wait</u> before you are sure of it. You will find me well & in good spirits when you come. You will see L [Lovelace] too, happy & satisfied as ever & I suspect you will leave us feeling pretty well satisfied yourself. –

All this is very incomprehensible I know, & must seem to you <u>queer</u> & <u>inconsistent</u>. No <u>possible</u> solution you can think of, can be a true one. Ainsi Monsieur, ne vous tormentez pas. It is all in vain. I am a <u>Fairy</u> you know; & there is no other way of settling the question. I don't <u>want</u> a mortal husband & he is a bit of an earthly <u>clay</u> now & then; but however I am his fairy guardian for his life, & must mind my business. And then I have my own <u>fairy</u> <u>resources,</u> which none can judge of.

Now, my good friend, pray be quiet and comfortable & think nothing <u>more</u> disturbing to you about me than that I am incomprehensible, & must be left to make myself happy in my own quiet & peculiar way. Yours ever

A.A.L...

To Woronzow Greig

Tuesday, 4 February [1845]   Esher

My Dear Greig. I write from my mother's. I had your most kind letter this morning...

Had you not touched on <u>one</u> terrible chord the other evening, you would have had no hint from me of my <u>life</u>-<u>less</u>

life. That chord was simply your allusion to comfort in little kindly offices, in matrimonial life, <u>especially</u> in <u>illness</u>. –

It seemed to me so cruel & dreadful a <u>satire</u>, that much was revealed by me before I knew what I was about hardly. I hope you will <u>not</u> renew the subject with me. No good <u>can</u> come of it; & much pain <u>would</u> come of it.

Do not think this unkind. I appreciate and understand <u>all</u> you <u>feel</u>, as well, as well as all you <u>express</u>. <u>My</u> existence is <u>one</u> <u>continuous</u> & <u>unbroken</u> series of <u>small</u> disappointments; – & has long been so. –

I must be at <u>work</u> again, I have been too <u>idle</u> lately. It never does for <u>me</u> to <u>repose</u> <u>upon</u> <u>existence</u>, or to have time for remembering <u>myself</u> & <u>feelings</u>. That is a <u>fact</u>.

I <u>hope</u> to live to make L – happier than I <u>have</u> done. It is not his fault that to <u>me</u> he is <u>nothing</u> whatever, but one who has given me a certain <u>social</u> <u>position</u>. . . He does <u>all</u> that his perceptions <u>can</u> enable him to do. He is a good & just man. He is a <u>son</u> to me. I have tried my very best to feel him to my mind. But it has been a hopeless case; & the less it is <u>dwelt</u> on, the better.

I <u>drive</u> it from my mind for <u>months</u> often. I have passed thro' <u>some</u> dreadful feelings at times. You don't know <u>half</u>, nor ever must. I have resources as you say; & I shall do well enough. I begin however of late to grow <u>unambitious</u>, & very <u>indifferent</u> to <u>everything</u>. – Were it not for the <u>necessity</u> of allowing myself no time for thought, I doubt if I should work much. But I <u>must</u>. –

Unfortunately, <u>every</u> year adds to my utter <u>want</u> of pleasure in my children. They are to me irksome <u>duties</u>, & nothing more. Poor things! I am sorry for them. They will at least find me a <u>harmless</u> and <u>inoffensive</u> parent, if nothing more. –

You will see me often gay & conversible as ever. –

I am no <u>worse</u> off than <u>others</u>. So do not unduly pity me. – <u>All</u> are more or less miserable. I believe. Ever yours,

A.A.L.

To Woronzow Greig

Sunday, 9 February 1845   Ockham

My Dear Greig. I really think you are angry with me, or at least
half angry. Now I hope this is not so. – As to some of the points
you now insist on, (such as that I do not know myself, &c), my
assertions & convictions that I do, can have no weight with you.
Therefore I feel it is useless & nugatory to express any such to
you. –

We must leave all to time to unravel. You are a wise man, &
will be ready & content to do so. –

I am sorry you think me so "changeable." – That impression
is a good deal caused by your seeing only so limited a part, of
me & my life & habits. The whole (could you see & know it)
would appear to you all one & of a piece.

But I know I cannot convey to you any conviction of this
being really so. Thus I must be content to seem as your eyes
alone see me; – a Will-o-the-Wisp, or any strange unenviable
kind of a non-descript creature! –

Only I do hope you are not angry. Certainly I am feeling
better in health than when you were here. So far, you perhaps
judge correctly. – Yours ever

                                                        A.A. Lovelace

To William, Lord Lovelace

1/2 past 9 o'clock, Thursday [1845 or 1846]

Dearest. What a kind kind mate ou is. Your sweetest letter
(just received) has almost made me cry. It is so wise, & yet so
tender.

I am going on more comfortably than expected. The head
improves every 6 hours & Locock was so impressed with the
change when he paid his yesterday's second visit the last thing
at night, that he did not administer the dose of Laudanum
which he had come expressly to give me himself. . .

My dear, I hope ou won't let people ride that horse. I suppose ou satisfied ou self first that Lord W [?] is a very good

rider. . . Give that message to Lord W – It will amuse him that the Avis is so chary of her animal. . .

To Mr. Wharton

Sunday, 17 August 1845   Brighton

Dear Mr Wharton. I return you the two documents, (signed by me yesterday on receiving them). –

I enclose you also 5 more bills from, Mr Beely; (Writing master), Hook (Shoemaker), Isidore (Hairdresser &c), Mardor (Bookseller), Landzelle (Dentist).

I have desired the following parties to call or send to you for their money:

1. Baillière (bookseller)
2. Superintendent of Royal Academy, (for Mr J. Thomas's half-yearly tuition);
3. Messers Wheatstone, (for price of a concertina)
4. Mr Egley, (bookseller):

These four are the most pressing. I will let you know when I desire the rest to apply. –

I enclose you a check for £30, just received from Lord Lovelace for payment of the children's masters. I explained to you that I intended to apply to him for £30 towards that purpose. –

If the whole of the bills should turn out to exceed £325, (the sum now in your hands), I will make up the remainder in cash. It is very possible there may be a matter of £10 or £20 above the £295. For instance, there is £7 of the Dentist's bill which is not for me to discharge, being the children's expenses.

I must ask Lord L – for that money when I return. The same thing may occur in one or two other cases. – With many thanks I remain, Most sincerely yours

                                        Augusta Ada Lovelace

To Charles Babbage

Tuesday, 2 September [1845]   Brighton

My Dear Babbage. I enclose you a note I have had from Mr
John Crosse the author of the Article in the Westminster. He is
in great distress at the infamous manner in which it has been
printed.

I have <u>leave</u> to mention his name to you, – & indeed to forward the enclosed to you, – for he is annoyed rather about <u>your
note</u> which you, so kindly furnished. It seems to have been
inserted in a way that does not do it justice, & that makes it
<u>irrelevant</u>.

He has been out of Town, & <u>is</u> out of Town, or he would I
dare say have called on you on the subject. –

I am recovering gradually, & well; – but have had a devil of
a job. I hope I may be the <u>better</u> for it eventually. I intend if I
continue to prosper, to go to Horsley about Weddy of <u>next</u> week,
for a <u>few</u> <u>days</u> <u>only</u>. I shall then return here again <u>till</u> <u>Octr</u>. . .

Let me hear please, <u>soon</u> from you. –

In haste, Yours ever   A.A.L.

To Woronzow Greig

Monday, 24 November [1845]   East Horsley Park, Ripley Surrey

My Dear Greig. I do not exactly know <u>what</u> you allude to about
my similitude to the wild <u>Ostrich</u> (I think it is the <u>Ostrich</u> that
hides its' head); – but I suppose it is that you think I <u>could</u> not
preserve an <u>incognito</u>. Yet I had the next positive <u>proofs</u> that I
did. –

Perhaps you misunderstand the <u>extent</u> of what I attempted.
I simply meant that nobody knew <u>where</u> I was in Brighton, &
then I was <u>unknown</u> at my <u>lodgings</u>. I so managed that I certainly <u>was</u> unknown; – neither did I seem to attract the <u>least
curiousity</u> in the lodging-house people.

My habits were too quiet & unobtrusive to do so, – & on the
contrary I was the <u>worst</u> <u>served</u>, from being supposed the <u>least
important</u>.

I know that you will not believe me; – Yet I know the <u>fact</u> that I certainly was thought a simple Mr Two-Shoes, – & scarcely <u>noticed</u> in <u>any</u> way.

Mrs Jameson & others <u>in vain</u> endeavoured to find me out at Brighton. But I had far more conclusive proofs than <u>that</u>, that no one suspected me. – Yours   A.L.

To Lady Byron

Saturday, 6 o'clock [Date uncertain, most likely 1845]

St James' Square

Dearest Hen. . . I have been very successful today in all business & engagements. I have had a delightful two or three hours chat with the old <u>Bab</u> [Babbage] who was very unusually agreeable. –

If I can but manage to secure the <u>Horse</u> [Dr Locock] this evening, <u>this</u> trip will have been completely the thing. The <u>last</u> was all cross purposes.

What a <u>nice</u> <u>meddling</u> old Hen you are! But I have ceased to be <u>afraid</u> of your influence, & am not quite sure that I do not, (mean-spirited tho' this may be), prefer it to that of the <u>romantic</u> school, which is deemed <u>deadly</u> <u>dull, flat, stale</u> & <u>unprofitable.</u> Besides which, I think that as one approaches that delectable age of 30 which I so vastly prefer to 20, one may <u>afford</u> to be <u>obedient</u> <u>with</u> <u>safety</u>.

At <u>40</u>, I think one might even adopt leading strings. – But seriously, it is not <u>worth</u> <u>while</u> to kick & run riot, when one reaches mature years. Those <u>independent</u> cracks & dreams are very <u>juvenile</u> performances.

To Lady Byron

[Before December 1845, Undated fragment]

. . . person not yet 30, (& with all my <u>sufferings</u>, I am yet vigorous enough I am sure), may do <u>anything</u>, if they will but go to school. It is no bad epoch of life to begin education from.

Are we d'accord now do you think, about poetry & music &

philosophy? – I don't consider that as yet I have made anything like full <u>use</u> of music; and often much foolish <u>abuse</u> indeed.

You will not concede me <u>philosophical poetry</u>. Invert the order! Will you give me <u>poetical philosophy, poetical science</u>? –

POETICAL SCIENCE is the leitmotif of this book. I found this letter, this fragment, after sitting three years at the Bodleian Library at Oxford reading Ada's letters. Poetical science is Ada's greatest strength – her metaphysical ability to see wholeness, to take disparate approaches of poetry and science and integrate them. Psychologically, it was not that easy for her. She could be "obedient with safety." She was resigned to her fate and that those "<u>independent</u> cracks & dreams" were very "<u>juvenile</u> performances," but then couldn't she be allowed "<u>poetical science</u>?"

There was no response from her mother to that plea. Her mother was constantly pressuring her to achieve intellectual feats; yet, Ada had to cope with everyday needs and demands of her mother, husband, and children. She focused on these real-life tasks, but dreams and curiosity about her father and his life were easily revived.

Ada sent Babbage cryptic notes, which biographers of Babbage and Ada have analyzed ad nauseam. A few of these notes included references to a woman thought to be Countess Teresa Guiccioli, Lord Byron's last mistress. That these notes were written to Babbage is no surprise. When Ada was seventeen, she went to lectures that Dionysius Lardner gave on Babbage's Analytical Engine. Lardner was not only Babbage's friend but a friend of Teresa Guiccioli's. Babbage had probably met the Countess Guiccioli. Unlike Lady Byron, he would not be concerned about Ada's meeting Teresa. In the following letters, Ada is probably referring to Teresa when she mentions Countess "Italia-Italia."

To Charles Babbage

Thursday, 12 February [1846]   East Horsley

The Militia vacancy Lord Torrington alludes to has been
already filled up by Lovelace. –

   I am in bed with a very severe cold, & can scarcely speak. –
I have had so <u>many</u> severe colds this last 4 months that I consider myself very ill used. –

   I hope <u>you</u> are better. – Ever yours   A.L.

I have mislaid Lord T's letter, – which I meant to send you back.

To Charles Babbage

Tuesday [18 March 1846]   Ockham

My Dear Babbage. You will <u>breakfast</u> with me in Town on <u>Satdy</u>
<u>morning</u> I expect, as near to <u>nine</u> as possible. –

   The Drummond visit stands thus: <u>He</u> comes, but neither
wife nor <u>daughter</u>.

   Still, I think it would be very desirable for you to make <u>his</u>
acquaintance; & it might lead to an invitation to <u>Albury</u> even, if
you manage well. – It is on Tuesday 25th. – Let me hear
directly from you. – Ever yours, Most <u>filially</u> &c &c

To Charles Babbage

Thursday 12 1/2 o'clock [18 June 1846]

I am at 52 George St, & shall be with <u>you</u> in a very short time.
Lovelace wants <u>you</u> to take me to call on Countess Italia-Italia;
so I hope you know her <u>address</u>. –

   Some one has told L – that Faustina is like <u>me</u>, which has
quite delighted him. – Yours &c   A.L.

To Charles Babbage

Thursday 3 o'clock, 18 June [1846]

My Dear Babbage. I am in despair about not finding you this
morning. –

In the first place <u>do</u> <u>you</u> dine with us on Monday? – I asked you this, – last Tuesday.

In the next place, I don't know what to do about Countess Italia-Italia & <u>Co</u>. Lovelace is dying to know her, – and for <u>me</u> to know her, – & desires me to ask her to dinner on Monday. – But is it not a great <u>liberty</u>, unless someone introduced me?

Then what am I to do about Baron B – ? – Neither I nor L – have any objection to countenancing him; – but will it get <u>me</u> into a scrape with my other <u>lady-guests</u>, or with <u>society</u> in general? –

In short I want to have 5 minutes talk with you. But there is no <u>time</u> to lose, – & that is the difficulty. –

I send you cards (of all kinds), – & if <u>you</u> could leave them for us this afternoon, it would perhaps do. L – thought that <u>you</u>, being so great a friend of mine, might take upon yourself to chaperone me, (or my <u>cards</u>), to Countess Italia's – & to explain to her the strong wish of Lovelace & myself to make her acquaintance, – & that we have but 4 or 5 days more in Town, which must be our apology to her for this hasty proceeding. – Ever yours.   A.L.

F ROM 1846 Ada was forced to face her financial problems. It is easy to assume that since Ada was a countess, the wife of a man with estates in Surrey and Somerset, and the daughter of a woman of enormous wealth, money would not be an issue. That assumption is wrong.

Her marriage settlement gave William one-half of the legacy she would inherit when her mother died. In exchange for that, from 1835, William gave her £300 a year discretionary income. To put that amount of money in perspective, Carpenter had received £400 per annum. Lady Byron's annual income at this time was £7000, and examination of Lady Byron's bank books reveals that she never gave Ada more than an occasional £30 to £50 a year from the time Ada married.

To find the truth about Ada's economic situation, I went to the bank books. From the £300 Ada received from William, she bought books, which were quite expensive at the time, and dresses for social occasions. According to her bank books, she paid for the dentist, the children's riding masters, the tuition for the Welsh boy at the Royal Academy, and various other expenses.

In addition to her financial troubles, Ada had to address the educational future of the children, her mixed feelings towards William, and the influence the drugs the doctors had prescribed were having on her state of mind. Ada headed to Brighton, thought about these issues, and decided to face all her problems as squarely as she could.

To Lady Byron

10 o'clock Saturday [undated]   Brighton

This is merely to say that I am alive. The lumbago is beginning to give way today. –

I can perceive nothing about my illnesses which is not <u>perfectly</u> accounted for as the simple result of long continued <u>mismanagement</u> (in the ignorance of <u>Dare-Devil</u> of youth) for some years, upon a very susceptible temperament; & nothing that long continued <u>judicious</u> management will not entirely remove. . .

Nothing is needed but a year or two more of patience & <u>cure</u>. Even <u>one</u> year will do much probably.

I have been injured at different times, by <u>3</u> <u>extravagant</u> agents: –

        1. extravagant <u>stimulating</u>

        2. extravagant <u>dosing</u>

        3. extravagant <u>exercise</u>

I have put them in what I also believe to be the order of <u>pernicious</u> influence. The <u>exercise</u> <u>alone</u> would scarcely have done very serious mischief. . . All the doctors say I am completely built for it.

To Lady Byron

Thursday, 19 November [1846]   Ashley

My absence has been well timed & fruitful in good results; independent of its' <u>direct</u> object – the <u>teeth</u>! The simple naïf joy of the Crow over my return is amusing & really touching. Just now I might do <u>anything</u> – absurd or ill tempered. I am <u>perfect</u> & really very much <u>overrated</u>. I believe he had fully made up his mind that I should <u>not</u> <u>return;</u> – & he certainly has <u>told</u> everyone so. – The main <u>practical</u> point of importance at present is that he is <u>very</u> just & reasonable about <u>children,</u> <u>tutor,</u> & all such matters. – ...

I am rather struck with one thing; – L's very increased & very obvious <u>deference</u> for the Thrush! –

Just now there is a violent fit of <u>petting</u> & <u>affection;</u> but there is something <u>beyond</u> this which has been growing gradually, ever since that desperate affair of the <u>boots</u>. – ...

17.
A Transition State
[1846-1850]

LADY BYRON OFFERED TO TAKE CARE of the children's education so that Ada could devote herself to her "profession," but problems quickly developed. Annabella was upset about living with her grandmother at Esher, and Ada had reservations about Annabella's governess, Miss Lamont. At Lady Byron's suggestion, Byron had been put in the care of the Kings in Brighton. That arrangement did not last long because Byron, as well as Ada and William, was annoyed by King's evangelical sermonizing. Byron was then sent to Lady Byron's Leicestershire Estates at Peckleton run by Charles Noel. To Ada, there always seemed to be another child's problem to deal with despite the help from her mother and the servants.

In addition to the children being in a state of transition, the Lovelaces' three homes were in a constant turmoil. In late 1845 they moved to the 4000-square-foot home at East Horsley Towers, a home designed by Sir Charles Barry, who built the Parliament buildings. William found the dwelling an inspiration for his architectural talents, and he started rebuilding, adding towers and tunnels, doubling the size of the mansion. Books and household items were constantly packed and unpacked as the building progressed. They moved from their London residence at St James's Square to temporary residences, at first Grosvenor Place, then Great Cumberland Street. With Babbage's help they finally found a home on Great Cumberland Place, a crescent-shaped street several blocks from Marble Arch and Hyde Park. William continued to transform Ashley Combe in Somerset. He added a "philosopher's walk" for Babbage, with small pink brick towers at either end. There were rose-colored glass windows in the towers through which one could see exquisite views of Bristol Channel.

Both Ada and William were delighted with Babbage's visits and discussions of the latest scientific developments of their mutual friends: Herschel, Faraday, Wheatstone, and Sir David Brewster, a pioneer in the field of optics. They encouraged Babbage to continue his work on calculating engines although Ada sometimes was frustrated that there was little acceptance of what Babbage regarded as his "imagined mission." The letters between Babbage and Ada at this time were cryptic, similar to today's email.

In December 1846 Ada received a letter from Richard Ford, Sir William Molesworth's brother-in-law, mentioning that he sat next to Babbage at a party and the main subject of conversation was Ada and William. Ford asked Ada to read an article he wrote and mentioned that Babbage praised William's architectural accomplishments. William was experimenting with making his own bricks as well as arching wooden beams by steam for the dining room at Horsley Towers. He wrote articles about some of his accomplishments, including an article on crop raising.

To Lady Byron

Sunday, 29 November [1846]   Ashley Combe

Your letter received <u>yesterday</u> anticipates some things I had inquired of you in mine of <u>Friday</u>. . . I ought to tell you that Lovelace had desired me a week ago to arrange with you about a yearly <u>contribution</u> towards Ralph's maintenance under your roof. He proposes £100: per ann. (annun): <u>without</u> <u>any</u> <u>enquiry</u> as to the <u>how</u> & <u>what</u> is spent upon him. L – is not so ignorant as to fancy that this £100 anything like <u>covers</u> Ralph's expenses, but he proposes to contribute that.

He would contribute <u>more</u> if <u>I</u> proposed it. But there are objections to doing so. <u>You</u> will have more <u>power</u> & <u>freedom</u> about the child, by L's feeling that <u>he</u> only contributes a <u>fraction</u> of the expenses for him. – This is <u>one</u> important point . . .

❧

FOR THE NEXT FEW MONTHS the letters were edged in black. Hester and her husband, Sir George Craufurd, had moved to Italy for his health. Hester died in April, very soon after she gave birth to a baby boy. Annabella was particularly upset. Later she recalled that the happiest moments of her childhood were spent with her Aunt Hester.

Ada continued to be displeased with Annabella's governess, Miss Lamont, whom Lady Byron liked. According to the bank books, Lady Byron had helped with Miss Lamont's salary. Ada knew her mother well. If Lady Byron did not choose the governess, she would not cover the expense. Ada turned to a neighbor, a banker, for financial help.

When Mr Currie loaned Ada money, which was repaid in full before she died, Ada used the money to hire Miss Wächter, a German woman, as the new governess for Annabella. Ada then turned her attention to finding a permanent solution for Byron. He was not happy living with Charles Noel.

In 1848 Ada loaned John Crosse money for furniture; however, the major financial burdens were finding the tuition for the children and William's never-ending architectural improvements. Ada realized that she needed to restructure her financial situation.

To Lady Byron

11 o'clock Wednesday [Undated]

I fancied you were at Esher, & I wrote <u>there</u> by yesterday's post...

As to any "reply to people about my not having seen you," I should think the <u>truth</u> was enough: viz, that I was going to sleep that day, being almost unable to speak, after <u>violent</u> <u>palpitations</u> <u>of</u> <u>the</u> <u>heart</u> – faint – & sickness &c. I have seen <u>no</u> one (excepting L –) before <u>8</u> <u>o'clock</u> <u>in</u> <u>the</u> <u>evening</u>. The last three evenings I have seen Byron & Babbage, at <u>that</u> hour. I could not have seen either of them in the daytime.

I never saw <u>Greig</u> <u>at</u> <u>all</u>, nor any other person excepting my son & Babbage in the evg... In the state in which my circulation is at moments, it is absolute cruelty of people to expect I am to see any one whatever; & I should not judge another invalid as to their fitness or unfitness to do so. . .

I only ask others to "do bye me as I should certainly do by them."

To Henry Currie

1 May 1848   19 Great Cumberland St

Dear Mr Currie. I have received £500 safely, & sincerely thank you for this very kind assistance. In order to prevent the possibility of future misunderstanding I will here repeat the terms we have agreed upon;

1st. I am to pay 5 percent Interest per ann: during the period that the loan shall continue; –

2nd. I am to repay you £100 of the Capital (May 1st 1849), and £100 every six months subsequently.

Thus the whole Loan will have been paid off this day three years hence (May 1st, 1851).

My present embarrassments originate in a very small sum (considering my inheritance and position), which was settled on me upon marriage. This sum has been totally insufficient to meet the expenses incidental to my position as Lord Lovelace's wife.

Very heavy expenses which are at this moment entailed on Lord L by his Buildings & some other circumstances, have made me feel that I should be wrong if I adopted your suggestion of applying to him (at present) for so considerable a sum as that for which I am now indebted to yourself. But I have the fullest ground for expecting from him henceforward those increased means which will preclude difficulties in future.

I believe you are fully aware that I have applied to you on two special grounds; Ist my conviction of your highly honorable character and generous feelings: 2nd It appeared to me very fitting to make such an application to a Banker, & in every way most proper & natural. Very faithfully yrs

Augusta Ada Lovelace

DURING THE SUMMER OF 1848 William was working on an article about the effect of sunlight on the growing of crops. Ada added two technical footnotes to the article, based on information she received from writing Sir John Herschel about a nebulometer, a simple hand-made device used to determine the amount of daylight.

Ada was worried that her children, no longer living together, would lose a sense of family, yet Lady Byron considered Ada's children a bad influence on one another. To convince her mother that this was a misconception, Ada defended her children. She described each child's individual personality with sensitivity and pride and showed that Annabella and Byron had a positive influence on one other. Ada's main concern was Ralph, who was living with Lady Byron.

Charles Babbage visited the Lovelaces at Ashley Combe and from the tone of Ada's letters to him, they were better friends than ever. They gossiped about their mutual friends and spent time discussing games, notations for mathematical games, and Babbage's idea for an automatic tic-tac-toe machine. Perhaps, he suggested, he would exhibit it at fairs to raise money for his calculating engines. Their friendship became even closer when Ada hired a personal maid, Mary Wilson, who had worked for Babbage's family. Ada writes about Ryan, Babbage's brother-in-law, and the Nightingales, friends of Babbage's and Lady Byron's. Everywhere Ada, Mary Wilson, and Babbage went, they were surrounded by dogs. Sirius and Nelson were Ada's favorites.

To Charles Babbage

Sunday, 27 August [1848]   Ashley Combe

Dear Babbage. I am delighted you have fixed <u>Weddy,</u> & your inside place from Bridgewater will be secured. –

Could you bring down <u>Herschel's Astronomy</u>? We have it at <u>Horsley</u>, but where it cannot be got at in our absence; & it would be rather useful just now. – Most truly yrs

A.A. Lovelace

To Lady Byron

Thursday, 21 September [1848]   Ashley

    ... Lovelace is anxious I should tell you how highly I think
of his digest upon certain meteorological facts in connexion
with agriculture. It is <u>admirably</u> done; & the subjects treated
are of a most complex nature; exceedingly difficult to deal
with. <u>I</u> am inclined to think it is the best thing he has done yet,
having more <u>form</u> & <u>system</u>, & more of <u>definite</u> <u>conclusions</u>,
than any of his former productions.

    It contains an immense mass of <u>facts</u>, remarkably well pre-
sented.

    The <u>language</u> too (& I have read it <u>out</u> <u>aloud</u> to test this) is
flowing, agreeable, & clear. It will do him great credit. His
literary powers improve rapidly. –

To Charles Babbage

<u>Saturday,</u> 30 September [1848]   Ashley Combe

Dear Babbage. The skies are weeping unceasingly over yr
departure. The morg you went, it <u>set</u> <u>in</u> wet; – & it has scarcely
intermitted for 10 minutes since. – You must have had a very
wretched journey. You cannot think how we miss you. – Even
the <u>dogs</u>, & the brace of Thrushes (Sprite & Harry), look as if
there was something wanting. –

    My <u>chief</u> reason for writing so soon is to mention that
Lovelace has been really quite <u>unhappy</u> because he was unfortunately <u>just</u> too late to see you on Thursdy Morg. He rushed
after you to the Lodge & saw you <u>driving on</u>. <u>He</u> shouted, <u>Mrs</u>
<u>Court</u> tried to <u>run</u> <u>after</u> the <u>two</u> <u>Pegasi</u>(!), the men on the <u>lawn</u>
& <u>terrace</u> (seeing there was something wrong), <u>all</u> yelled &
shouted. – But in vain. Neither you nor the beasts would hear;
– tho' I really wonder that the <u>latter</u> did not run away again,
thro' the <u>fracas</u>. – Lovelace is afraid you must think he
neglected you. – ...

Sometimes I think en passant of all the Games, & notations for them. If any good idea should accidentally strike me, I will take care to mention it to you. But this is not likely.

I believe the Molesworths will come here on the 10th Octr, for a day or two. I am very anxious to hear from you. –
Ever yrs   A.A. Lovelace

P.S. The Nightingales say you must write to them. But (as you can't sing & hate music) I wonder how you will manage to send them any intelligible song! –

To Lady Byron
Sunday, 1 October 1848

. . . A great deal has been done for A [Annabella] latterly by indirect means. I take care that she has intellectual difficulties to overcome, – & her presumption seems to be more lowered by her finding out experimentally how little she can do, then by any direct precepts. –

I look after her Algebra & her music. Not daily, but quite sufficiently to answer every purpose. . . She finds I explain agreeably & give animation & zest to the subjects. But I take care to let her find out her great ignorance and imperfection. . . I think A – most wonderfully clever; – & her judgement as sound, as her perceptions rapid. A remarkable union of powers. . .

To Lady Byron
[10 October 1848]

. . . I suppose that Byron will go to Sea in about two years. It will be a question whether he is to remain with C. Noel after another year or whether he should then go to some Naval Seminary. Or again, whether Mr P [Pennington] is a sufficient adjunct to C. Noel, supposing Byron does remain on at Peckleton till he enters the Navy.

Annabella seems very different indeed from a month ago.

Still I cannot expect her agreeable state to last uninterrupted. But her excellent understanding gains <u>experience</u> with wonderful rapidity. I like Miss W [Wächter] better & better. – You would be pleased with A's whole <u>look</u> now. She is not like the <u>same</u> girl.

To Lady Byron

Sunday, 15 October [1848]   Ashley

. . . Delighted also that you agree with me, in thinking L's essay on temperature &c, his best. Some time ago I wrote you word how highly I thought of it. His literary progress seems to me to be very considerable. . .

Yr communications to A [Annabella] (whether Sea-weed, Book, note of Birrach's . . .) are <u>so</u> useful. The greater <u>variety</u> of interests she has, the better. Our large family of <u>dogs</u> even, do her much good. She generally has at least a couple (out of the 4), with her, in her walks & rides. <u>All</u> the dogs love her, & rush round her in an ecstasy when they see her. . . Her taste for <u>Natural</u> <u>History</u>, & her <u>love</u> for <u>animals</u>, I encourage to the utmost.

In this Miss W [Wächter] is all I could wish; & an immense merit it is, which I should not easily find. . . A – is looking remarkably <u>well</u>, & wonderfully <u>happy</u>.

Miss W– tells me that tho' the <u>immediate</u> effect of Byron upon A's manners & ideas, is bad; yet she thinks the real & more lasting effects of B – upon his Sister very valuable. I think Miss W– shows much profound observation (like many of the <u>Germans</u>) upon this & other points.

By the bye I never told you how respectable & amiable Byron <u>always</u> was to Miss Wächter, whom he certainly <u>liked</u>. I doubt not we shall <u>at</u> <u>times</u> find A – very troublesome however. But she certainly is an interesting charge, – & <u>well</u> <u>worth</u> trouble. . . My <u>love</u> to Ralph, & tell him that all <u>Sea-weeds</u>, shells, &c, will be thankfully received. . .

To Charles Babbage

18 October [1848]   Ashley

Dear Babbage. I hope you got Lovelace's Packet, (& also a subsequent letter from the Birds).

The Life-Preserver is safe here. What shall I do with it? – It
certainly can't go by Post, (until there is a yet further extension
of the Postal system). –

I hope you are as pleased as I am with the account of you &
your engines, in the last Athenaeum. – We think it very just &
impartial. Let the Government answer it, if they can! –

I am vexed to think of your returning to unwholesome dull
London. Do frequent us a little more, at Horsley; which is
come-attable. –

You say nothing of Tic-tac-toe – in yr last. I am alarmed lest
it should never be accomplished. I want you to complete something; especially if the something is likely to produce silver &
golden somethings. . .

Write to me again directly; – or the Birds will be angry, &
won't sing. –

Sirius is becoming a little steadier. But, do what he will, he
continues the universal favorite. Nelson hates him worse than
ever. –

I have much more to say, but I hear the fatal Horn which
(like Death), waits nobody's pleasure. – Yrs ever   A.L.

To Charles Babbage

Thursday, 2 November [1848]   Ashley Combe

Dear Babbage. . . Have you noticed the account (in the
Athenaeum of the 21st Octr.), of the American Astronomer,
Mitchell? – It is very interesting, & there is in it a good remark
about Science never having been over patronised by royalty. –

We leave on Weddy next. I for Leicestershire for a few
days. –

I do not know what to do about the Transit. I don't wish to
lose it. It seems it is at a convenient Hour enough, – 11 o'clock

fore-noon. But we have no conveniences here. – I suppose one can see it with the naked eye, (thro' <u>smoked</u> glass). Any directions you can send will be valuable. –

I have had 2 or 3 more letters from my son, really <u>very</u> promising; & showing much accurate habit of observation, & <u>excellent</u> sense too. Also a facility for <u>caricaturing</u> which is quite a <u>talent</u>, but which is doubtless one of some danger. He is however, I suspect the <u>Tortoise</u> who will get before the <u>Hares</u> by & bye. –

"<u>Sirius</u>" has been obliged to submit to a muzzle, whenever he goes on expeditions. He pertinaciously attacked the <u>Gallinacea</u>.

But he is everybody's favorite, & wins all hearts – from the stern <u>Earl's</u> (his master), downwards. Always well received, & made much of! –

Old "<u>Nelson</u>" has ceased <u>active</u> interference concerning his son, & looks <u>philosophical</u> & <u>saturnine</u> – but pays great court to <u>me</u>. – Nelson will always be <u>judicious</u>.

How is <u>Polly?</u>

Conceive my maid being so mad as to petition taking <u>Sirius</u> (on a pleasure-expedition) to <u>Leicestershire</u>! – Imagine the bother one should have with that spotted scamp, at <u>Inns, Stations,</u> &c; – not to mention the (almost) <u>certainty</u> of his killing Mrs. Noel's fowls, & playing the very deuce <u>there</u>. – But I believe Mary thinks the dog more wonderful & perfect than ever! – Ever yrs   A.A. Lovelace

To Lady Byron

Wednesday, (5 o'clock) 15 November [1848]   East Horsley

I arrived here last evg quite well & safely . . . I am extremely pleased with all the arrangements here. They certainly approach perfection. All today we have been wholly occupied in moving & arranging <u>books</u> & furniture; an occupation which will be daily renewed for some little time. – I shall enter my (<u>most</u> <u>delightful</u>) new rooms in a day or two. They are quite warm & dry.

I find Annabella looking remarkably <u>well</u>, & she has made several clear sketches of various things, during her week away from me. I think she has something very like <u>genius</u> for drawing & painting. I am surprised at the talents not only for <u>representing</u>, but for <u>combining</u>; & it is an occupation so good for her, & which enables her to do many little <u>kindnesses</u> <u>to</u> <u>others</u>. . .

I am anxious to talk to you about Byron's joining Ralph . . . at Xmas Holidays; partly <u>here</u>, & partly <u>chez</u> <u>vous</u>. – We have several reasons for strongly desiring this, <u>which</u> I can better explain when we meet.

The <u>main</u> reason is that, in consequence of Byron's entering the Navy, the brothers will be <u>almost</u> <u>entirely</u> separated for very many years; – & we think it important therefore for <u>both</u> of them, that the Holidays should now be passed <u>together</u>, – during the year or two which yet remains. – I cannot think it would injure either brother. . .

Ralph ought to write & thank me for the <u>Book</u>. He has not done so. – Indeed he has not written <u>at</u> <u>all</u>, for a very long time; tho' I answered his <u>last</u> letter to me almost immediately.

To Charles Babbage

Sunday, 17 December [1848]   Horsley

Dear Babbage. The further account in today's *Athenaeum* is certainly <u>excellent</u>. The <u>one</u> little error about what you said to Lord Melbourne, is put so very <u>slightly</u>, that it is of no importance. –

I scarcely think there is anything one could wish altered.

I <u>believe</u> we shall have room for you next Satdy.

The starling don't <u>talk</u> as yet. –

I hope you will come next Satdy. Yrs, ever   A.A.L.

Don't forget to let me have a heap of yr reprints as soon as you can. I can make good use of them. –

B Y EARLY 1849, despite Ada's loan from Henry Currie, her money problems continued. She appealed to Greig to help her but had reservations about doing so because Greig was Lady Byron's friend as well, and he had a tendency to gossip.

Ada went off for a few days to Brighton and had an engagement to meet Charles Dickens. He wrote her on 18 February 1849 that strange things were happening at his hotel. He wondered whether Ada was "haunting" him, and if so: "I hope you won't do so." Dickens had just completed *Dombey and Son* and *The Haunted Man and the Ghost's Bargain*.

Lady Byron was still involved in her own "strange happenings" in mesmerism. She encouraged Ada to support the remarkable effects of mesmerism, writing her about the unusual experience with mesmerism that Mrs Charles Lamb (her cousin) had experienced. Ada was skeptical.

To Woronzow Greig

5 January 1849   Brighton

Dear Greig. For the reasons I yesterday told you, I <u>ought</u> to see you before my mother enters on <u>business</u> with you. . .

Supposing however that you <u>cannot</u> come, remember the following points: –

1. You <u>must</u> <u>not</u> let out about <u>debts</u>; or <u>money</u> having been borrowed. I trust to you to give <u>no</u> hint of <u>this</u>.

2. Bear in mind that <u>I</u> <u>have</u> told my mother I consulted <u>you</u> some months ago, & laid before you the expense I have incurred as to the <u>main</u> <u>points</u>. I said <u>you</u> advised me to ask for an <u>increase</u> of £200 per ann: – which I acted on; – but the party declined to <u>bind</u> himself to <u>any</u> <u>sum</u> <u>regularly</u>, – but agreed to pay for Court-Dresses, & <u>did</u> pay <u>one</u> such Bill for last year.

This is the <u>whole</u> my mother knows, she must not know more.

Her reason for speaking to you now, is because <u>I</u> had been <u>complaining</u> of the <u>marriage</u> <u>settlement</u>, & speaking very strangely as to the <u>great</u> <u>difficulties</u> I have, to <u>scramble</u> on, – unless a decided & <u>regular</u> increase is allowed me. –

But if she knew of the <u>debt,</u> it would do irreparable mischief in more ways than one. I have told her that <u>books</u> & <u>music</u> are <u>the</u> two things which have made me <u>overflow</u> at times; & that <u>perhaps</u> I <u>might</u> have done <u>without them</u>, tho' that would have been a <u>great</u> pity.

I think I have explained to you now. – ever yrs &c

To Charles Babbage

Sunday, 11 February [1849]   Horsley

Dear Babbage. I will send you the <u>book</u> on Tuesdy, & it can be left with you till <u>Friday</u> I believe. –

I want to get you to have a proper <u>visiting list</u> made out for me. If I send you my books of visitors, can you get it done, – & for what price about? –

On <u>Tuesday</u> I believe I am going to Brighton, till Friday.

I wish you had been here now; for we <u>have room,</u> which was quite unexpected. We thought we should be <u>full</u>. – ever yrs

A.A.L.

To Lady Byron

Monday, 12 February [1849]

. . . As for Mesmerism: I gave no positive information whatever; – but an assent or dissent was pressed for at (almost) every step of importance. . . But I have since been told by three legal people (of whom Greig is one), that it is sufficient or at least that it might be. –

The more I reflect on the subject, the less I can believe. I am more disposed to believe even in error of my own senses, & in being my self-deceived than in what is so contrary to all previous experience & philosophy. . .

I don't mean that no evidence could convince me. But it would require very strong, & I think repeated evidence. –

Now I think I have explained clearly.

To Woronzow Greig

Tuesday Evening, 13 March 1849   Esher

Dear Mr Greig. . . I have stated my <u>own</u> opinions & feelings
upon the subject of property & money, in a very decided way to
Lovelace, in <u>writing</u>; as respects the <u>past</u>, the <u>present</u>, & the
<u>future</u>; being entirely determined that the past & <u>present</u> state
of things must <u>not</u> <u>continue</u>, & <u>never</u> <u>ought</u> <u>to</u> <u>have</u> <u>existed</u>.

I of course have said nothing unkind or offensive to <u>him</u>
<u>personally</u>. Not only will it be unwise, but I do <u>really</u> <u>acquit</u>
him of all <u>intentional</u> wrong; & think that <u>ignorance</u> has been
the cause of the discomfort & difficulties I have been allowed
to experience.

<u>The</u> point of difficulty is: that Lovelace entirely <u>denies</u> that
anything unusual or unjust has been done; & indeed I believe
he considers the <u>miserable</u> <u>pittance</u> allotted to <u>me</u>, as <u>most</u>
<u>liberal</u>: (<u>even</u> the £<u>300</u> <u>per</u> <u>ann</u>: out of the future £7,000 (!) per
annum: which <u>he</u> is to enjoy to my exclusion!)

I scarcely however think it <u>possible</u> that he can, consis-
tently with <u>honor</u>, resist <u>that</u> which I have never <u>put</u> <u>in</u> <u>writing</u>
to him.

Had he agreed to my <u>oral</u> request last year, this further (&
more decided) measure would not have been requisite. In some
haste, Most truly yrs   A.A. Lovelace

ADA HAD SEEN her father's best friend, John Cam Hobhouse,
in 1846. At that time he wrote in his diary that he was impressed by Ada's candor and intelligence in discussing subjects
like immortality, that "few men & and rarely any women" discuss. He observed that Ada's health appeared frail.

In June 1849 Ada visited John Murray, who was another one
of her father's friends, as well as his publisher. She became ill at
John Murray's home.

During the summer of 1849 Byron [Lord Ockham] went off
to sea, and the rest of the Lovelace family headed for Ashley
Combe, inviting Babbage to come in late September. In addition

to the children at Ashley Combe, there were dogs, birds, and other animals who followed everyone about. Continual cryptic references to the "book" appear in Ada's letters to Babbage, which led one biographer to come to the mistaken conclusion that Babbage was involved in gambling on the horses with Ada.

Lady Byron became ill, and Ada, as a dutiful daughter, went off to attend to her mother, but she was not pleased about playing that role any longer. She complained to William. Previously, he had supported Ada's sacrificing her own interests to help her mother, but in 1849 he was annoyed that Ada had to go to help her mother when she should have been watching her own health and her own family. Qualms about having put Ralph in Lady Byron's care surfaced in Ada's letters to her mother (by repeating Babbage's criticisms of Ralph's manner). Ada tried her best to step back from her mother's influence over her life. She attempted to get Ralph back for at least short visits and began to feel more comfortable about handling the children herself.

To John Murray

<u>Thursdy</u> <u>Evening</u>, 14 June [1849]   Great Cumberland St

Dear Mr Murray. I must thank you for yr kindness & <u>excellent judgement</u> yesterday.

It is "<u>Spasms of the heart</u>" that I am subject to; – & I have been so at times, more or less, for about 20 years; but this <u>last year</u> much more. It is of course (<u>to the sufferers</u>) like a mortal struggle between life & death, tho' I believe not really dangerous under proper treatment. –

I have not had a return today, only I am very weak & ill & feel 20 years older than one did 3 days ago. – This is always the case. –

I think it is, as regards <u>sensation</u>, the most frightful thing anyone <u>can</u> have; & one has to call in <u>reason</u> afterwards to reconcile oneself. It might be worse; some organic disease, cancer, unsound lungs. – God knows what, for unhappily diseases <u>abound</u>.

I have never quite been able to decide whether <u>life</u> is most desirable or alarming! It is a nice question. At this moment, (just <u>after</u> an attack) the sense of the <u>alarming</u> is strongest. By & bye I hope the <u>desirable</u> oscillation will come round.

I am very sorry that I was fated to go thro' the "<u>valley of the shadow of death</u>" in <u>yr</u> house. However you brought me successfully to life again. I must go as soon as able to see Mrs Murray, or else she will certainly think I am only a <u>ghost</u>, & a very troublesome one too! – <u>Many</u> thanks & am very truly yrs

A.A.Lovelace

To William, Lord Lovelace

Wednesday, 5 September [1849]   Esher

Dearest L. . . I hope you found the bottle of Quinine. I remember afterwards that it had been just opened once by me. I think you want <u>some</u> tonic. . .

I think my Mother is doing pretty well. . .

I <u>long</u> to get to Ashley, <u>if</u> it be safe &c.

I am sick & weary of the life here, – & I think it affects my spirits in reality a good deal, within myself; – tho' it don't show externally.

To Charles Babbage

Thursday, 20 September [1849]   Horsley

Dear Babbage. We propose to be down at Ashley on <u>Thursday</u> next – this day week; – & both L & I agree in urging you to come <u>there</u> during Octr, as the best possible rest & refreshment for you. Our house is not like the <u>Somerset</u> house, & I think we are now more regular even than we ever were.

You can have a <u>pony</u> all to yourself, & never need walk a step except on the terrace – the "<u>philosopher's walk</u>."

I propose to sleep in <u>Town</u> on Weddy next & go down by express train on Thursdy. Will <u>you</u> come back & go <u>with</u> me? –

Don't forget the <u>new cover</u> you promised to bring for the <u>book</u>. The poor book is very shabby, & wants one.

There is a great deal I want to explain to you, which can't be <u>by letter</u>. I can't decipher satisfactorily some <u>indications</u> in the work in question. –

Is not the above <u>medallion</u> a very pretty thing? – ever yrs truly   A.L.

<u>P. S.</u> I forgot to say that we have had <u>more</u> news from Ockham [Byron], round by <u>Holland</u>, – of a date 15 days <u>earlier</u> than the letter from the equator! . . . <u>All</u> <u>well</u> <u>&</u> <u>merry</u> & the letter is a very charming one.

To Charles Babbage

Friday, 28 September [1849]   Ashley Combe, Porlock, Somerset

Dear Babbage. At <u>present</u> coaches are running <u>daily</u> both from <u>Bridgewater</u> & from <u>Taunton</u>, to <u>Porlock</u>. –

I do not think they will continue to run <u>daily</u>, for <u>above</u> a <u>fortnight</u> longer. But you will be with us long before <u>that</u> I hope.

And at any rate if there is any <u>change</u> I will <u>immediately</u> let you know.

It is the <u>express</u> Train (9:50, Paddington Station) which meets the coaches.

We must ask you to do us the favor of bringing us down a package; – & also of going to Gt Cumberland St to select some things which <u>Lovelace</u> wants out of a <u>parcel</u> which is there. – Of all this I will write to you fully, in a day or two; & I will take care <u>so</u> to arrange it as to give you the <u>least</u> <u>possible</u> trouble.

I was so hurried & bothered the evg you came, (not <u>expecting</u> you in the least), that I could scarcely speak to you. Yet I was <u>particularly</u> glad to see you, – even in that uncomfortable way; – & it was a <u>very</u> good thing as regarded the <u>book.</u> –

I think your visit to Paris has been a most excellent step; very pleasant. –

I hope you will soon come, to <u>people</u> the "philosopher's walk!" – Don't forget to pay respects to <u>Pearce</u> en passant, – & pray enquire after his (young) "<u>Nelson.</u>" He was an own brother of <u>Rover's</u>, one of Flora's <u>first</u> litter; – & it has turned out splendid, the <u>best</u> of the lot in fact! – It is called "<u>Nelson</u>" (junior), & it's – very like <u>Papa</u>. – Yrs ever truly   A.L.

To Lady Byron

Friday, 9 November [1849]   Ashley

We have only just heard of Mrs Greig. She is settled at Edinburgh for the winter, to be under Dr Simpson's care. I do not
think that her <u>life</u> is to be feared for, but she is in a very
wretched state.. There is an "<u>inversion of the womb,</u>" but this
is curable. . . . Greig is just returned to Lambeth, where he says
he is very <u>lonely</u> & <u>miserable</u>. . . . I continue to be very much
better, & I have a little <u>hope</u> now of surviving yet a few years.

18.
Descending into the Grave, Resurrection, Be a Gypsy, Doomsday
[1850-1851]

BY 1850 THE LOVELACES had taken a firm step back from their involvement with Lady Byron. Annabella came back to live with them under the tutelage of Miss Wächter, Byron joined the Navy and was off at sea, and they continued to complain about Ralph. Financially, however, they could not distance themselves from Lady Byron. Their new home in London, at 6 Great Cumberland Place, needed many repairs. Lady Byron wrote that she would help by giving Lord Lovelace a loan of £4500 secured by his life insurance policy in her favor. According to the bank books, she gave them £1500 in 1850. Money is discussed, but inspection of the bank books reveals differences.

The Lovelaces were involved in a busy social scene with Babbage, their scientific friends, court activities, and racing. Greig reported the latest gossip to Ada. She replied, and then without a pause continued at a frenetic pace. After the Derby in 1850, she paid her mother a duty call on 6 June. A few days later on 10 June, she gave a party for fifty of her scientific friends, on the 20th she went to a ball where she saw Queen Victoria, and on the 21st she went to the opera. However, the big event of 1850 was the trip Ada had anticipated taking with William for years to forbidden territory, to racing friends, and to Newstead Abbey, her father's ancestral home.

Many letters in this chapter have been used by biographers to imply that Ada had a "vice" or an obsession, gambling on the horse races. This interpretation probably was due to the fact that Lady Byron, after Ada's death, made a big issue of Ada's interest in horses and gambling.

Ada, like her father, delighted in flouting conventional rules and evoking the "bad and mad" image. She wrote, perhaps seriously, perhaps in jest, phrases like "scorn and fury," "a fairy in your service," "her total ruin," and at a later time, making Annabella her "slave."

To Lady Byron

Your Birthday 1850   [17 May 1850]

. . . Dear little Miss Boutell has just been here with me for some time; so much improved, & impressing me very highly. –

I have ceased any belief in summer which I regard as a dream & a poetical fiction. –

Where had I better send a card of invitation to Bob Noel for Monday 27th I am anxious he should be here that evg, so I hope it may suit him to return to Town by that time. Do you know his present whereabouts? –

I am afraid you will take no interest in what interests me much just now, – viz: the winner of the Derby (May 29th). Indeed I am in danger of becoming quite a sporting character. The 2 horses I care about are Lord Zetland's Voltigeur, & Lady Albemarles' Bolingbroke.

To Lady Byron

Thursday, 30 May [1850]

I have such a horrible head today (owing of course to despair at the great pecuniary losses I have sustained by betting) that I can't write the long letter I intended. I hope to do so tomorrow, for I have very interesting things to tell you. –

. . . You will however see in the Papers: – "total ruin & suicide of the Earl of – – owing to the gambling of the Countess &c &c &c." –

What else could you expect?

We are delighted at Zetland's triumphant victory yesterday.

Voltigeur galloped to the winning post gloriously & with perfect ease.

No one expected it & the "King (?)" is half ruined! – They have all been <u>done</u> by the <u>North-country</u> men, which is rather delightful. : .

To Lady Byron

Friday, 21 June [1850]

. . .<u>Yesterday</u> was the <u>Drawing Room,</u> from which we only returned just in time to prepare for the <u>Opera</u> where we went last evg; – the <u>only</u> time I have been yet. So my day was <u>brimful</u> yesterdy, or I should have written. –

We are nothing short of <u>enchanted</u> with <u>Sontag</u> whom we went to hear as <u>Miranda</u> in Halevy's opera the <u>Tempest.</u> I think Sontag <u>far</u> superior to Lind. Her voice is deliciously sweet – quite <u>angelic</u>; – & her <u>execution</u> <u>and</u> expression are the ne plus ultra of perfection & refinement. There is likewise such <u>certainty</u> & <u>facility</u> – such absence of all effort – as I never heard equalled. – There is a <u>grace</u> in Sontag's person & <u>movements</u> which is far more satisfactory then the <u>angularity</u> & <u>jerkiness</u> of Lind. In short I can hardly perceive in her one single <u>shortcoming</u>. She is so <u>simple</u> & <u>harmonious</u>. . .

Lovelace is very much struck & charmed, & he is not easily pleased by even the best performers. . .

I have been very much <u>better</u> lately, – from some additional care & precautions.

The Queen looked <u>pleasant</u> yesterdy, which she <u>very</u> <u>rarely</u> does. She really looked <u>smiling</u>. –

We are going to the Ball on Weddy, & she has asked us <u>again</u> for <u>July 10th</u>. I consider that we ought to come up <u>for</u> it, which would be <u>very</u> easy – & rather convenient than otherwise in some respects. But L – swears he <u>won't</u>, which I think is a mistake. These sorts of <u>omissions</u> are likely to cause our being neglected. I am trying to persuade him. . .

I hope you are <u>furious</u> about the <u>Post</u> stopping entirely on Sundays. Everyone <u>I</u> know is, & yet all are submitting quietly, & letting the Saints have their way. <u>Dickens</u> is frantic about it. Look for his next Number. He has written something.

ADA WROTE A LONG LETTER to Greig about the rumors circulating about her behavior: "I very much regret that you
should allow such an absurdity to give you a moment's anxiety.
In general society every one is grossly slandered at times, & I am
sure if you heard all I hear about other people, of the same nature, you would see how little moment it is . . ."

She recognized at this time that she had become a victim of
her own naivete in having confided in Sophia DeMorgan. She
concluded her letter to Greig: "My character can't be mended
now. It was utterly gone before I was 26. I believe I owe much of
this to Mrs D. M [De Morgan] but I owe it also to other causes. –

"Pray understand that I have written all this entirely on yr
account, – & because I am extremely vexed to see you take the
matter so much to heart, & feel sure that if you knew all the past
you would view it differently."

Her attention switched once again to Babbage.

To Charles Babbage

Tuesday, 23 July 1850

Dear Babbage. It is possible that I may go to Town on Thursdy
evg or Fridy morng (early), – & to return here on Saturday
afternoon. I shall not be able to decide about this till
Thursday, – but I think it as well to give you timely notice in
case. If you would be so kind as to find out if I could see the
diamonds at the Exhibition d' Industrie, on Friday or Satdy, – it
would help me. yrs   A.L.

I am anxious to learn the progress of yr Nebulous Theory. I
suppose it depends on the mathematical laws of the condensa-
tion & expansion of Gases; the gases being supposed subject to
certain initial conditions, for instance gravitation, rotary
motion, &c. . .

MRS GREIG OFFERED to take Annabella on her first continental excursion. Ada filled her letters to Annabella with lightness but also gave firm instructions on how Annabella should behave. Ada kept Annabella informed of all the latest family developments, especially Byron's exploits at sea.

Ada and William finalized their plans for the tour of northern England. Their first stop was to visit the author Bulwer Lytton, later Lord Lytton. Little did Ada or Annabella realize that their two families would be joined in time. Annabella's daughter would marry Bulwer Lytton's grandson. After Ada and William visited the Lyttons, they travelled to see Captain Byron, Ada's cousin, and went on to see Reverend Gamlen in Yorkshire. Ada was particularly excited about their next stop, to the Earl and the Countess of Zetland in Aske, where she could have a good look at the famous horse, Voltigeur.

However, the highlight of the trip was Newstead Abbey, which had been bought by Colonel Wildman from Ada's father before he died. As poignant as Ada's letters are, they can only give us a glimpse of what she must have felt. She worded her letters to her mother very carefully, most likely recognizing that her father, even after almost thirty-five years, still evoked strong feelings in her mother. If Ada intended her letters to be an unemotional travel plan, she was not successful. Serious problems developed between Ada and her mother.

To Annabella

11 August 1850   Horsley

Dear Annabella. You will be glad to hear that we have heard very favorable reports of Byron, <u>from</u> <u>three</u> different sources. 1st The Lt of the Swift has returned to England & told a friend of Dr Lushington that Byron was a <u>general</u> <u>favorite</u>, learned his <u>duties</u> very <u>quickly</u>, & conducted himself extremely well. . .

Thank Mrs Greig for her letter for me. It was very acceptable.

We should have written to you before, but we really have
had <u>nothing</u> to say. – How much you seem to be enjoying yourself You must regard it as a <u>Holiday</u>, like what <u>School</u> boys &
girls get for a few weeks. And if you <u>work</u> <u>very</u> <u>hard</u> & <u>behave</u>
<u>very</u> <u>well</u>, during the next winter & spring, – we can perhaps,
manage to give you some <u>other</u> Holiday sometime next year.
But this must all depend 1st on what I see of the <u>effects</u> <u>on</u> <u>you</u>
of the present trip & next on what we can afford.

Yr sketches are very nice. . . Pray draw some of the <u>oxen</u>, as
there are no <u>horses</u> to draw! What a sorry land for an <u>eques-</u>
<u>trian</u> like you. . .

My injunctions for you: <u>don't</u> <u>get</u> <u>over-excited</u>, <u>don't</u> <u>talk</u>
<u>loud</u>. <u>Do</u> sketch, & <u>do</u> talk <u>German</u>.

I am forming schemes against <u>yr</u> <u>liberty</u>, & some very deep
designs for making you a <u>greater</u> <u>slave</u> than ever. So you had
better persuade Mrs Greig to keep you as long as possible, – for
– when you come back, you don't know all that may happen to
you. . .

There is a <u>gigantic</u> <u>Tortoise</u> now at the Z. Gardens, indeed I
believe they have several new things there. – yrs very Affectly
                                                              A.A.Lovelace

To Lady Byron

Monday Night, 19 August [1850]   London

We believed you to be at Brighton still, till we received yr two
<u>afternoon</u> letters just before I set out today. I had been intend-
ing to write to you tonight to <u>Brighton</u>. – . . .

We leave on <u>Thursday</u>, for Sir E. Bulwer Lytton's <u>first</u>,
Knebworth – Herts; then the G. Byrons in Nottinghamshire;
then the <u>Nightingales</u>, Derbyshire, then <u>Gamlen</u>; then the <u>Zet-</u>
<u>lands</u>; then the <u>Cumberland</u> <u>Lakes</u> about <u>Sepr</u> <u>6th</u>; for 10 days
or so. Then (I <u>believe</u>) we shall cut across the country again to
<u>Newstead</u> for a day or two, (the Wildmans not being there now,
& proposing to us the middle of Septr instead), half-way to Bristol & Ashley, where we purpose to be by the . . .18th Septr. But

we cannot afford to move the <u>family</u> &c to Ashley this year, so only L – & I . . . for perhaps about 3 weeks. – Perhaps we may linger there by way of <u>economy</u>, for a certain time.

I have had a bad <u>rheumatic</u> attack in one shoulder, which <u>Chloroform</u> cured.

To Annabella

Sunday, 25 August 1850

Dear Annabella. I hope this will be in time still to find you at Schwalbach. Papa wrote to you last Weddy from London. – We are at this moment at my relations Captain Byron, in Nottinghamshire – at a place called Thrumpton – about 8 miles from Nottingham. We have been visiting a very distinguished man in Hertfordshire, who has written many books which <u>you</u> will hereafter read (as thousands have) with delight, – Sir Edward Bulwer Lytton. He is a friend of ours', but I do not think you have ever seen him. He has a great reputation all over the world, & I think I have heard Miss Wächter say that the <u>Germans</u> have a high admiration for his works . . .

We cannot afford to move the whole family, horses, luggage &c to <u>Ashley</u> this year. So Papa & I (with John & Miss Wilson) will be there. No one else. Rents are half paid, & we are in some difficulty. . .

We are glad that the new <u>Admiral</u> just appointed to the <u>Pacific</u> <u>Station</u>, is an old friend of ours, & most <u>intimate</u> friend of Mr Knight's & Mr Halliday's, Admiral Moresby. It may be of use to Byron. Tell this to Mrs Greig. Tell her also that the red Shawl she gave me is <u>very</u> <u>much</u> <u>admired</u> & very <u>useful</u>. It is the most comfortable Shawl I ever had.

I hope to find that your manners are quiet and those of a lady. When you return; & that you <u>speak</u> quietly & gently, & not as if you had been in a <u>hurry-scurry</u>, & state of over excitement. . . Most affectly   A.A.L.

To Lady Byron

Sunday, 8 September [1850]   Newstead Abbey

I received yrs at Bossall & gave Gamlen yr message If I <u>was</u> to be ill I could not have chosen so good a hospital as the <u>Zetlands</u>, & I am thankful it happened there. I should scarcely have been as well off at <u>home</u>, & they are in some danger of my going to them I think as to a <u>Hospital</u> – whenever ill. – Their <u>doctor</u> was successful with me also.

I cannot imagine <u>what</u> it is in my late letters which has set you speculating! I cannot remember having said anything whatever that could do so. –

We came <u>here</u> yesterday. I have not yet been over the <u>whole</u>, nor much about;- but it is <u>grandly</u> monastic, & <u>everything</u> speaks of the past history of the <u>place</u> & of the <u>Byrons</u>, for centuries. The repairs & restorations are most <u>admirably</u> done, and certainly no <u>Byron</u> could have afforded to do such justice to this antique & historical residence.

I feel as if, however, it ought to belong to <u>me</u>; & altogether horribly low & melancholy. All is like <u>death</u> round one; & I seem to be in the <u>Mausoleum</u> of my race. What is the good of living, when <u>thus</u> all passes away & leaves only cold stone behind it? There is no <u>life</u> here, but cold dreary <u>death</u> only, & everywhere – The death of <u>everything</u> that <u>was</u>! –

I am glad to <u>see</u> the home of my ancestors, but I shall not be sorry to escape from the <u>grave</u>. I see my <u>own</u> future continuing visibly around me. <u>They</u> <u>were</u>! I <u>am</u>, but shall not be. Alas ! Well, so it is – & will be <u>world</u> <u>without</u> <u>end</u>. –

We ought to have been happy, rich, & great. But one thing after another has sent us to the 4 winds of Heaven. The Civil Wars destroyed the estates & fortune, which <u>were</u> immense till the Roundheads seized it all. Only a <u>very</u> <u>small</u> part was restored to the Byrons afterwards.

They tell <u>such</u> tales here of "<u>the</u> <u>Wicked</u> <u>old</u> <u>Lord</u>" as he was called commonly, – my father's <u>predecessor</u> & great-uncle, the one who killed Mr Chaworth.

I have not yet seen <u>my</u> <u>father's</u> rooms. No one is here but the Hamilton Greys, & we are perfectly quiet, & just like Goody Two Shoes!

Only I feel as if I had become a stone monument myself. I am petrifying fast.

To Lady Byron

Sunday, 15 September [1850]   Radbourne

Yrs of the 14th received this morg. We came here last evg after a most delightful & successful tour of 3 days to see all the Beauties of Derbyshire. A completely <u>nomad</u> life suits me wonderfully. –

On Weddy we slept at Bolsover Castle & saw Hardwick Hall. On Thursdy we went to Castleton (30 miles), a drive which is one continued series of varying & romantic views. We saw the <u>Peak</u> Cavern, the old Castle (<u>Peverils</u>), & other wonders at Castleton; & on Friday went by Bakewell to see Haddon Hall, – & on to <u>Downdale</u> in the evg. Yesterday morg early we saw <u>Downdale</u> & <u>Flan</u>, – then went 10 miles to see Alton Towers (Earl Of Shrewsbury's) & came on here (22 miles) in the evg. –

My <u>first</u> & very melancholy impressions at Newstead, gradually changed to quite an <u>affection</u> for the place before I left it. I began to feel as if it were an <u>old</u> <u>home</u>, – & I left it with with regret & reluctance, – & feel that I <u>must</u> go back to it before a year is over. –

Col Wildman is a man of talent, feeling, & good taste. There is no <u>profession</u> in him, but he <u>acts</u> & <u>lives</u> in devotion to my father & my race. He knew my father only in his <u>very</u> <u>young</u> days, – Col W's profession as a Soldier entirely withdrawing him afterwards.

Col W's <u>own</u> history is in some points singular, & he is full of <u>originality</u>.

It has been the <u>salvation</u> of <u>Newstead</u>, that <u>he</u> has had it. No one else in the world would have <u>resuscitated</u> <u>it</u>, & all its <u>best</u> reminiscences, as <u>he</u> has done.

And no <u>Byron</u> could have <u>afforded</u> even to preserve the edifice from actually tumbling down. – The outlay requisite has been enormous.

There is an old <u>prophecy</u> that the place was to pass out of the family <u>when</u> <u>it</u> <u>did</u>, & which further adds that it is to <u>come</u> <u>back</u> in the present generation!

Altogether it is an <u>epoch</u> in my life, my visit there. I have lost my <u>monumental</u> & <u>desolate</u> feeling respecting it. – It seemed like descending into the <u>grave</u>, but I have had a <u>resurrection</u>. – I do love the venerable old place & all my <u>wicked</u> <u>forefathers</u>!

On Tuesday I go to <u>Doncaster</u> to see the races; & at the end of the week we go to Aske (the Zetlands), & then <u>across</u> <u>York-shire</u> to <u>Kendal</u> & <u>the</u> <u>Lakes</u> for a week or two.-

I think <u>yr</u> <u>Fund</u> will <u>not</u> be touched <u>this</u> year; & will let you know in a weeks time...

L ADY BYRON COULD NOT ALLOW Ada to entertain any pleasant images of her father. She replied to Ada's letters about Newstead by accusing Ada of harboring a "mythic image" of her father. Lady Byron was suspicious that she was the topic of conversation at Newstead. Ada tried to convey to her mother that she had no illusions about her father. According to her information, he left what remained of his estate to his half-sister, Augusta Leigh. Lord Byron had assumed that since Lady Byron was always complaining that she was on her death bed, she would die early and Ada would be left well off. That assumption turned out to be inaccurate.

Ada tried to put all these thoughts in the back of her mind as she prepared to see the greatest of all races at the Doncaster Cup. The competition was between the favorites – Flying Dutchman and Voltigeur. William missed the first day of the races, but he was there for the big event and was the unfortunate victim of a pickpocket.

To Lady Byron

Monday, 23 September [1850]   Aske

The <u>second</u> victory of <u>Voltigeur</u> on Friday, when he won the
Cup, beating the <u>invincible</u> Flying Dutchman – who it was supposed <u>no</u> horse could equal, – is the greatest triumph ever
achieved in racing ! – It was a magnificent struggle between
these two <u>greatest</u> of Horses! – Like single combat between two
heroes. – I am glad to have seen this greatest of Races which
will be <u>historical.</u> I believe that no horse has yet won the Derby,
the St. Leger, <u>and</u> the Cup – especially against such a Cham-
pion as the Flying Dutchman.

I feel some difficulty in replying to your enclosure of yesterday – because it seems to me as if addressed to a Phantom of
something that don't exist. No feeling or opinion respecting my
father's <u>moral</u> <u>character</u> or yr relations towards him, could be
altered by my visit to Newstead, is by any <u>tone</u> assumed by any
parties whatever. –

I am confident however that no tone of the kind you conceive, exists with the Wildmans. One may feel the deepest
<u>interest</u> in persons & characters whom one cannot (morally
speaking) <u>admire</u>. –

Nothing passed while I was there which could, directly or
indirectly, bear the slightest relation to his <u>matrimonial</u> history,
or to any of the <u>indefensible</u> points of his life. I am persuaded
that there is nothing of the <u>Partisan</u> about Col. Wildman; & if
<u>all</u> my father's friends had been of Col. W's sort it would have
been well for him. But after school days they lost sight of each
other.

<u>Mrs</u> <u>Leigh</u> & her children are no <u>favorites</u> at Newstead.
Indeed it is some years since <u>she</u> has been there. I heard a
good deal about <u>that</u>.

So far from having a <u>mythical</u> veneration for my father, I
cannot (to adhere only to <u>personal</u> considerations) forget his
conduct as regards my <u>own</u> self, – a conduct <u>unjust</u> & <u>vindic-</u>
<u>tive.</u> –

I write all this <u>off</u> <u>hand</u> and in a hurry. Probably I shall
write again & more fully on the subject. –

To Lady Byron

Thursday, 26 September [1850]   Aske

I am delighted to find that <u>you</u> think of Sontag as I do. I do not think she is even appreciated as she ought to be, – for she has not created a <u>Lind</u> <u>furor,</u> altho' she is greatly admired. – . . .

I will secure for you a <u>good</u> picture of Voltigeur. None of the prints yet out do him justice. –

He is a very remarkable animal, in <u>character</u> as well as performance.

A most <u>earnest,</u> <u>conscientious,</u> sort of horse, – & a very gentle & amiable.

We are much distressed at a few words in yrs to Lovelace today, which we do not <u>understand;</u> an allusion to "agitation <u>of late.</u>" Surely nothing <u>we</u> have done or said can have been the cause of any <u>agitation</u> or <u>anxiety</u>! –

I only wish you could know all we have <u>really</u> thought & felt. You could not but feel entirely at rest, if you <u>did</u>. Do <u>pray</u> let us at least know the whole. I cannot <u>bear</u> the idea of yr going on under a <u>mis</u>-apprehension so painful, & (I can most positively & truly assure you) so <u>unfounded</u>.

I believe that <u>writing</u> often leads to misunderstandings. Only <u>certain</u> <u>special</u> points start out prominently in correspondence, & are falsified by not forming <u>part</u> <u>of</u> <u>the</u> <u>whole</u>. –

It seems to me so impossible that what L – or I <u>wrote</u>, was of a nature to suggest any ideas of our views that could <u>seriously</u> <u>agitate</u> you, – that I cannot help apprehending lest some <u>misapprehension</u> may have been made to you. I cannot conceive that there are <u>always</u>, & in <u>all</u> cases, persons ready to make mischief; – and generally from entirely some unsuspected quarter. –

We stay here 2 or 3 days longer, & then go to the Lakes. <u>No occasion</u> for the <u>£30</u> this year. But <u>next</u> year, it will be very acceptable.

❧

AFTER TRYING TO COME TO TERMS with the emotion that the Newstead visit evoked and the illness she had experienced at the Zetlands, Ada decided that her mother's plans for her destiny just would not do. She was now at a critical juncture in her life and decided on the path she must take.

Concerned about Ada's chronic ill health, Babbage tried to get her to do something about it. When she arrived in London, she in turn prodded him to attend to the problems he faced. Their problems aside, they were both excited and delighted with the plans under way for the Great Exhibition in May of 1851, an exhibition of the fruits of the Industrial Revolution. Babbage was writing a guide, *The Great Exhibition of 1851*, which was due to come out before the exhibition. The highlight of the exhibition was the Crystal Palace, a prefabricated glass building being built by Paxton to house industrial and technological displays.

To Lady Byron

Tuesday, 22 October [1850]   Ashley Combe

Please to forward Byron's letter to <u>Annabella</u>. . .

I have such a formidable arrear of letters, – & my <u>writing</u> powers are always so <u>very</u> limited – that I cannot write you the letter I wish, until next week. I am anxious to tell you the conclusions I have come to about my health & the plans necessary for it, – & also more of the opinions of me of a most sensible man (the Zetland's Doctor Malcolm) who was with me constantly for so long, & who had also the advantage of seeing me so <u>very</u> ill with my heart. . .

<u>Writing</u> he above everything prohibits, – beyond a very small amount, – He says that <u>now</u> is my turning point, & if I do not follow out the right plans for the <u>next</u> <u>two</u> years, I shall <u>not</u> have a long life or a prosperous one; - whereas in his opinion, I am calculated for a <u>vigorous</u> old age, if I am saved <u>now</u>. –

Nature seems to point out the course very plainly. I ought to be a <u>Gypsy</u> very nearly.

More of all of this hereafter. I <u>never</u> expected to be as well as I <u>now</u> am, & it is thanks to my roving life of late. –

Pray how are <u>you</u>? . . .

To Lady Byron

28 October [1850]   Ashley Combe

We must regard it as more important for Ralph to acquire a just
& intimate knowledge of <u>Nature</u> & her exact <u>laws</u>, than of the
<u>conventionalities</u> of <u>man</u> & of <u>civilization</u>. <u>Language</u> is not
<u>knowledge</u>, tho' a very valuable acquisition for its' own proper
objects & purposes. The very excitable intellect & imagination
of Ralph is trained & soothed by the acquisition of true <u>science</u>
& by the cultivation of <u>exact</u> <u>reasoning</u> power, – this last cultivation being <u>peculiarly</u> necessary to his sensitive & passionate
nature- & best attained thro' that <u>mathematical</u> course of study,
which will also <u>aid</u> him to comprehend the . . . laws of the Universe. We could not think Ralph properly educated anywhere
where <u>routine</u> should be predominant, or where <u>memory</u> should
be cultivated in preference to <u>reason</u>. It is true that a young
child ought <u>not</u> to be much tried as to the <u>reasoning</u> faculties.
But a clever boy of <u>twelve</u> will certainly reason (<u>wrongly</u> & <u>pre-
sumptuously</u>), if not <u>trained</u> to reason <u>rightly</u> & <u>guardedly</u>. It is
therefore desirable to take the lead, & not to let the strengthen-
ing faculties go blundering or without full direction & surveil-
lance. –

To Charles Babbage

Friday, 1 November [1850]   Ashley

Dear Babbage. I have delayed writing, intending to send you a
<u>long</u> letter. I have not time to do this yet, so I had better delay
no longer letting you know the invalid is certainly <u>better</u> from
Erasmus Wilson's medicines. But the health is so utterly broken at present, that I wish to follow the plan you suggest; & to
have the examination & enquiries by <u>yr</u> medical friend – as
soon as return to Town shall admit of it.

I think this of great importance. Some very thorough remedial measures must be pursued, – or all power of getting any livelihood in <u>any</u> way whatever, will be at an end. – Yrs in haste

A.L.

To Annabella

Tuesday, 5 November [1850]   Ashley

Dear Annabella. You have never told me [?] about <u>Nelson</u>, – which I very much wonder at! – Nor indeed about <u>any</u> live thing. The <u>animal</u> department has been much neglected. I hear you have got your <u>Starling</u> back! – Miss Wilson has just lost <u>her</u> dear Starling, here. –

I enclose your communication from the Zoological Society, which came 2 or 3 months ago for you. Mind you <u>understand</u> it.

There is a Birthday present which you will have after our return: none the worse I hope for being after date. –

While you were abroad I looked for several books which you had had in London but they could not be found either at Horsley or London. The <u>Handbook</u> <u>of</u> <u>Games</u> was one; & the <u>Horsemanship</u> in 3 vols (Mr. H. Babbage's) <u>another</u>, & Staunton's Chess Books.

By the bye I wish you would read the <u>Horsemanship</u> carefully. –

Could you find me the Dice (in the Backgammon Board), & send by post. . .

Ever yrs affectly   A.A. Lovelace

To Agnes Greig

Thursday, 21 November [1850]

Ashley Combe, Porlock, (by Taunton) Somerset

Dear Mrs Greig . . . Will you come for Xmas? How is yr health now?. . . Pray let me hear soon & pray get <u>all</u> you can from Mrs Fanshawe. Would she be so <u>very</u> kind as to write <u>me</u>?

We must still settle <u>accounts</u> about Annabella; – add some money I think. I have never yet paid you for the things you got for Byron, – & also some expenses Mr Greig paid for <u>Ralph's</u>

journey last year, & which have just occurred to me that we owe
him. –

A thousand thanks for all yr kindness to Annabella, in
which Lovelace desires to join. Very sincerely yrs

A.A. Lovelace

To Lady Byron

Monday, 23 December [1850]   E.H.P.

I had made the arrangements for Ralph's going to Esher tomorrow & returning. I am glad he did not suffer for his Journey on
Friday. He had to go outside as far as Leatherhead. It is
(Alas!) very <u>unusual</u> that our Coach is so filled. I do not think
he was properly provided with Rugs & Wraps for <u>outside</u>, & I
was rather alarmed. I believe the Coachman lent him something...

How does this weather suit you? ... I went to the Glass
House, where I spent some <u>hours,</u> – & was not the worse, tho' it
was a most trying day, & <u>bitter</u> cold & <u>fog.</u>

I think we shall let our house in May, & go to the <u>Pyrenees.</u>
I am not joking. I reflected on yr suggestion, & soon got accustomed to it. It frightened me at first.

It would <u>set</u> <u>me</u> <u>up</u> for years, (& set our <u>purses</u> up too). –

THIS LAST REFERENCE is an enigma. William had written
a description of Newstead Abbey to Lady Byron. His description read like a current-day real estate agent's assessment
of a property. He analyzed the income from tenants, the size of
the property and need for repairs, and supplied a list of what
needed to be done. The whole letter conveyed the impression
that he was interested in buying the property.

At this time the relationship between the Lovelaces and
Lady Byron was very fragile. The Newstead Abbey visit, which
revived old wounds, was not the only reason. Lady Byron was involved with a popular evangelist, Mr Robertson, which further

alienated the Lovelaces from Lady Byron. By April, Ada no longer minced words about her feelings towards her mother. After her visit to the Zetlands, she expressed her increased interest in horses and racing. William reported to Lady Byron that Ada even considered breeding race horses (a destiny fulfilled by Ada's descendants).

Certain events in Ada's life in early 1851 can only be guessed at because no letters survive from Ada to her so-called "sporting friends." The few letters to Ada that survive about horse racing evoke illusions that Lady Byron, and later Ralph, were very anxious to promote after Ada's death. There are letters that leave enticing images from Richard Ford, a friend of Babbage's, mentioning John Crosse, Malcolm (not the Zetlands' physician), Childs and Fleming, and the Nightingales (who were also close friends of Lady Byron's).

The information that remains about Ada's gambling comes from a secondary report, though in many biographies it is quoted as a primary source, leaving the reader to assume that the report was written by a witness. It was not. It was written by Ada's son Ralph decades later (he was eleven years old at this time), based on information garnered from some of Ada's so-called sporting friends after she died. Ralph was brought up by Lady Byron and considered himself her defender. He blamed Ada and William for all his problems and rarely spoke to his father after Ada's death. The "sporting friends" alleged that Ada had owed them money, but both Greig and Lushington, Lady Byron's attorney, thought they were a pack of liars. Greig encouraged William, distraught over Ada's death, to sue the lot of them. In fact, Ada was involved in gambling on horses and was very successful. Greig reported later that she had won £1000 in early 1851.

The following letters indicate, I believe, that Ada's involvement in betting on the horses was not addictive, though it does make a good story or "myth" to sell even scholarly books. It appears she was involved, but not to the point that it was the motivating force in her life. Her interest was similar to the kind of interest that many people today have in investing in the stock market, hoping that careful analysis might give them a better than random chance; both activities involve the manipulation of numbers. Today, both the stock market and legalized betting houses in Great Britain use sophisticated statistical techniques, such as regression analysis, to predict performance outcome. When I was studying those techniques at Berkeley, someone in my class used such variables as the weight of the horse, past performance, genetic background, and many other variables to predict the winner of a race. But horse racing, like gambling, is not just numbers; it is passion, and that passion came from Ada's Byron heritage.

Ada's grandfather was an addictive gambler. It led to his financial ruin. Although Ada's father had renounced gambling because he could not afford it, he liked gamblers and found the activity exhilarating. He wrote: "I have a notion that Gamblers are as happy as most people, being always *excited*. Women, wine, fame, the table, even Ambition, *sate* now and then: but every turn of the card, and cast of the dice, keeps the Gamester alive . . ."[1]

Ada found excitement in letters from a man, most likely Malcolm, in January 1851, who wrote her: "I am anxious to hear what is definitely proposed about Childs, I don't quite know if opening a list means taking an office & giving the odds after the Davies fashion." Davies was a prominent bookmaker at the time.

The following Monday, the writer made excuses about not calling on Ada because "Your uncertain invitation & £3000 this year! How my mouth waters at such draught. But by what magic is such a sum to be obtained and how has Childs become so suddenly combined with depository of thousands from not having half a penny. I will call you tomorrow morning between 10 and 11 to hear the solution of this golden mystery." The following letters do not answer the mystery because other events were occurring in Ada's life.

To Lady Byron

Thursday, 10 April [1851]   Gt C. Place

I was distressed & shocked by yr few lines recd last evg, – altho' far from <u>surprised</u>. Indeed in my heart I <u>expected</u> as much.

I have been <u>extremely</u> busy the last week upon matters connected with our worldly & pecuniary affairs, (& <u>still</u> am so); & between this, & the daily expectation of hearing from <u>you</u> about the <u>Interview</u>, I think I have not written to you for a century. –

I am sorry <u>that</u> Interview has even taken place, & (as you must have seen) I was uneasy & <u>vexed</u> even, about it from the first. –

I almost wish now that I had ventured on what I did <u>not</u> think right towards a <u>Parent</u>, viz: strongly to urge & remonstrate. I never felt so tempted to step out of all the usual bounds of filial propriety – I feared so for yr <u>health</u> & peace.

<u>That</u> <u>filial</u> relation is always hanging like a Mill-stone round my neck.

But I believe that even if I could have <u>succeeded</u> in persuading you, you were already <u>committed</u> when you first told me about it.

Pray do not be angry at my having the <u>idea</u> (never likely to be practically attempted) of ever <u>persuading</u> you to anything! It is only an <u>idea</u>, – a wish! –

I am rather unhappy about it all.

Every year of my life of late years I have been <u>happier</u>, so on the whole I think I do very well, & I dare say <u>shall</u> do very well. –

I really don't <u>exactly</u> know what I <u>do</u> or do <u>not</u> believe. How <u>can</u> one?

These are not matters upon which we can get at <u>certainties</u>. I think my own belief goes <u>only</u> so far as this: I do not see <u>certainty</u> where a good many do, but I feel there <u>may</u> be a certainty tho', <u>I</u> do not see it.

Besides which, at present I am rather occupied in <u>living</u>, & find <u>that</u> quite enough to do. – When I <u>do</u> die, I have no doubt I shall be occupied with <u>that</u>, heart & soul (if I <u>have</u> any then) –

But I am sure I could find out nothing certain about it by occupying myself now with the <u>dark</u> <u>page</u> (as it is to <u>me</u>)! –

By the bye am I to come on <u>Satdy</u> or Sundy?

To Lady Byron

21 April [1851]   London

I have been so ill with cough & influenza, & <u>am</u> so ill, – that I scarcely can put pen to paper. I have also an awful amount of <u>writing</u> to do at present, & sometimes have scarcely time to recollect my own existence. This great pressure is owing to particular circumstances at present, which will not endure for ever.

There is great probability of my letting the house on the 20th May, but nothing is yet settled.

Admiral Dundas speaks of Byron as "<u>an</u> <u>active</u> <u>zealous mind,</u>" – & from another quarter we heard it had been said he was likely to be an "<u>ornament</u> <u>to</u> <u>his</u> <u>Profession</u>."

Miss Smith's character of me from the writing is I suppose pretty good, excepting the <u>absence</u> of <u>imagination</u>, which I think quite wrong. God knows I have enough of it, & a great plague it often is. –

Oh! I am such a sick Wretch! I shall soon be <u>better</u> now I suppose...

IF ADA WAS INDEED the addictive gambler, as many biographies picture her, why was she talking of renting the house from the beginning of the racing season?

To Lady Byron

(<u>Doomsday</u>)

17 May 1851

I scarcely like to recollect or allude to <u>today</u>, with my views of life & death &c &c! It is a dreadful thing to <u>get</u> <u>on</u> thus towards extinction. And yet, as I hope to <u>live</u> <u>as</u> <u>long</u> <u>as</u> <u>possible</u>, I must hope to be <u>as</u> <u>old</u> some day as you are.

The Voltigeur defeat distresses me less than <u>yr</u> <u>age</u>. I was a good deal prepared for it, & expected that the Flying Dutchman <u>would</u> have it this time, & in fact strongly <u>expressed</u> this opinion to some of the party. –

I hope to go down to you tomorrow <u>afternoon</u> (to return to Town by the late train in the evg), unless I am <u>countermanded</u> by you, for which there may be causes unknown to me.* – Ralph looks very well. Perhaps I may bring down Annab. tomorrow.-

Pray believe how sincerely I commiserate you. In <u>all</u> respects at this moment you appear to me to be a lamentable example of <u>my</u> blackest views of life! –

*You know I always <u>believe</u> myself to be in the way, unless there is strong demonstration of the contrary.

19.

Catch a Comet,
Not £5 in My Purse,
Give the Despots a Shove
[1851]

THE MONTH OF May 1851 was an extraordinary month not only in Ada's life, but in the history of the Industrial Revolution. Thomas Hardy in *The Fiddler of the Reels* described the Great Exhibition that opened that month "as an extraordinary chronological frontier or transit-line." Several books describe this great event. Asa Briggs's magnificent *Iron Bridge to Crystal Palace, Impact and Images of the Industrial Revolution* summarizes in words and pictures as Hardy did in words the importance of this event in the history of civilization.

I have developed a time line of Ada's and William's activities during this month because Ada's biographers have taken this month out of context, focusing on her downfall at the races and totally ignoring her joy, and her friends' and family's joy – at the opening of the Great Exhibition.

The month could not have started with greater promise for Babbage, Ada, William, and Annabella. They were all involved. Babbage had already shown Ada the Crystal Palace when it was under construction in Hyde Park the previous December, and on 1 May the Great Exhibition opened. It was the largest display ever gathered of the fruits of the Industrial Revolution. The Crystal Palace was constantly filled with huge crowds viewing everything from jewels to machine tools. William won an award for brick making. Annabella wrote Byron long letters about her many visits. The Great Exhibition symbolized the hopes and aspirations of the Industrial age. Ada and all her friends – Babbage, Brewster, Faraday, and Crosse were caught up in the excitement. It was a month that Ada would not forget.

The week of 13 May began with Ada's attendance at the York races. The *Times* vividly described that event, noting that such excitement had never been seen before and perhaps never would be seen again. The roar of the people could be heard for miles.

Ada's social activities continued non-stop. On Saturday evening Lord Lovelace attended the Royal Society dinner along with Sir David Brewster, Dr Locock, Babbage, Wheatstone, and Quêtelet. The next day Ada paid a duty call on her mother, bringing along Sir David Brewster. She did not stay long for that evening was "the Gala occasion" – Queen Victoria gave a ball at Buckingham Palace in honor of the Great Exhibition. More than 2000 people attended. The dancing started at 10:00 p.m. with the Great Exhibition Quadrille. Dinner was served at midnight, and people did not leave the palace till dawn. Ada and William were listed as attending, as were their friends the Zetlands and the Bessboroughs.

The Derby was held on 21 May at Epsom Downs. It stated in the *Times* that the Zetlands and Bessboroughs were present, but there was no mention of the Lovelaces being present. Teddington, a chestnut horse, won a surprising victory by a length. According to Ada's son Ralph, she lost £3200. She settled the losses a few days after the Derby. Exactly how she covered them on her annual income of £300, which appeared to be covering other expenses, I am not sure. She borrowed £600 from Ford, and according to Greig, she had won money throughout the spring. How much money was involved is not known.

A few weeks after the Derby, Ada had massive hemorrhages. Her physician wrote Lord Lovelace of the severity of Ada's condition. On 20 June William, totally distraught, went to Leamington Spa, about 100 miles from London, to see Lady Byron, who was ill and taking a cure. The letter dated 19 June was dated in handwriting other than Ada's. The date is incorrect. Wednesday was written in by Ada, and Wednesday that year was the 18th.

I have included the next two letters to Babbage because they contain a reference to a book thought to be a Mathematics

Scrapbook; however, according to one biographer, Maboth Mose-
ley, it might have referred to a "book" in gambling terms. The
British Library dated these two letters in either late 1844 or
1845. I believe they are incorrectly dated. Ada mentions Sir
David Brewster, who, in addition to being a pioneer in the field
of optics, was the author of the *Martyrs of Science,* biographies of
scientists who sacrificed themselves for the sake of science.

To Charles Babbage

11 1/2 o'clock, Monday morning, [most likely May 1851]

Dear Babbage. I cannot <u>spare</u> the book at all today, which I am
very sorry for. I want it for a constant reference, – but I think
you can have it <u>tomorrow</u> evg, – & you could send it down to
Horsley per coach on Weddy.

    Could Sir D. B. [David Brewster] call on me at 10 1/2
o'clock tomorrow (Tuesdy) morg. Yrs   A.L.

To Charles Babbage

10 minutes to 11 o'clock [May 1851?]

Dear Babbage. I quite fully engaged this morg – but I will send
you the Book <u>directly,</u> & you can say, when you receive it, how
long you will want to keep it.

    I will let Sir D. B. [David Brewster] know this afternoon. I
must communicate with others before I can settle the day. Yrs

          A.L.

To Charles Babbage

Tuesday morning, 27 May [1851]   G. C. P.

Dear Babbage

    We want you & Sir D. B. [Brewster] to <u>dine</u> with us today to
meet <u>Quêtelet</u>.

    Pray manage this.

    No party.   A.L.

To Lady Byron

Wednesday Night [19th June 1851]

I am not surprised to hear of yr illness. That is to say I am never surprised. –

I think there is a very marked change in the local state in me. My <u>general</u> health is by the bye no means much affected, – I think rather improved by the great rest & care necessitated.

I cannot comprehend what you allude to, as regards my exciting habits for <u>long past</u>. I never was so careful, so regular, so quiet, in anything, as during the whole of last year. There is in the <u>Spring</u> always the miserable East Winds, which always <u>must</u> affect me & indeed many others; & there is also the <u>high-pressure</u> of the present age & epoch & state of society. But of all my life, the last 2 years have been those <u>least</u> addicted to anything of stimulants & over excitements. My <u>hours</u> alone, have been so perfectly regular & natural, – & no <u>extremes</u> of exercise, or diet, or anything. –

You know that ever since those <u>Heart</u> attacks, I have not dared take liberties; & perhaps their <u>best</u> result was thoroughly <u>frightening</u> me. –

It is evident that Dr Locock is managing the present case most admirably. Everything turns out exactly as he predicts, & I am disposed now to hope that cure will go on steadily; – altho' the treatment <u>appears</u> to do harm sometimes. . .

W HEN WILLIAM INFORMED Lady Byron of Ada's illness and betting losses, which he clearly stated had been covered, Lady Byron chose to ignore the gravity of Ada's illness. She filed a statement with her attorney blaming William for Ada's gambling and further stated that she knew nothing of Ada's involvement with gambling. That is why the letter dated the 19th, but really the 18th, makes little sense.

Lady Byron then reiterated her suggestion to Ada that she had made several weeks before during the visit with Sir David Brewster. Ada should embark on an intellectual endeavor, perhaps with one of her scientific friends. Lady Byron's suggestion for a scientific treatise was for Ada to examine the work of Rutter, a phrenologist and mesmerist whom Lady Byron admired. As sick as Ada was, she tried to comply with her mother's wishes and hold on to family ties.

To Lady Byron

Saturday Morning [21 June 1851]   Gt. C. Place

I am very much obliged by your kind note. Yr suggestion (made at Esher) has been already followed up by me – & is going on daily. – It does not give me any undue trouble or excitement. Faraday has kindly engaged to come & pass next Weddy evg with me, or purpose to give me <u>his</u> ideas on the subject. . . I hope in a few months to have a tolerably well expressed MS fit to submit to <u>yr</u> criticism.

The two doctors decided yesterday that on account of the <u>haemorrhages</u> about every 5th day, which necessarily result from the extensive <u>sloughing</u>, I must not at present leave Town.

I believe they are now quite satisfied that a favorable progress is going on, tho' of course such a case must be <u>slow</u>. – I feel much better on the whole.

I forgot if I mentioned that Faraday has both <u>spoken</u> & <u>written</u> to me in very high terms of Annabella, & also of Ralph.

To Annabella he has given a <u>Book</u>.

To Annabella

Sunday, 22 June [1851]

Dear Annabella. Papa has doubtless told you that my medical men do not just now think me in a state to be out of their sight.

It will please me very much if you will read some of Sir Harris' little Book, so as to be prepared for my examining you upon it. Do not try to read a great <u>quantity</u>, but let me find that you <u>completely</u> <u>study</u>, & <u>have</u> <u>at</u> <u>command</u> what you have read whether this be 6 pages or 20.

If you have not already written to Mr Faraday, already pray do so.

He is coming to spend Weddy evg with me. – yrs affectly

A.A.L.

To William, Lord Lovelace

Thursday, 24 July [1851]

Dearest L –. I am very glad of yr letter – & perhaps a <u>little</u> glad that you "<u>miss me</u>"!

It shows at least that I have not become irksome or odious to you. If you will <u>have patience yet</u> a <u>little longer,</u> you will <u>rejoice that you had</u> patience. –

Now as to my health: I do not agree with you that the progress is <u>slow</u>. When we consider that I have <u>not</u> been quite <u>2 months</u> under treatment, for a most serious complaint which had existed (more or less) for upward of a year, – I think we cannot call the present state other than <u>very</u> satisfactory. Not only is there an improvement in <u>nerves</u> & in general health which is obvious to everyone, & is most of all felt & known to myself,- but the <u>local</u> condition is no longer <u>vicious</u>. Dr Locock explained to me yesterday how threatening & how morbid it <u>had</u> been. –

He said that tho' now there is still an extensive deep seated <u>sore</u>, yet it is a <u>healthy</u> sore. . .

He [Dr Locock] is shortly going away, & will have to leave me under Dr <u>Cape's</u> care & this is one reason why very peculiar attention from him (Dr L) is right at <u>this time</u>, in order that he may leave Dr Cape in full possession of all that is desirable during the 5 or 6 weeks of Dr L's absence. <u>This transfer</u> to Dr Cape is to me extremely distressing & unpleasant, but it is inevitable.

To Lady Byron

[Undated Fragment]

The week <u>after</u> next, I hope the intended visit to you <u>may</u> be accomplished at last. And I am very anxious to see the <u>experi-ments</u> of Mr R's, [Rutter] if you can arrange that. I have been thinking about the little I gathered on the subject, & I am disposed to think that not only would Faraday be much disposed to give full attention to the facts, but that possibly important results might ensue from his doing so. – . . .

To Lady Byron

Saturday [2 August 1851]

I rather fear Sir D. Brewster will have left Town, but if not the idea is a good one, & I will see about it. Faraday is however much more (in my opinion) the right kind of mind, – & is far more of a <u>Philosopher</u> in many respects. Moreover Rutters' experiments are in Faraday's own peculiar line of subjects, & I think they are just the particular facts which Faraday has been looking out for. –

I believe I shall go down on Tuesdy evg. –

I feel pretty well today. What has occurred is nothing but a necessary part of the <u>cure</u>.

Ralph seemed very pleased to see me, & delighted with a kind message from his father.

But he was agitated, & much like a <u>blushing</u> <u>Miss</u>.

To Lady Byron

Sunday, 3 August [1851]   E.H.P.

In consequence of a note from Dr King, Sir D. B.[David Brewster] & I propose to reach Brighton by the <u>12 o'clock</u>, or else the <u>1 o'clock</u>, Mid-day train on <u>Tuesdy</u> & to be at Mr. Rutter's at <u>4 o'clock</u>. –

I have written to Dr King to say so, & have added that I think he, Mr R–, Sir D. B. & I might all adjourn together to an <u>evg</u> <u>meal</u> (under yr hospitable roof) about 7 o'clock; – & pass the evg in discussion.

Sometimes I am too ill in the <u>morg</u>, to take a journey. But we must hope this will not be so on Tuesday. . .

Sir D. B. is now <u>here</u>.

Dr Locock <u>gave</u> <u>me</u> <u>over</u> to Dr Cape yesterday morg – & his account in my presence to Dr Cape of what my state <u>had</u> been really made me <u>shudder</u> retrospectively. <u>You</u> had not seen me for 3 or 4 weeks, if you recollect . . . & I suppose I had altered much & rapidly. Dr L – said there was more <u>death</u> than <u>life</u> in my face, & that my <u>hands</u> were like "<u>Birds'</u> <u>claws.</u>"

He says I appeared to him to be <u>going</u> hourly & <u>rapidly</u> down the hill. . .

Dr Locock . . . wrote to Lovelace that he "<u>believed</u>" the case, "serious tho' it was," to be perfectly curable.

The plain fact is that he had as much <u>doubt</u> as hope, & feared it was just too late. – The <u>painless</u> nature of the case was nearly my destruction. I believe the <u>worst</u> cases are these painless ones. . .

D R LOCOCK PUT Ada back on laudanum, and she floated in and out of reality. The Great Exhibition was drawing to a close. The Royal Commission reported in November that over six million people visited the exhibit. Annabella sent Byron the floor plan and descriptions of the many exhibits. Ada, like all of her family and friends, had great hopes for the future of a world in which Babbage's "imagined mission" to build an Analytical Engine might materialize. Ada wrote many of her letters on Great Exhibition stationery. In the background Lady Byron was still encouraging (or pushing) Ada to perform more intellectual feats, but Ada was running out of money and time. Some of the letters Ada wrote at this time are particularly strange because of her description of herself as a general. She has now come to represent a computer language developed by the U.S. Department of Defense and named in her honor.

To Lady Byron

Sunday, 10 August [1851]

. . . They say that "coming events cast their shadows before."

May they not sometimes cast their lights before?

The gathering of the "drops" proceeds, & bright & beautiful drops they appear to me to be; – not tear drops, but sparkling with life & light! –

Whether any others will find the beauty in them that I do, remains to be seen. We cannot ourselves always judge of the impressions our own ideas & productions may make on others. . .

To Lady Byron

Saturday Morning, 16 August [1851]

. . . Will you be so kind to send me back the two Rutter M. S.'s, by the Bearer. I wrote to you by last evg's post, to say I would send for them today. –

The gathering of the drops proceeds – & is not even intermittent, altho sometimes the flow is greater, sometimes less, but never dried up. They are prismatic drops full of bright & various hues. . . I think almost (some of them) like the Magic Crystals of which they talk now-a-days. –

I think I am getting on well as to health, & that the flow of the drops contributes, & is sunatory. –

By the bye, Dr Cape said last time, that my complaint such as it was, must have injured my mind, & greatly impaired its power & its clearness; – because that for months previous, there had been as it were a continuous current drawn off from the Brain. – I often feel great confusion & difficulty in concentrating my ideas; & also as if I could only perceive one idea at a time. At other times I felt also as if I were dulled & indifferent. –

He tells me that death would have been preceded by total failure of mind; in short the successive fading first of everything human, & then everything vital! Give me a spasm to kill me at once, sooner than such a dreadful fate. I was (partially) dead there is no doubt; And I have come to life again. This is all very melancholy, but it might have been yet worse! –

All will yet be well. –

But what a fearful thing is an insidious painless disease, that undermines before one knows it. – Locock was very blamable in Febry. I believe that none of the things that have happened would have happened, – had my state been discovered! . . .

To Charles Babbage

Friday Morning, 22 August [1851]

Dear Babbage. I unfortunately forgot a very principal thing I had to say to you last evg, & which can be less well explained in writing. It is to ask you if you would be so very kind as to see a gentleman (one of the Leighs) on Tuesdy next at 11 o'clock, – who wants to sell to me, a Rifle & a pair of Pistols which he declares to have been my father's. –

He is in great distress, & obliged to sell everything he has, – . . . I have promised that no mention shall be made of his circumstances, in application to me. He writes that it is of the utmost moment to him to keep his affairs private.

It will be a great favor to us, if you will see him, – & see the articles, – & examine how far they are likely to be genuine, – & worth the price he may ask. –

I have written him a note to desire him to call on you on Tuesdy, but I shall not send it till I have yr consent. It is most unlucky I forgot this yesterday. – Yrs   A.L.

To Agnes Greig

Saturday, 29 August [1851][1]   E.H.P.

Dear Mrs Greig. I am miserable about Miss Wächter . . . Hawkins says she has a Cancer in the breast, which is beyond all hope – even from an operation. She is wholly unconscious, & thinks she has a little lump of no more importance than a Wart! – It is to me most afflicting to hear her speaking of the

<u>future</u>, just as usual; – unconscious of her horrible doom! –

Ask Annab: to show you my letter to her about Miss W. Annab: ought to be prepared for the sad misfortune.

We wish to <u>give</u> Annab: a <u>dress</u>; – I think a very nice silk dress; to be made up by a good Paris Milliner. Will you be so very kind as to manage this. She had better have what ever she likes best. – Could she not have a <u>low</u> dress; with also a <u>Polka</u> <u>of</u> <u>the</u> <u>same</u>, to make it a morning dress? –

This fate of Miss W is a dark <u>cloud</u> over us, & so it will be to you. – Very truly yrs   A.A. Lovelace

To Lady Byron

Monday, 1 September [1851]

I think that Ralph's visit has been as delightful to <u>him,</u> as it has been agreeable to others; – & I hope he will generally come on Satdy. He is like a gush of warm rays from the <u>rising</u> sun, dancing & revelling in their own growing radiance and <u>coming</u> <u>glories</u>! –

I begin to feel that I <u>am</u>, & <u>can</u> be, of <u>use</u> to Ralph. He <u>lis-</u> <u>tens</u> to me, & pays more attention to many considerations which I suggest, – than I could have hoped or expected.

And I <u>do</u> a little hope that I may have some <u>guiding</u> & <u>sug-</u> <u>gestive</u> weight with him. – No one can be <u>so</u> fit to catch a <u>Comet</u>. <u>Set</u> <u>a</u> <u>Genius</u> <u>to</u> <u>warn</u> <u>a</u> <u>Genius</u>. And set a <u>Byron</u> to rule a <u>Byron</u>! – For Ralph is a Byron, – three-quarters at least. There is a curious sympathy growing up between him & me. – I may be wrong, but something seems to tell me that I can <u>save</u> Ralph a great deal; & it is perhaps this protective sympathy, which makes him so very interesting to me. –

Well, – we shall see! – You know you are to <u>live</u> to see at any rate <u>some</u> great changes. – Whenever you are ill, I shall always say to you the one word:

"<u>Remember</u>"

The "drops" are flowing fast & thick. Do not suppose, (because you <u>hear</u> no more of them <u>quite</u> <u>just</u> <u>yet</u>), – that <u>that</u>

stream can be stilled. It is a very steady even current, that flows from an <u>infinite</u> source. –

When you <u>do</u> see & hear, – I wish it to be in order that you may feel <u>certainty</u>, not merely <u>hope</u>. I wish to present to you not more <u>indications</u>; but a certain solid <u>reality</u>, upon which to <u>judge</u>, rather than to <u>hope</u>. –

You have lived upon <u>hope</u> long enough; – for many a long year indeed! –

Have patience (you were an "Ass" you know when I was but 5 years old), yet a <u>little</u> longer. And perhaps the time may come when you maybe permitted to be something <u>more</u> than an Ass.

But prick yr long ears as yet, & don't try to get rid of them. – <u>Be</u> a donkey still! –

P. S. This is a dreadfully <u>mischievous</u> letter. – But you <u>must</u> forgive it.

To Lady Byron

Wednesday, 15 October [1851]   London

I have been very unwell, & am getting better again; But still everything seems difficult & troublesome. The last "<u>drop</u>" today is <u>serene</u>, (which is more than I think the <u>writer</u> of it is).

<u>Life</u> <u>is</u> <u>so</u> <u>difficult</u>. I must say that the <u>least</u> difficult part of existence I have ever known, is the <u>flow</u> <u>of</u> <u>the</u> <u>drops</u>. The only thing I have ever done in my life, which did not give me the idea & feeling of striving after something beyond my grasp!. . .

I wonder if <u>any</u> one personally laments Mrs Leigh?– A sad end, to a sad life. I suppose a <u>bad</u> life is generally a <u>sad</u> one.

But I do dread that horrible <u>struggle</u>, which I fear is in the Byron blood. I don't think we die easy. – <u>I</u> should like to "drop" off, gently, but quickly, some 30 or 40 years hence.

To Lady Byron

1 1/2 o'clock, Tuesday [October 28 1851]

Maria has given £1 to William. I have not £5 in my purse. –

I am a good deal better & refreshed, & had a tolerable night. <u>Many</u> thanks for yr letter this morg; but I feel quite incapable of <u>shifting</u> <u>about</u> to different places at present & of going to <u>Inns</u> particularly.

You are <u>mistaken</u> in <u>one</u> thing; it is not my <u>inner</u> life. Alas! but my <u>outward</u> life, which is wearing me. If I could follow the <u>inner</u> life more fully, it would be well. But a thousand fatigues & worries <u>tear</u> my wretched nervous system to pieces. – I never have peace for 3 <u>days</u>. Somebody is <u>ill</u>, or somebody is <u>coming</u>; – or somebody is something or other. Those eternal <u>arrangements,</u> without which life cannot <u>go</u> <u>on</u> in any way; <u>crowd</u> on me at times; – & have done so lately to a pernicious extent. I wish I <u>could</u> <u>rest</u> <u>on</u> <u>my</u> <u>perch</u>, in <u>solitude</u>, for even a fortnight; – provided I were not pursued by this medium of the past, by the unceasing <u>dropping</u> <u>on</u> <u>the</u> <u>stone</u> which drives me nearly mad. –

And yet no <u>one</u> person or thing is the cause. It is the combination of the whole. . . .

To Lady Byron

Wednesday Afternoon, 29 October [1851]   London

Some of the conversation between us this morg on general topics, has been like a genial <u>watering</u> to a certain seed which is sprouting, (but as yet has not reached the <u>surface</u> of the soil)! –

If I <u>could</u> ever help to give the <u>despots</u> a <u>shove</u>, I should certainly feel that I <u>had</u> <u>not</u> <u>lived</u> <u>in</u> <u>vain</u>. –

Your hope, and <u>expectation</u> almost, that such a day may arrive, gives me great encouragement.

I think, when you <u>do</u> by and bye, see certain productions, you will not even despair of my being <u>in</u> <u>time</u> an Autocrat, in my own way; before whose <u>marshalled</u> <u>regiments</u> some of the iron rulers of the earth may even have to give way ! –

But of <u>what</u> <u>materials</u> my <u>regiments</u> are to consist, I do not at present divulge. I have however the hope that they will be most <u>harmoniously</u> disciplined troops; – consisting of vast <u>num-bers</u> & marching in irresistible power to the sound of <u>Music</u>. Is not this very mysterious? Certainly <u>my</u> troops must consist of <u>numbers</u>, or they can have no existence at all, & would cease to be the particular sort of troops in question. –

But then, <u>what</u> are these <u>numbers</u>? There is a riddle.

20.
The Dragon and the Rainbow
[1851-1852]

> I feel persuaded that you do <u>seriously</u> intend . . . to exact
> all furys.
>
> Ada

> The greatest of all blots on human nature appears to me the
> conduct of civilized man to his <u>un</u>civilized brethren. . .
>
> Ada

M OST OF THE TIME Ada was confined to the sofa at her
home in London. When she felt strong enough, she went
out for short excursions in an invalid chair and could see Marble
Arch just a block away. Mrs Greig came to help, but Ada still
had to attend to family problems. William was very busy with
the duties of a lord and spent most of his time at East Horsley
Towers, involved with his many agricultural and architectural
duties. He was giving a hunt breakfast at Horsley, and Ada
needed to find a hostess for him. Though William had not seen
Lady Byron since June, Ada still dutifully wrote to her mother,
who was ill at Esher.

Byron was sending home tales of his exploits, and Ada was
disturbed by his descriptions. Furthermore, Byron was not sure
whether a career in the Navy was for him. Ralph contracted
scarlet fever. Annabella sent delightful riddles to her mother
and brother Ralph. Money problems simmered in the background, yet Ada tried to keep her balance, at least for the children's sake, and some sense of humor.

To Lady Byron

Thursday [13 Nov 1851]   London

. . . We sent you yesterday a letter from Byron. There is
another (to Ralph), which you will have in time. It is clear that
he has written some letters which we have never recd.

In the letter to Ralph, he gives an account of an engagement they had with the Indians, in which they killed 2 or 3
hundred Indians, & burnt their village. They only had 2 men
slightly wounded. The Indians had murdered some English, &
refused reparation. I suppose the Daphne was sent to demand
it.

What a very odd mind Byron's is! He is delighted with the
Scalps, & wanted to get some to bring home!

. . . I am now nearly confined to the Sofa, & various new
measures are going on. It seems to be a most obstinate case. But
then, I have moved so much, too much. They seemed surprised
that on the whole I am not more gloomy, or else savage . . .

To Byron, Lord Ockham

Saturday 15 November 1851   6 Gt Cumberland Place

Dearest Byron. . . I now send you several Illustrated News, containing articles that will interest you.

My health is at present very delicate and infirm, & I am
obliged to be chiefly in Town; for surgical advice, – & to lie up
on the Sofa almost entirely.

I am rather appalled at yr idea of bringing home scalps! I
hope you have not become quite a barbarian. ever most
affectly yrs   A.A. Lovelace

To Annabella

Friday, 21 November [1851]   London

Dear Annabella. Ralph is ill at Brighton with the Scarlet Fever.
Pray write to him. I hope he is going on well, but I fear he suffers a good deal. He was delirious at one time, & I felt rather

anxious. But I had a better account of him, by the <u>Electric Tele-graph</u>. And this morg I heard again by post.

Have you attended to <u>Sprite</u>? He ought to be kept as <u>warm</u> as possible.

I expect Mrs Burr next week. The doctors keep me almost entirely now to the <u>Sofa</u>, which ought to have been done months ago.

You really <u>must</u> practise <u>leaping</u>. Do speak to the groom about it. I felt myself <u>blush</u> when I read yr account.

But really, it <u>is</u> a nuisance not to be able to take fences. Yrs affectly   A.L.

I am glad we have escaped the <u>Scalps</u>.

To Annabella

Saturday, 22 November [1851]

Dear Annab: I have sent yr very annoying little vignettes to <u>Ralph</u>. It made me laugh. I send you the account I recd of him last evg. . .

Papa will be down at Horsley tomorrow afternoon. I showed him yr letter this morng, and he was <u>very</u> <u>grave</u> respecting the consequences of having too many pets, & his gardeners' time being taken up in <u>parrot-hunting</u>. I had not foreseen this view of the case, & I might have judged wise to with-hold the communication. But it made me laugh so much, that I thought <u>he</u> would laugh too.

I am afraid too that he did not quite approve of the lamentation over the <u>oaks</u>, (which I should certainly allow to remain there). Papa considers that they take a great liberty in shrouding the <u>Tower,</u> & he is not pleased with anyone who dares to defend them. You know that the <u>Tower</u> is decidedly Papa's <u>first born</u>, & dearer to him than kith or kin or life itself.

You must take my place on Satdy, at the <u>Hunt</u> <u>Breakfast</u>, and make yourself as agreeable & useful as you can instead of me. Papa will want you with him, to receive his guests as they come in. You are quite old enough & experienced enough, & it is also good practise for your probable hereafter. If you marry, you will be the better wife; & if you <u>don't</u> marry young, why you will be the more useful to <u>me</u>, for I can tell you I mean (unless you <u>escape</u> by marrying) to make a Slave of you, & that you shall be my Vice-queen in everything.

To Annabella

28 November [1851]

Dear Annabella. Mrs Burr sends her love to you, & is very busy about her <u>fancy</u> <u>Ball</u> & we are deciding on the weighty matter of a dress for you. You are I believe to be a young Spanish Lady in <u>Mantilla</u> &c. And as the dress is entirely <u>black,</u> & not at all gay, we do think it may meet with yr demure approbation. We <u>had</u> an idea of yr being the Infante Isabella (daughter of <u>the</u> Isabella of Castille) but we found her dress so hideous, so like a <u>Hag</u> in <u>armour,</u> that we gave it up in horror. You know Papa is <u>condemned</u> to this ball & considers himself a <u>martyr</u>, especially as it is intended he shall be in his <u>Albanian</u> dress, (in which he is most striking looking & attractive). . .

Will you tell Papa that Dr Locock has been today, & gives a <u>decidedly</u> better account, – & that he attributes the improvement to my very quiet life & abscence of moving.

Do not forget this, for Papa was a good deal discouraged at what Dr Locock told him, at the same time we must not hope too much yet. Very Affectly yrs   A.L.

To William, Lord Lovelace

Tuesday [December 1851]

I hope you will not <u>disappoint</u> the Burrs about going to their Ball Jan 8th.

It is an old promise that A – is to go, but they reckon on you most particularly, & Mrs B [Burr] has begged me to use all my persuasion. The <u>Camarrons</u> are expected. Annab: is to be a <u>Spanish</u> Lady with <u>Mantilla</u> &c. This is <u>Wilkinson's</u> wish, who

thinks she will be irresistibly pretty & sparkling, in that cos-
tume, which will particularly suit her.

If you <u>have</u> refused Mrs B, (which however I can scarcely
believe possible), pay respect.

It would also be a pleasure to you to see how handsome and
admired <u>yr</u> <u>daughter</u> will be! . . .

To Lady Byron

Sunday Night, [25 January 1852]

You will perhaps be <u>uneasy</u> about me if I don't write tonight. I
have a rather bad <u>cold</u>, which does no good. I am not so very
<u>weak</u>. I <u>can</u> crawl; tho' with difficulty & terribly <u>bent.</u> But I am
full of a <u>malaise</u> that is indescribable. . .

Babbage is so uneasy at the state of things, & at this frightful liability, that he has (for his own sake & satisfaction) been
consulting <u>Sir</u> <u>J.</u> <u>South</u> about me, who thinks that some further
advice should perhaps be had, unless there is more decided
reason shortly, to be satisfied. . .

I consider that, tho wretchedly uncomfortable & shattered,
I am <u>better</u> than one could have hoped. But more downhearted
& less hopeful. Still, I have no thing that the doctors <u>call</u> low
spirits. They say most people <u>cry</u>. . .

To Lady Byron

Saturday, 6 March [1852]

It is is even some little encouragement to find that you have
<u>some</u> <u>faith</u> in <u>my</u> <u>want</u> <u>of</u> <u>faith</u>! – But I had better not write
another long letter. The last gave me a restless night . . .

Will you give my love to Ralph, & tell him that the greatest
of all blots on human nature appears to me to be the conduct of
civilized man to his <u>un</u>civilized brethren . . .

🙶

A T THE BEGINNING OF 1852, the Lovelaces' financial problems worsened. William had not received the payments Lady Byron had promised on the note he had signed for the repairs that he was doing at Great Cumberland Place. Ada needed nurses day and night to take care of her.

Lady Byron informed her attorney, Dr Lushington (who lived at the Lovelaces' Ockham estate), that she would consider paying the debts if Ada supplied a list of the debts owed. When Lushington went to see Ada in April, he was shocked. Ada looked much worse than he had imagined. She was frail, bedridden, and on drugs to relieve the agony. Lushington received from Ada a detailed account of the money she owed. Lady Byron reviewed the list, questioning a hairdresser's bill, and suggested that Ada use a mesmerist instead of opium.

Lady Byron was writing one thing to Ada and another to Lushington about the issue of a new rector for Ockham. Ada wanted her old friend Reverend Gamlen to be appointed the new rector. Despite the appearance that her mother supported the selection, Lushington wrote to Lady Byron: "why won't you let Gamlen come here?" Even stranger is that Robert Crosse, the brother of Ada's alleged lover and gambling accomplice, John Crosse, was appointed rector instead of Gamlen.

In discussing Ada's financial obligations, Lushington wrote Lady Byron on 30 April that an unauthorized use was being made of Ada's name for "motives of gain," and powers had been delegated, but without Ada's knowledge. What that cryptic reference meant and to whom he was specifically referring are not known. Charles Babbage was Ada's executor.

Lady Byron had not visited her daughter for months. On 19 and 21 May, Lady Byron paid in total £2800 to cover Ada's obligations. Lady Byron stated specifically that none of the money covered any gambling obligations. In exchange for the money Ada agreed to see her mother. Lady Byron did not like the way Dr Locock was handling Ada's case and pressured her to hire other physicians, thereby minimizing Locock's influence. Dr Locock wrote to Ada, "why won't they leave us alone?"

Ada's support system was slowly being eroded by Lady Byron.

To Lady Byron

[Early 1852]

I have heard a deal about Cannabis from Sir G Wilkinson who is very familiar with it. It is not a thing to trifle with, but the effects . . . are <u>very</u> <u>definite</u>. I have got back to my old friend <u>Opium</u> & thankful enough. It seems mesmerism is powerless when I have my <u>real</u> pains, & not merely some slight cramps. . .

To Lady Byron

[Undated <u>Monday</u> <u>Evening</u>]

If I had a little less <u>brains,</u> I should & would be a good Catholic, & cling to that <u>certainty</u> which I do long for. However I don't wish to be without my brains, tho' they doubtless interfere with a blind faith which would be very comfortable.

When I find that not only one's whole being can become merely one living <u>agony</u>, but that in that state, & <u>after</u> it, ones <u>mind</u> is gone more or less, – the impression of <u>mortality</u> becomes appalling; & not of mortality merely, but of mortality in an <u>agony</u> & a <u>struggle</u>. . .

The more one suffers, the more appalling is it to feel that it may all be only in order to "<u>die</u> <u>like</u> <u>a</u> <u>dog</u>" as they say. . .

To Lady Byron

Sunday, 28 March [1852]

. . . My love to Ralph, & tell him I am sorry he has such a sick <u>Mama</u> & <u>Grandmama</u>, both! –

P.S. I can't help telling you of a funny speech of <u>Babbage's</u> to me just now. He said; "Why! you are a capital subject for an illness. <u>As</u> <u>patient</u> <u>as</u> <u>if</u> <u>you</u> <u>had</u> <u>true</u> <u>religion</u>"! He knows I am writing you word of this. Is it a <u>Concept</u> or not? –

To Byron, Lord Ockham

8 April 1852   6 Great Cumberland Place

Dearest Byron... We are very much disappointed at not hearing from you... If you have recd <u>our</u> <u>numerous</u> letters to you, during the last year, you will be aware that I have been in bad health. I regret to say that this has been prolonged, & that I am quite an invalid – obliged to live in 2 rooms on the ground floor, & only able to go out in a Wheel Chair (with <u>Indian</u> <u>Rubber</u> Wheels)... They give me every hope of a recovery, but I am in great fear that I may still be a cripple on yr return to land, – which would be a sad distress to me during the few weeks you would probably remain, I should wish to be strong & <u>active</u>.

Mrs Greig, who has been very kind is nursing me. <u>Annabella</u> grows much, & develops a wonderful <u>genius</u> (nothing less) for drawing & painting.

<u>Ralph</u> <u>is</u> very amiable & much improved in everything. Grandmama is very unwell down at Brighton. She has had a very bad winter as to health.

Old <u>Sprite</u> & dear old <u>Nelson</u>, alive & well. Ever, Dearest Byron, Most Affectly yrs

Augusta Ada Lovelace

To Byron, Lord Ockham

Friday, 7 May 1852   London

My dearest Son. I am quite a cripple & an <u>invalid</u>...

I am sadly distressed to think that during the few weeks <u>you</u> are likely to be with us, you will have a <u>sick</u> <u>Mama</u>, whom I fear a handsome active young fellow like you, will regard as a bore. Yet I think you are too good, & too aware of my <u>affection</u> <u>for</u> <u>you</u> & of my anxiety to see you again to be otherwise than my <u>affectionate</u> <u>son,</u> whether I am ill or well. <u>I</u> resign myself to my present state & I trust will others.

Your most <u>affectionate</u> <u>Mother</u>

To Lady Byron

[Undated]

. . . There is nothing that can be very painful to <u>you</u>, that I have to communicate. Nothing can either shock, or startle, or alarm you; – tho' to <u>me</u> there is much that is most harassing & anxious.

If I were in any <u>urgent</u> way in difficulty or compromised, I would <u>at</u> <u>once</u> & without any instant delay tell you so, & beg to be rescued.

A year ago I would have <u>died</u> – literally & really sooner than owned to you or have asked you for even the <u>merest</u> <u>trifle</u>. So that there is <u>indeed</u> a difference in my feelings, at all events.

I have an earnest wish to use my <u>brains,</u> & I feel as if I could do so <u>now</u> <u>that</u> I <u>am</u> <u>an</u> <u>invalid,</u> – (were I but in ordinarily favourable circumstances). The freedom from <u>outward</u> <u>inter-</u><u>ruptions</u> more than balances <u>sickness</u>.

To Lady Byron

10 o'clock Monday morg [undated]

I think you would like to know how I have slept after my <u>ac-</u><u>couchement</u> <u>of</u> <u>the</u> <u>Dragon</u>, (which considering its <u>adamanative</u> nature was certainly no trifle).

I have had a very good night, & much less pain yesterday than is usual, on the other hand there is a greater than usual discharge, which accounts for the lessened pain.

I am much relieved to have told you, the Dragon, <u>at</u> <u>last</u>. I had felt that I was not acting quite fairly towards <u>you</u> while it was reserved. If one asks & accepts the assistance of anyone, under certain circumstances that is, – it seems wrong to keep from them the point of most importance. . .

I am anxious to see you after the communication of the Dragon, – that I may be finally satisfied <u>you</u> won't devour me.

To Lady Byron

[Undated]

I am so very glad to have seen you at last that I can't help saying so. . . . I was very <u>anxious</u> about our meeting. I cannot endure any longer the past state of things, & if the sort of <u>glacier</u> which has somehow been accumulating <u>can</u> be thawed why <u>better</u> <u>later</u> <u>than</u> <u>never</u>.

I think I had better almost say to you anything & even <u>any</u> <u>disagreeable</u> thing than <u>nothing</u>! . . .

To Lady Byron

Tuesday, 1 June 1852

In yr last, 3 or 4 days ago, you say, "<u>There</u> <u>is</u> <u>much</u> <u>virtue</u> <u>in</u> <u>plain</u> <u>speaking</u>." But on the other hand: <u>What</u> <u>is</u> <u>once</u> <u>said</u> <u>never</u> <u>can</u> <u>be</u> <u>unsaid</u>, & <u>this</u> is a formidable drawback from resolutions to be perfectly frank. It is a <u>kill</u> or <u>cure</u> & it requires much courage to run the risk (if one sees it) of <u>kill</u>, instead of <u>cure</u>!

At all events there is always imminent danger in plain speaking, when under the influence of <u>excited</u> & <u>passionate</u> feelings, & before reflection has time to interpose. It is of course less so when there has been ample time for consideration.

I feel persuaded that you do <u>seriously</u> intend what you have however put in a rather <u>jocose</u> way & viz: to exact all <u>furys</u>.

There are unhappily <u>associations</u> now connected specifically with <u>you</u> extremely painful to me, & which have weighed hard on me throughout my illness, so that I cannot but feel some agitation in first seeing you. And yet I desire <u>extremely</u>, perhaps beyond everything else that we <u>should</u> meet. – . . .

AND LADY BYRON DID INDEED exact all furies. On 11 June Ada notified her mother that she had given a diamond parure to John Crosse to pawn. Lady Byron retrieved the parure of diamonds for £800 plus £100 interest. Ada agreed to her mother's suggestion to see the mesmerist on 17 July; there was no improvement in Ada's health.

Just at this time, William discovered that John Crosse was a married man, though Crosse had never mentioned that fact or brought his wife to social engagements. That was a severe breach of etiquette at the time. When William confronted Crosse with this information, he hemmed and hawed. Crosse went to visit Ada on 4 August, and once again she gave him the diamond parure, which she did not remember doing until 11 October.

During August, Henry Phillips, the son of Thomas Phillips, R.A., who had painted two famous portraits of Lord Byron, painted a portrait of Ada seated at the piano. Ada played duets on the pianoforte with Annabella. She was pleased to see Byron home from sea and asked Lady Byron to have Ralph come home from DeFellenberg's school in Switzerland. He returned home at the end of August.

Ada told William she wanted to be buried next to her father and asked him to inform Colonel Wildman and make the proper arrangements. Babbage came to visit on 12 August, and Ada, suspecting the doctors' prognosis of the case that came from the doctors the next day, pushed a letter into his hands.

Babbage later stated that Ada had no control of her house or life from that day forward. I agree with Babbage and have only included one letter after that date because the content of the letters after 12 August is suspect. Both Babbage and John Crosse were barred from seeing Ada again. Lady Byron took complete control and moved into the house on 20 August.

To Lady Byron

Sunday Night [Early August 1852]

You must be prepared to see a <u>very</u> <u>handsome</u> <u>young</u> <u>man</u>! No longer a Boy! Tall & stout, the voice formed & manly; but really he is so splendidly <u>handsome</u>. I am quite amazed!

He was much agitated at meeting <u>me</u>, & quite upset at

<u>alteration</u> which he remarked; altho' he controlled himself in a very manly way.

<u>No</u> want of <u>feeling</u> in him. Quite the contrary. And indeed he seems to be all one could most desire.

To Byron, Lord Ockham

9 August 1852

My Dear Child. We have had so little conversation of late that I had best write to <u>you</u> in place of Papa. . . I have felt <u>better</u> & <u>stronger</u> all of today than for many weeks, (or indeed months past). . .

I think <u>yr</u> arrival has given me quite a new life – especially as you seem to me to be <u>all</u> <u>I</u> <u>could</u> <u>wish</u>.

I am so thankful to see you again & I feel myself full of hope for the future. I shall be so glad to see your dear face again. . . Yr Affectionate   <u>Mother</u>

To Lady Byron

[Early August 1852]

The two M.D.'s came. I like Dr West very well, & he is so gentle in <u>manipulating</u> that he causes as little pain as possible.

Lovelace saw them afterwards, & they seem to have made him <u>fully</u> <u>aware</u> of the grave nature of the case. So much so, that Lovelace himself has expressed the hope I will leave nothing <u>unsettled,</u> that I might wish to settle. He says the doctors evidently spoke with much grave seriousness; nor could he in any way elicit <u>one</u> <u>word</u> of positive hope or encouragement.

Tomorrow morg don't come, till after 2 o'clock. From <u>two</u> <u>to</u> <u>five</u> will suit.

To Lady Byron

[Early August]

Tomorrow at 12 o'clock will be best. . .

For I shall <u>never</u> get thro' all I have to do unless I have

more leisure. Lovelace <u>will</u> not let me alone, tho' I often send
him away. But he returns like a <u>dog</u> to his master.

I shall be quite glad when he goes away.

To Charles Babbage

12 August 1852   6 Great Cumberland Place

Dear Babbage. In the event of my sudden decease before the
completion of a Will I write you this letter to entreat that you
will <u>as</u> <u>my</u> Executor attend to the following directions; 1stly you
will apply to my mother for the sum of £<u>600</u>; to be employed by
you as I have elsewhere privately directed you. 2ndly you will
go to the bankers Messrs Drummond's and obtain from them
my account & Balance (if any) and also all of my <u>old</u> <u>drafts</u>.

3rdly You will dispose of all papers and property deposited
by me with you, as you may think proper <u>after</u> <u>full</u> <u>examination</u>.

Any <u>balance</u> in money at my bankers you will add to the
£600 above named to be similarly employed.

In the fullest reliance on yr faithful performance of the
above, I am Most sincerely & affectionately yours
                                    Augusta Ada Lovelace

To Lady Byron

[Middle August 1852]

Tolerably comfortable <u>now</u>, & being let down <u>very</u> <u>easy</u>. I begin
to understand <u>Death</u>; which is going on quietly & gradually
every minute, & will never be a thing of one particular <u>moment</u>.

I shall send for you at any minute, but we have still a <u>little</u>
<u>time</u> before us. I want <u>Ralph</u> back.

To Mary Wilson

18 August 1852   6 Great Cumberland Place

Wilson: I rely on <u>you</u> to keep all quiet & right for my comfort
during the few months or weeks which in all probability remain
to me, and you will without delay receive from me a <u>token</u> of

this confidence. You have been a faithfull & attached servant to me thro' Life & I wish to place this upon <u>record</u> while I can.

I hope that God will yet grant me a certain time in order to fulfill all I wish but in case this should not be so, I lose not a moment in writing my present note to you. I hope that whenever your own hour comes you will feel all the <u>trust</u> and gratitude & thankfulness which I do in a <u>Higher</u> <u>Power</u>. Yrs

<u>Augusta</u> <u>Ada</u> <u>Lovelace</u>

ON 19 AUGUST Ada requested Charles Dickens to come and read the death scene of the little boy from *Dombey and Son*: "Now the boat was out at sea, but gliding smoothly on. And now there was a shore before him. . . The golden ripple on the wall came back again, & nothing else stirred in the room. The old, old fashion! The fashion that came in with our first garments, and will last unchanged until our race has run its course, and the wide firmament is rolled up like a scroll. The old, old fashion – Death! Oh, thank God, all who see it, for that older fashion yet, of Immortality!"[1] Dickens walked out of her room, impressed and touched by Ada's courage and bravery. He was the last non-family member, other than Lady Byron's friends and physicians, to see her alive. Lady Byron moved into Great Cumberland Place the next day.

On 1 September at Lady Byron's prompting, Ada confessed her sins to William. He walked out of the room devastated and remained silent about what was revealed to him until his death. William's handwriting was normally like a pigeon's scrawl, and yet, in very clear handwriting he wrote that if he was absent it should be known that "Lady Byron is the Mistress of My House." And Ada was no longer "<u>Our</u> <u>Bird.</u>"

After she dismissed Mary Wilson, Ada's personal maid, Lady Byron sat, very virtuously, at Ada's side believing that Ada's suffering was a pathway to paradise. Dr King wrote Ada, at Lady Byron's suggestion, a several-page sermon on the virtue of suffering as a means of absolving sin.

Ada's suffering continued for almost three more months. She did not die until 27 November 1852 at 9:30 p.m. Ada had asked William to arrange for her burial next to her father. The father she had never known in life would now be her companion in death.

Ada was laid to rest next to her father on 3 December in the small church near Newstead, at Hucknall Torkard. Lady Byron did not attend Ada's funeral. Ada's coffin was covered in violet velvet; the handles were solid silver; and at the head and foot of the coffin were massive silver coronets. Upon the lid was an escutcheon of the Earl of Lovelace with the Lovelace motto: LABOR IPSE VOLUPTAS (LABOUR IS ITS OWN REWARD).

Ada asked that this sonnet that she wrote be inscribed on her tombstone:

The Rainbow

Bow down in hope, in thanks, all ye who mourn
Where'en that peerless arch of radiant hues
Surpassing earthly tints, – the storm subdued,
Of nature's strife and tears 'tis heaven-born
To soothe the sad, the sinning and the forlorn;
A lovely loving token; to infuse;
The hope, the faith, that Pow'r divine endures
With latent good the woes by which we're torn.
'Tis like sweet repentance of the skies,
To beckon all but the sense of sin opprest,
Revealing harmony from tears and sighs;
A pledge, – that deep implanted in the breast
A hidden light may burn that never dies,
But burst thro' storms in purest hues exprest.

Appendix I

Glossary

Analog: a smoothly changing variable or indicator such as the hands of a clock. Singing is analog. For additional information read Anthony Hyman's *The Computer in Design*, Studio Vista, London, 1973.

Digital: something in discrete, separate lumps. Morse code and on-off switches are digital.

Objectivism: experiment, reason, digital skills, scientific tradition. For more information read George Lakoff's *Metaphors We Live By*, University of Chicago, 1986, readily available in paperback.

Subjectivism: imagination, "higher truth," metaphor, poetical tradition, also in Lakoff.

Poetical Science: the integration of poetical and scientific skills. Ada's prescription for science, which applies to general analysis of information as well.

Quantum: referring to a concept of modern physics. The concept highlights how the subjectivity of the observer affects the objectivity of the observation (see Chapter 8 of this book). Some people have extended this concept to mean that everything is an illusion. For additional information on this subject, and one of the most thoughtful analyses I have read of quantum theory, read Danah Zohar's *The Quantum Self*, Quill/Morrow, 1990.

FOOTNOTES

Introduction

1. Zohar, Donna, *The Quantum Self*, Quill/Morrow, 1990.
2. Lakoff, George, *The Metaphors We Live By*, University of Chicago, 1986. The ideas in this paragraph represent my understanding of this book.
3. Marchand, Leslie, *Lord Byron, Selected Letters and Journals*, Harvard University Press, 1982, p. 65.
4. Marchand, Leslie, *Byron, A Portrait*, John Murray, 1971, p. 171.
5. Marchand, op.cit., *Letters*, p. 109.
6. Moore, Doris Langley, *The Late Lord Bryron*, J. P. Lippincott, 1961, p. 233.
7. Elwin, Malcolm, *Lord Byron's Family*, John Murray, 1975, p. 131.

Chapter 7 - [1841]

1. Hyman, Anthony, *Charles Babbage, Pioneeer of the Computer*, Oxford, 1982, p. 185.

2. This is the first line of Byron's *Childe Harold*.

3. Holmes, Richard, *Coleridge, Early Visions*, Viking, 1989, p. 1.

Chapter 12 - [1843]

1. Brooks, F. P. Jr., "No Silver Bullet: Essence and Accidents of Software Engineering." *Computer* 20, 4 (April 1987), pp. 10-19.

2. Baggi, Dennis, "Computer-Generated Music." *Computer* 24, 7 (July 1991), p. 6.

3. Parnas, D. L., and H. Wuerges, "Response to Undesired Events in Software Systems." *Proceedings of the 2nd International Conference on Software Engineering*, 13-15 October 1976, pp. 437-446.

4. The immense importance of this capability can be illustrated by imagining the work required to add to a manually maintained and already page set telephone directory a block of fifty new names beginning with "A." Such is the task of making changes to software systems if facilities like the *Ada* language are not used as separate concerns.

5. Dubbey, J. M., *The Mathematical Work of Charles Babbage*, Cambridge University Press, 1978, p. 211.

6. British Library Add MSS 37197-215, 14 June 1857.

7. *Charles Babbage and His Calculating Engines, Selected Writings of Charles Babbage*, edited by Phillip and Emily Morrison, Dover Publications, New York, 1961, from the reprint of *Passages*, p. 68.

8. Op.cit, p. 142.

9. *A Computer Perspective, Background to the Computer Age,* The Office of Charles Eames, from the Introduction by I. Bernard Cohen, p. 7.

10. Beer, Stafford, *Pebbles to Computers, The Thread*, Oxford University Press, 1986, p. 89.

Chapter 18 - [1851]

1. Marchand, L., *Portrait*, op.cit., p. 52.

Chapter 20 - [1852]

1. Dickens, Charles, *Dombey and Son*, Everyman Edition, 1997, pp. 220-221.

ANNOTATED BIBLIOGRAPHY

The purpose of this bibliography is to provide a reliable starting place for the reader whose interest might be peaked by some of the characters or the background of the story. The following lists contain only a fraction of the primary and secondary sources I have read. All the letters in this book are from primary sources, unless noted. Specific quotations from published books, secondary sources, are cited in the above footnotes. Anyone wanting to quote the primary sources in this book must cite this book and not the original sources that this book is derived from; that way mistakes can be easily traced. Where quotations of more than 100 words are used, the writer in print and electronic media must apply for permission to copyright owners. For the convenience of scholars who wish to consult the primary sources that I have used, the following information is included:

Primary Sources:

1. Lovelace-Byron Papers, Bodleian Library, Oxford University (catalogued by Mary Clapinson. Catalog is found in Room 132). All letters in this book are dated and addressed so that they can be easily found in the catalog.

2. Somerville Papers, Bodleian Library, Oxford University (also found in Room 132). The files used were SP 206, 355, 367, 369.

3. Babbage's correspondence is found at the British Library, London. All letters from Ada to Babbage are quoted and can be found in: Additional MSS-37189: 281. Add MSS 37190: 386-7. Add MSS 37191: 87-8, 127, 134, 343-4, 532, 566-568, 572, 591, 632, 633-634, 691-2. Add MSS 37192: 75, 126, 129, 237, 278, 335, 337, 339, 342, 348, 349, 355, 357, 360, 362, 364, 370, 379, 382, 386, 388, 390, 393, 399, 401-3, 407, 414, 422, 429. Add MSS 37193: 132, 134, 176, 228, 232, 238, 239, 252, 257, 259, 263, 286, 287, 550. Add MSS 37194: 14, 176, 184, 196, 203, 207, 214, 230, 232, 237, 250, 252, 256, 309, 317, 334, 358, 361, 363, 415, 430, 438, 444, 532. An additional letter was from a private collector.

4. Wentworth Bequest, British Library, London.

Secondary Sources:

1. *Scientific Memoirs*, Selections from The Transactions of Foreign Academies and Learned Societies and from Foreign Journals Edited by Richard Taylor, F.S.A., Vol III London: 1843, Article XXIX. *Sketch of the Analytical Engine invented by* Charles Babbage *Esq. By* L.F. Menabrea, *of Turin, Officer of the Military Engineers*. [From the Bibliothèque Universelle de Génève, No. 82, October 1842].

2. Additional letters are from an article written by Cornelia Crosse in the *Argosy*, November 1869.

BOOKS ABOUT ADA, CHARLES BABBAGE, AND HISTORY OF COMPUTERS

Malcolm Elwin's *Lord Byron's Family,* John Murray, 1975, and Doris Langley Moore's *Ada, the Countess of Lovelace*, John Murray, 1977, are good places to begin reading about Ada and her family. Velma and Harry Huskey's article, *Lady Lovelace and Charles Babbage*, found in the *Annals of the History of Computing,* Volume 2, No. 4, October 1980, is an excellent introduction. In 1986, Joan Baum's *The*

Calculating Passion of Ada Byron was published by Archon Books. Baum began the task of rectifying the new myth about Ada – that she did not write the Notes describing the Analytical Engine and was merely Babbage's secretary.

There are several biographies of Babbage; the best is Anthony Hyman's *Charles Babbage, Pioneer of the Computer*, Oxford, 1982. Charles Babbage's *Passages from the Life of a Philosopher*, his autobiography, published by Longman Green, 1864, is a gem, and the most important excerpts from *Passages* are found in Hyman's biography of Babbage. Hyman's *Science & Reform: Selected Works of Charles Babbage,* published by Cambridge University, 1991, explores the very sensitive and important relationship between scientific innovation and government. Pickering and Chatto, London, published in 1989 an 11-volume edition, *The Works of Charles Babbage* edited by Martin Campbell-Kelly which includes Babbage's *Passages* and is found in many university libraries. *Charles Babbage and His Calculating Engines, Selected Writings of Charles Babbage*, edited by Phillip and Emily Morrison, Dover Publications, New York, 1961, also contains Babbage's autobiography *Passages*. The Science Museum in London had a major exhibition in 1991 to commemorate Babbage's birth, and Doran Swade's *Charles Babbage and His Calculating Engines*, a beautiful guide to the exhibit, is available from the Science Museum in London. Also Dubbey's *The Mathematical Work of Charles Babbage,* Cambridge University Press, 1978, has an excellent section on Ada's Notes. There are many books on the history of computing devices; two of the best are *Engines of the Mind* by Joel Shurkin, Norton, 1984, and *Pebbles to Computers, The Thread*, Oxford, 1986, beautifully photographed by Hans Blohm, written by Stafford Beer, and with an introduction by David Suzuki. Three books highlight thinking skills in the computer age: *Descartes' Dream* by Paul Davis and Reuben Hersh, Harcourt, Brace and Jovanovich, 1986, *Electronic Life: How to Think About Computers* by Michael Crichton, Ballantine Books, 1984; and *Things That Make Us Smart: Defending Human Attributes in the Age of the Machine* by Donald Norman, Addison-Wesley, 1993.

WEB SITES ABOUT ADA, CHARLES BABBAGE, AND HISTORY OF COMPUTERS.

You can obtain the latest information by performing a search. At this time pictures of Ada can be found at the "Ada picture gallery," http//www.cs.kuleuven.ac.be; check out the "Ada Project" at Yale University by going to http//www.cs yale and then follow the trail to the "Ada Project" and from there to "Women in History." The picture of Ada is from the picture on my bookcover, and the text is from my sources. Another source highlights the issue that IEEE put out on "Women in Computing," http//www.ieee.org/ieee-women in eng, and the other site is http//www.alephO.clarke.edu. For Babbage, check out "The Babbage Pages" at http//www.ex.ac. uk/Babbage/

BOOKS ABOUT LORD AND LADY BYRON

There are so many. Start with Leslie Marchand's *Byron, A Portrait*, published by John Murray, 1971. It is readily available in paperback as is Marchand's *Lord Byron, Selected Letters and Journals*. My edition is Harvard Press, 1982. Malcolm Elwin's *Lord Byron's Wife*, Harcourt Brace, 1962, is a brilliant scholarly revelation of the duplicity of Lady Byron. Lady Longford's biography of Byron is excellent. The many other books by Doris Langley Moore, Malcolm Elwin, Peter Quenell, and Michael Foot about Byron are also excellent. One of my favorite biographies, not easily available, is John Drinkwater's *The Pilgrim of Eternity*, Hodder and Stoughton, 1925. Byron's poetry and prose are found in most bookstores and libraries; consult those bibliographies for more references. An essential history of this period, from Lord Byron to Lady Anne Blunt, is Asa Briggs's *The Age of Improvement 1783-1867*, Longman Paperback, 1979.

WEB SITES ABOUT BYRON

There are many, but the best one I have found is John Leys's at http//www.geocities.com/athens/acropolis/8916/

BOOKS ABOUT ADA'S DAUGHTER, ANNABELLA, LADY ANNE BLUNT

Lady Longford's biography of Annabella's husband, Wilfrid Scawen Blunt, *A Pilgrimage of Passion*, published in paperback by Granada, 1979, is good reading. Part of that biography covers the journey they made without servants through Arabia on horseback. Lady Anne Blunt was one of the first European women to do so. She wrote and illustrated a chronicle of that journey, *A Pilgrimage to Nejd*, which was first published by John Murray in 1881 and now is reprinted in paperback and readily available in the travel section of most bookstores. Her journals, *Lady Anne Blunt, Journals and Correspondence, 1878-1917*, were edited by Rosemary Archer and James Fleming and published in 1986 by Alexander Heriot.

ADDITIONAL WEB SITES

For Charles Dickens try http//www.dspace.dial.pipex.com; for Michael Faraday try http//www.astro.virginia.edu; and for Mary Somerville http//www.mala.bc.ca and the "Ada Project" at Yale University.

EPILOGUE AND BIOGRAPHIES

A short note about what happened to Ada's family after she died. Lady Byron blamed Lord Lovelace for Ada's gambling. Lord Lovelace and Lady Byron never spoke again, and their correspondence was through lawyers. Lord Lovelace remarried in 1865 and spent the rest of his life building towers and tunnels; Ashley Combe ended up looking like a toy fortification.

Byron, Lord Ockham, went back to sea, ended up deserting the Navy, and worked under an assumed name in a Liverpool shipyard. He died of consumption in 1862, two years after Lady Byron's death. Ralph then inherited the Wentworth title, and took the name Milbanke (Lady Byron's father's name). He published *Astarte*, a book that was a selection of letters meant to defend his grandmother, but instead, for many intelligent readers, revealed hints of duplicity. Ralph considered all of his problems due to his mother and father. He was an avid mountain climber and had one daughter from his first marriage, who died without issue. It was Annabella who was responsible for carrying the family's heritage forward. In 1869, at the age of 32, she married Wilfrid Scawen Blunt. They are credited with bringing the Arab horse to England and establishing the Crabbet Stud. Her life was so fascinating and complex that it is well worth reading the books about and by her. She had a long life and died in Cairo in 1917. Her only child, Judith, married Lord Lytton, and continued the family's interest in horses and mathematics. She is reputed to have used a binary system to trace the lineage of racing horses. Her son, the late Lord Lytton, who died in 1985, was an eloquent writer. The current Earl of Lytton is Judith's grandson, who, from the few letters I have received, carries forward the family's gift for writing excellent letters.

BABBAGE, Charles (1791–1871) He was a widower, 42 years old, when he met Ada, a young woman of 17. Babbage's many accomplishments include his ideas for the penny post, the oscillating light used by lighthouses, tables used by actuaries for decades, experiments with colored pages and print, etc. & etc. Babbage and De Morgan ended their friendship as a result of Lady Byron's moving into Ada's home and "taking over."

BREWSTER, Sir David (1781–1868) Scottish physicist and natural philosopher noted for research into the polarization of light. He is generally credited with the invention of the kaleidoscope, which Ada collected, and so do I. According to Ada's bank book, it was one of her last purchases.

CROSSE, Andrew (1784–1855) Englishman who performed experiments with electricity. He specialized in the field of electro-crystallization. He lived at Fyne Court, Somerset, about 20 miles from the Lovelace estate at Ashley Combe.

DE MORGAN, Augustus (1806–1871) British mathematician whose main field of study was logic. He spent much of his time writing about mathematics, philosophy and antiquarian matters. He was a professor at the University College, now part of the University of London. His letters to Babbage were filled with cryptograms. Their friendship ended when Ada died because his wife, Sophia Frend, was a staunch critic of Ada and defender of Lady Byron.

FARADAY, Michael (1791–1867) English chemist and physicist who discovered benzene and invented the dynamo. His most important work was in electricity and magnetism. He discovered electromagnetic induction, which led to the development of a simple electric motor and the first electric generator, and recognized that the energy in magnetism was in the space around the iron bar, not in the bar itself. This theory (the Field Theory) was ridiculed, and Faraday died before it was respectfully proved by James Clerk Maxwell (1831-1879).

GAMLEN, Samuel (1783–1855) He matriculated at Oxford, Balliol College, 1805, and received his M.A. in 1811. He was the vicar at Bossall, Yorkshire, and in 1854 after Ada had died, Lady Byron appointed him the rector at Kirkby Mallory, at her estates in Leicestershire. Lady Byron appeared to like him, but did not want him too near Ada in 1852. Even though Ada, at one point, regarded him more highly than she regarded Babbage, and certainly as one of her closest friends, every biographer has mistaken his occupation and relationship to Ada.

GUICCIOLI, Countess Teresa (1799?–1873) One year after marrying a wealthy but eccentric man, the countess met Lord Byron (April, 1819) and fell desperately in love with him in Venice. He became her "Cavalier Servente," and, after the Pope granted her separation from her husband, Lord Byron continued in "the strictest adultery" with her (his words).

MELBOURNE, William Lamb, 2nd Viscount (1779–1848). British prime minister from July to November 1834 and from April 1835 to August 1841. He was Lady Byron's first cousin and Queen Victoria's chief advisor from April 1837. His mother was a confidante and close friend of Lord Byron's and the sister of Lady Byron's father. Caroline Lamb, William's wife, further entwined these characters. She had had a celebrated affair with Lord Byron and most likely was the origin of the "incest rumour." Lord Melbourne went to visit Lady Byron in January 1838, and whether his influence or

William's service in the Ionian Islands before he met Ada was the reason, William became an earl in June 1838. Babbage's relationship with Melbourne is described in Anthony Hyman's book.

MOORE, Thomas (1779–1852) One of Byron's closest friends. In 1830, during the time that Lady Byron accused Ada of "conversational litigation," Lady Byron was busy gathering arguments in opposition to Moore's *Life and Letters of Lord Byron,* which portrayed Byron's view of the separation.

MURRAY, John (1778–1843) The first John Murray founded a bookselling and publishing business in Fleet Street in 1768. His son, John Murray II, became one of the most prestigious publishers in London. His reputation was enhanced by the publication of Lord Byron's *Childe Harold* and the poet's succeeding works.

SOMERVILLE, Mary (1780–1872) Mrs Somerville's scientific accomplishments are described in the narrative. What I find remarkable is her humanity and her understanding of the pressures Ada had to cope with. Mrs Somerville tried to get Ada to balance her life, to think of her own needs and health. Mrs Somerville was not explicit about Lady Byron until Ada was dying. She heard about Lady Byron's behavior from her son, Woronzow Greig, and evidently wrote a letter criticizing Lady Byron's possessive attitude. That letter does not remain; however, Lady Byron's response was her typical self-justification, this time blaming "that widower," meaning Babbage, for all of Ada's problems.

WHEATSTONE, Sir Charles (1802–1875) English physicist who, with W. F. Cooke (1806-1875), patented in 1837 the first electric telegraph.

Dr Betty Alexandra Toole attended the University of Chicago and received her bachelor's degree and doctorate from the University of California at Berkeley. While obtaining her doctorate, she worked full-time to support the development of a technological innovation and was co-owner of a Silicon Valley company. She enjoys doing presentations about Ada, and loves being with her children and grandchildren, trading options, teaching computer science, and Greek dancing.

Leah Schwartz, the author of *Leah Schwartz, the life of a woman who managed to keep painting*, designed the cover. She has lived several lives – wife, mother, house manager, domestic drudge, and passionate artist.

Strawberry Press publishes reference books for the succulent world including *The Euphorbia Journal* Volumes 1-10, *Caudiciform and Pachycaul Succulents*, *A History of Succulents*, and *Succulent Compositae* by Professor Gordon Rowley, *Des Cactées* by Charles LeMaire, and *Succulents of Madagascar*, Volumes 1 and 2 by Professor Werner Rauh. Strawberry Press published *Leah Schwartz, the life of a woman who managed to keep painting*, an autobiography that includes full color reproductions of 284 color paintings, as well as the original hard cover edition of *Ada, The Enchantress of Numbers: A Selection from the Letters of Lord Byron's Daughter and Her Description of the First Computer*, which includes 80 illustrations. All Strawberry Press books are printed on the finest quality paper, with laser scanned reproductions of the highest quality. These limited editions are sold throughout the world. The Web site of Strawberry Press is http://www.shell2.ba.best.com~spress

Strawberry Press • 227 Strawberry Drive • Mill Valley, CA 94941